THE ROLE OF THE POET
IN EARLY SOCIETIES

Morton W. Bloomfield and Charles W. Dunn

D. S. BREWER

First published 1989 by D. S. Brewer, Cambridge

D. S. Brewer is an imprint of Boydell & Brewer Ltd
PO Box 9, Woodbridge, Suffolk IP12 3DF
and of Boydell & Brewer Inc.
Wolfeboro, New Hampshire 03894-2069, USA

ISBN 0 85991 279 5

British Library Cataloguing in Publication Data
Bloomfield, Morton W. (Morton Wilfred)
1913–
The role of the poet in early societies
1. Society. Role of poets, 1100–1500
I. Title   II. Dunn, Charles W. (Charles
William), 1915–
305.3'381
ISBN 0-85991-279-5

Library of Congress Cataloging-in-Publication Data
Bloomfield, Morton W. (Morton Wilfred), 1913–1987
The role of the poet in early societies / Morton W. Bloomfield and
Charles W. Dunn.
    p.   cm.
  ISBN 0-85991-279-5 (alk. paper)
  1. Poetry, Medieval—History and criticism.   2. Poets in
literature.   3. Literature and society.   I. Dunn, Charles W.
(Charles William), 1915–   .   II. Title.
PN688.B5   1989
809.1'02—dc19   89-30069
                                                                CIP

∞ The paper used in this publication meets the minimum
requirements of American National Standard for Information
Sciences – Permanence of Paper for Printed Library Materials,
ANSI Z39.48–1984.

Printed in Great Britain by
St Edmundsbury Press, Bury St Edmunds, Suffolk

Dedicated to our seminar students
who joined us in search of the wisdom of poets.

M.W.B.
C.W.D.

Fochen aí,
ingen soïs,
siur chélle,
ingen menman,
miadach, mórdae!

Hail poetry,
Daughter of wisdom,
Sister of reason,
Daughter of prudence,
Noble, revered!

Old Irish *Ode to Poetry*

CONTENTS

ILLUSTRATIONS

1. (p. 164) A Gaelic bard authenticates the claims of Alexander III as King of Scotland in 1249. (*Scotichronicon*, XVth century, paper Ms. 171, 11½″ × 8″, half-page drawing, fol.205, Corpus Christi College, Cambridge, by kind permission of the Master and Fellows.)

    [For description, see *Facsimiles of National Manuscripts of Scotland*, ed. Sir William Gibson-Craig, II (Southampton, 1870), intro. Cosmo Innes, item 85, pp. xviii, 68; and M. R. James, *Descriptive Catalogue of the Western Manuscripts in Christ's College Cambridge* (Cambridge, 1905), I, 390–395 (item 171). For translation of the relevant passage, see *Chronicle of the Scottish Nation*, ed. W. F. Skene (Edinburgh, 1872), II, 289–290.]

2. (p. 165) *The Bard*, a Romantic view of the solitary poet painted by a Welsh artist, Thomas Jones (1742–1803) (canvas 45.5″ × 66″), by kind permission of the Director and Curators of the National Museum of Wales, Cardiff.

PREFACE

It is with much regret that I must undertake alone to write the preface to a book which sprang from a warm-hearted academic collaboration between two friends. My fellow author, Morton Bloomfield, died on April 14, 1987, shortly before our book had reached the publisher. Here I must trust that I am speaking on behalf of both of us.

As colleagues in medieval studies at Harvard, Morton and I decided some years ago to join forces in presenting a series of seminars devoted to some specific problems connected with the interpretation of early poetry. We were using the word 'poetry' in the broadest possible sense, and we were not immediately concerned with the philological problems that once faced medievalists and are now being solved by the advancing skills of linguists and lexicographers. Rather, we were concerned with questions relating to the original *overall meaning* of individual works within the body of what is called 'medieval literature'. In attempting to find some satisfactory answers, we therefore centered our attention on the role and functions of the poets within the societies to which they belonged, and this book presents our conclusions.

Our discussions regarding our topic were widened by the coincidental fact that both Morton and I, despite our special absorption in medieval studies, had always seized the opportunity to study present-day 'folk-cultures', or – to use the more accurate terminology – 'pre-modern' or 'pre-literate' cultures. Here our principal field-studies differed widely in scope. Morton became especially interested in the native cultures of Africa, whereas I investigated the Scottish Gaelic culture surviving in the Highlands and Islands of Scotland and in certain Scottish settlements in Canada.

The results of our studies presented here are thus somewhat particular, but they are, we trust, none the less significant. We argue that in early Western European cultures the 'poet' has served as a functionary within the tribe (Chapters 1 and 2). We illustrate the operations of this function by an examination of the poet in the role of interpreter of the past, present, and future within Early Irish and surviving Scottish Gaelic cultures (Chapters 3 and 4) and Welsh (Chapter 5) and Norse and Old English (Chapter 6).

We argue that the basic role of the poet has been to serve as a carrier of tribal wisdom (Chapter 7), and we provide an illustration of the ubiquity of the role by means of a broad based survey of wisdom literature (Chapter 8). Finally, returning to our original quest for appropriate guidance in the interpretation of the records of the past, we examine, by way of example, the Romantic view of the Middle Ages (Chapter 9).

For readers who might be curious, Morton was the author of Chapters 1, 2, 7, and 8, along with his characteristically exhaustive annotations. I was the author of Chapters 3, 4, 5, 6, and 9. Each of us read, and commented on, and freely reworked the other author's chapters.

In the publication of this book, we are deeply indebted to a wide range of people. In our seminars we enjoyed the stimulating companionship of independently-minded graduate and undergraduate students, several of whom have already published in fields related to our seminars. In devoting our heart-felt dedication to them in the forefront of this book, we can only hope that we have not borrowed from them without paying them credit.

The senior academics who as presences in our lives have influenced us particularly – to mention only a few – would include the late Professor R. W. Chambers, the late Professor Fred Norris Robinson, the late Professor Kemp Malone, and our esteemed friends Professor B. J. Whiting, Professor Kenneth H. Jackson, and Professor John V. Kelleher. Only one of the aforementioned has read some preliminary pages of our present work, and he is of course entirely exempt from any blame that may be associated with our errors and misinterpretations.

In a most practical way, we are also indebted to William J. Mahon (Ph.D. in Celtic Studies, Harvard) for his assiduous and well-informed scrutiny of the text, style, footnoting, and format of our manuscript. In preparation of the manuscript for publication, we are deeply indebted to the skill and sympathetic cooperation of Margo Granfors (Administrative Assistant, Department of Celtic Languages and Literatures, Harvard). Also, in terms of marital patience and support, we have been totally dependent on our much beloved wives, Caroline Bloomfield and Elaine Dunn.

Signed on behalf of Morton W. Bloomfield, late Arthur Kingsley Porter Professor of English, Emeritus, Harvard University.

Charles W. Dunn

(Margaret Brooks Robinson Professor of Celtic Languages and
Literatures, Emeritus, Harvard University)

CHAPTER 1

THE POETIC FUNCTION

1. INTRODUCTION

We have undertaken this study in order to define the role of the poet in medieval society. Our basic question is, How best can we understand, interpret, and appreciate the poetry[1] of a vanished past? Obviously the usual critical methods are all relevant and can be illuminating. Philology can unlock the linguistic secrets of an ancient poet's word-hoard. Surviving poems can, like the artifacts discovered by an archaeologist, be arranged in chronological sequence that may reveal something of their meaning within an evolutionary development. Individual poems may be ascribed to a particular place and time within this sequence. The analysis of the structure of a poem may reveal such subtle matters as, for instance, a distinctive pattern of recurrent images that reflects the poet's intent. Aesthetic analysis may reveal the beauties that lie within a poem, at least in the eye of the contemporary beholder; philosophical analysis may reveal its inner meaning; and psychological analysis may reveal its specific significance for the poet. Yet these familiar approaches, whether applied individually or collectively, hardly suffice to answer our fundamental question; and we have therefore, imitating as it were the social anthropologist rather than the archaeologist, attempted first to define the functions of poetry in society. This endeavor has in turn led us to consider the functions of various kinds of verbal utterances, whether 'poetic' or not, that seem to appear repeatedly in the kinds of cultures, both medieval or pre-modern, with which we are concerned.

We have all been influenced deeply by the Romantic movement with its emphasis on the divine poet and the importance of artistic creation. The soul

[1] Whenever the word 'poetry' is used in this book, it should be understood as embracing all forms of verbal art except conversation. It is difficult to find an accurate word to cover these forms in early societies because verbal art is so closely woven into its culture. 'Literature' implies something separate from other social activities and is too elitist a term, although we occasionally use it. Some 'poetry' will of course include what we normally mean when we use 'prose' as opposed to 'poetry'. Not all early 'poetry' is in distinctively patterned form.

1

of the poet has been elevated into a kind of absolute, whereas the audience and the social ambience have been neglected because the art of poetry has in the last two centuries become in large measure alienated or at least separated from the mainstream of Western society, and the poet has been forced back, so to speak, onto himself. It is true that a new emphasis on the text has arisen in the past fifty years, an emphasis that is different from the positivistic unit approach of traditional philology and that embraces wholes as well as the building blocks of wholes. But as our continuing interest in confessional poetry and literary biography shows, we still elevate the creator of these texts into a very special position.

The theoreticians of the Romantic movement elevated art and the artist into an autonomous position, often even taking over religious terms and attitudes to describe them.[2] They also emphasized the particular at the cost of the universal, and uniqueness at the cost of the general. Counting the stripes on the petals of a tulip, an undertaking which Dr. Johnson had repudiated, once more became the fashion in the arts. Society, developing the powerful tools of scientific knowledge and technology, displaced man from his central position in the cosmos and the animal kingdom. Industrialization continued apace, and industrial and monopolistic capitalism flourished. The peasants, the farmers, and the artisans of an older society became less and less important, and many of the traditional cultural activities like the composition of poetry became less extensively practiced and were no longer integrated into societies. In spite of voices of protest such as, in England, those of Ruskin, Arnold, and Morris and their later descendants, the split between poetry and 'real' life widened and deepened.

The notion of the particular was extended to cultures and 'races', with great emphasis on different human modes of thinking and acting and on the characteristics of higher and lower 'races'. In some sense, these distinctions are valid, but their extension to a hierarchy of races dominated and directed by their innate powers led to insensitivity and pride and even to violence and destruction. The desire, in literary students, to find the Germanic qualities of early Germanic history and poetry created a myth out of the useful notion of a native soul that would account for every feature of older Germanic cultures. Poetry revealed, as Vico and Herder had earlier pointed out, the primeval element of life and the souls of various peoples.

Yet this same period gave rise to a greater and more accurate knowledge of other peoples and languages than the past had ever previously possessed and opened up to the West the treasures of other cultures in sound texts and accurate translations. It saw the rise of modern scholarly techniques that stood

[2] See M. H. Abrams, *The Mirror and the Lamp* (New York, 1953). Wimsatt is reported to have said in class, 'A poem is a verbal expression which has no end except to be known' (David Bromwich review of Wimsatt's *Day of the Leopards* in *TLS*, June 25, 1976), the most extreme statement of the autonomous and non-functionalist view of poetry.

2

beside the scientific advances of the nineteenth and twentieth centuries. Through Hegel, in particular, it made possible a new awareness of history and historical development. If Arnold could say of the eighteenth century that it was 'indispensable', we today can certainly apply his term to his own century. The nineteenth century provided us with the tools to transcend its own limits, even at the cost of losing certain valuable ideas. We hope it will also be possible in the twenty-first century to say the same of our present century.

Poetry in the West, in the past two centuries, has been praised for its beauty, its sincerity, its sweetness, its light, and its power, but it has seldom been praised for its usefulness. Poetry lost in large measure its social utility and has become decorative or self-sufficient. It is confined to our recreation (if in America we prefer it to TV or bowling). Occasionally it does affect ordinary life, but with the break-up of an integrated society, poetry has today little to do with the real concerns of everyday life. England still has a poet laureate who dutifully turns out a poem now and then for a public event involving the queen or the nation, but his role is in no way essential to the occasion, whether it be a birthday, wedding, coronation, or death. We retain some place for poets to write jingles or scenarios to help sell objects, places and products, but this activity is relatively minor and does not provide a livelihood for more than a fraction of our writers. Those who are so employed usually feel defensive or guilty, or both, about the commercialism in their jobs.

If we move to contemporary authoritarian societies, we do find poets who still have a function by giving themselves up completely to praising the regime and to encouraging the masses to forego luxuries and to work harder for a happier and ever-distant future. They are bureaucratized and differ from their praise-singing ancestors, although they are closer in spirit to them than to most poets in the West.[3]

What kind of poetry did early societies prefer? While sharing some political characteristics similar to those of Communist or authoritarian countries, the social context of traditional African and early Western poetry is very different. These societies believed in the power of the word, and in an otherworld peopled by spirits, gods, and, in especial, by the souls of ancestors. These were the social environment they favored – not a bureaucratic domineering machinery, nor a philosophy based on materialistic principles, nor a so-called dictatorship of the proletariat. Without a knowledge of the social context in which poetry is written, especially older poetry, we are hampered in our approach to the understanding of it.

Much early poetry is didactic, and even today one can argue that by far the

---

[3] 'Most of the literature [of classical Hindu Society] was written by men well integrated into their society and with few of the complex psychological difficulties of modern literary man.' A. L. Bashan, *The Wonder that was India* (London & New York, 1954), pp. 415–416, quoted in Jack Goody ed., *Literacy in Traditional Societies* (Cambridge, Eng., 1968), p. 82.

greatest portion of world literature is still didactic, although somewhat less so than, say, five centuries ago. Teaching has always been recognized as an important function of poetry. Early poets were teachers, diviners, prophets, and preservers of tradition. Part of their sacred office was to admonish and warn rulers and subjects alike, and to hand on the accumulated wisdom of the past. Because of the seriousness of their duty, they resorted to the potency of verbal magic and the hypnotically fascinating manipulations of word. Part of their didactic function has been taken on by historians, sociologists, and popular science writers on behalf of the educated classes.

Poetry even in the West, especially in popular or folk art, still teaches and enables humanity to face destiny and existence. This is a role which many poets, often looked down upon by their more exclusive colleagues, still fill – in comics, in folk songs, in films and TV programs, and in columns of advice to the lovelorn or unhappy. Yet even here most of the educated pay little attention to such activities, and usually the name of artist is withheld from such a creator.

Although we are concerned with the function of poets in early societies and with their continuing role, we are aware that function is not all. Functionalism does not provide criteria of judgment except for effectiveness. Functionally, a patriotic song is judged by the utility of its patriotism. Other criteria are needed, but because the function of early poetry has been so largely neglected in the past, we are emphasizing it in this book. We do, of course, realize that other criteria besides effectiveness in attaining a goal must have a strong role in literary judgment. Indeed, in early societies, the audience sometimes makes distinctions in artistic excellence between two poems which have identical functions so that these instinctive critics themselves use other, often more aesthetic and psychological, criteria. Yet if we, as modern readers, look beyond aesthetic evaluation, the discovery of the social function of poetry can help us to appreciate the genre used, the rationale for the form and emphases of the work, and even at times, its vocabulary and style. The circumstances necessary, even if not sufficient, for a work of art can help us understand it in various ways.

Functionalism in anthropology and other humanistic disciplines has come under severe criticism in recent times.[4] When other disciplines seem to be abandoning it, or at least minimizing it, it may seem odd that we should here be arguing for its use in the study of pre-modern literature. We do so because its application has rarely been applied to the verbal arts.[5] Although it has its

---

[4] See, e.g., Ruth Finnegan, *Oral Literature in Africa* (Oxford, 1970), pp. 38ff and 330ff.
[5] In the last part of the nineteenth century and early part of this century, some literary students like Gummere and Olrik did try to see early literature as functional even if they did not always use this term. See also Chapter 2, 'Literature as Magical Art', in Hugh Dalziel Duncan, *Language and Literature in Society, A Sociological Essay . . .* (Chicago, 1952), pp. 20ff. On contests, see Robert Elliott, *The Power of Satire* (Princeton, 1960) and

limitations as a method, it also has its strengths. It is especially helpful in studying integrated and relatively small societies, societies which are now being disrupted and are even disappearing in the face of modernity. Anthropologists in the early twentieth century tended to overuse the technique and method and to overstress the political function of early literature. Furthermore, it is easy, if one wishes, to dig up functions, and some are so extremely general that they can explain anything. Function is a tricky concept, and everything to some extent has a function, even if it be amusement. If, however, functions are carefully defined, and if we recognize that they have their limits, just as any teleological explanation has its limits, functionalism can be a very valuable tool. We must therefore use the method for what it can give and not expect complete answers. Ultimately, the effectiveness of the method will be judged from the point of view of literary study by the success it engenders in understanding literary works. The method must be judged by its fruits.

It should also be pointed out that in the West music, painting,[6] and the dance have also, in varying degrees in the last few centuries, lost much of their social and religious functions. Music, perhaps, has held on more than its sister arts to its social functions, but even so, it has given up much. Poetry, then, is only one of the arts and activities which have become more or less socially otiose. We, of course, shall here be concerned with poetry.

There is another way of looking at the functional element in early art. All art has an element of both the useful and the decorative or beautiful in it. In early societies the role of the tribal craftsman tended to dominate that of the individual artist (even if the same person). As societies lost their cohesion, if ever they had it, an aristocratic leisured class grew more and more important, and the distinction between the two roles of craftsman and artist grew. The popular arts took over the functions of tribal craftsmen, to produce enjoyable objects in a social context, as in work songs, styles of clothing, and so forth. In modern Western societies, except perhaps for architecture, the 'fine' arts (or *beaux arts*), since the late eighteenth century, have tended to provide their audience with solitary enjoyment through books, tapes, records, and museums. The Bauhaus School is a good example of a failed modern attempt to re-unite popular crafts and high art.

We have devoted this introduction, so far, to discussing the concept of function and its relation to poetry, but we would be amiss if we did not refer, at

Chadwick (note 30 below), p. 88.

'Comparative studies of oral and written literatures are illuminating because they show that what has happened in one society may well have happened in another. What they can never show is that any practice observed in one society *must* have occurred in another.' G. L. Huxley, *Greek Epic Poetry from Eumelos to Panyassis* (Cambridge, 1969), p. 191.

[6] On painting, see André Malraux's *Voices of Silence* (in French), trans. S. Gilbert (Garden City, N. Y., 1953).

least briefly, to the relation between function and audience. To ignore this subject completely in an age which is gradually rediscovering the importance of the role of the audience in the literary situation would be negligent in the extreme.

The audience whether in social or in individual contexts brings to a literary situation certain expectations. In oral cultures, the audience expects certain aspects of these anticipations to be more or less satisfied. The story, if it is a story, is usually well known; the social function, if it is occasion for praise, blame, instruction, complaint, lamentation, or consolation, is usually expected. In each case, however, a fine oral poet would also introduce something new, not because of a failure of his memory, but because a slight or even extensive variation increases the pleasure of the audience, provided, of course, the composition is not completely new and not unattached to its proper tradition.

In other words, poetic functions can be looked upon as rhetorical modes. A poet's social functions are determined in some large measure by the occasion at which he performs and by the expectations of his audience. The oral poet has certain limits imposed upon him by tradition. Women, for instance, are often limited to performing lamentations or funeral songs. These limitations are accepted by the poets. They know what their audience expects.

Not all rhetorical functions are equally important among all cultures. Praise, blame, and lamentation are the most common rhetorical aims. The Xhosa among whom one of the authors has worked emphasize the praise poem above all types. These rhetorical aims, which can include a large number of variations, provide merely another way of looking at the functions of poetry. The audience plays a role in all literature, but in oral literature, because of its actual presence, it plays a great role and, indeed, perhaps the final, determinant role. Even though function is the term we use, we are inevitably talking also about rhetoric, especially the rhetoric of early and comparable pre-modern societies.

2. SOME CHARACTERISTICS OF EARLY SOCIETIES

Inasmuch as poetry is heavily, even if not completely, integrated into early societies, some notion of their characteristics is a necessity if we are to explore its functions. In order to understand early societies we must take a fresh point of view and, as far as possible, rise above the immediacy of our own society.

Early societies are much smaller in population and physical boundaries than modern societies. Even the smallest modern country is larger than the normal traditional society by measure of hundreds of thousands as opposed to hundreds. The dynamics of traditional societies are based upon status and role. Public aspect is important; and the emotions of honor and shame are the important social forces. Celebration and rite give a rhythm to life and existence. Unless excluded because of senility, illness, or shameful conduct, everyone participates in these occasions. Eloquence, self-respect, and reverence towards superiors and the clan's ancestors are the highly admired virtues. There is a quiet objectivity which rules people's lives, and although, occasionally the personal psyche rebels, normally there are traditional ways of treating exaggerated individualism. Boasting, comparisons of merit, and contests are often indulged in. These are demanded by a sense of public honor.[7] One's activities are largely determined by status and tradition.

Honor and shame are guardians of the tradition. One has a strong sense of one's honor and what one can do and what is due to one. If someone said to the Irish hero Cú Chulainn, 'Give me your spear', he would immediately put it between his victim's eyes. One's public role is important. Praise and blame are the natural concomitants of a strong sense of role, whether the role be high or low. The poets are the creators of public opinion and public judgment and hence are of great social value. As Julian Pitt-Rivers writes, 'the significance of the presence of a person is highly relevant to his honour. That which is an affront if said to his face may not dishonour if said behind his back. . . . What is offensive is not the action in itself but the act of obliging the offended one to witness it.'[8] Thus the threat of public humiliation by the tribal poet is a potent inducement to live up to the demands of one's role. It should, however, be emphasized that all traditional societies emphasize honor and employ shame to some degree, but in the pre-modern societies with which we are concerned these qualities are fundamental. In some societies, too, honor is transferrable, and a victory over an opponent in public, either by word or deed, increases one's own honor to the extent that the conquered had already possessed it. An important hero in an honor-shame society will not bother to combat, openly and on equal terms, a person whose honor is so small that a victory over him would add nothing to his own. Such a person is done away with quickly.

As Dumézil points out, the virtue of praise or blame will not work unless it is true. It is not a matter of praising or blaming *anyone*; the claim must, above all, be true. A desire for accuracy or truth in praise or blame can be seen, as he points out, in the ancient Roman census, which is basically taken to situate a person, act, or opinion in its proper hierarchical place.[9] We shall discuss the

---

[7] Cf the Old Norse *mann-jafnadr* (comparison of men). See L. L. Schücking, 'Heldenstolz und Würde im Angelsachsischen', *Abh.d. sächs. Akademie der Wiss.* Philos/ Hist Klass 42,5 (Leipzig, 1933): Jan de Vries, *Altgermanische Religionsgeschichte* (Berlin, 1956), I, p. 505; H. Pedersen in *Festskrift J. L. Ussing* (Copenhagen, 1900), pp. 165–192.

[8] See 'Honour and Social Status' in *Honour and Shame: The Values of Mediterranean Society*, ed. J. C. Peristiany (Chicago, 1966), pp. 25–26. The essays in this book are useful for the understanding of honor and shame as social correctives and rewards. See also Paul Friedrich, 'Defilement and Honor in the Iliad', *Journal of Indo-European Studies* (1973), pp. 115–1126.

[9] See Georges Dumézil, *Servius et la fortune, Essai sur la function sociale de louange et de blâme et sur les éléments indo-européens du cens romain* (Paris, 1943), pp. 241ff.

notion of praise or blame in more detail later,[10] but here we wish to emphasize its relation to one's public position and image in society.

The strong emphasis on roles in early societies means that by their very positions human beings have certain well-defined activities demanded of them. Praise and blame are thus easy to apportion in such societies, because failure and success can be more accurately estimated and apportioned than in industrial societies. In early societies, a man is largely judged by two criteria: the status of his ancestors and his aptitude in fulfilling the demands and expectations of his role. If a man is a coward in battle, he damages his image in his role as a warrior. Nor do these failures have to be voluntary. If a wife cannot produce children, she too has in some way failed in her role.

The ancestors of the clan or of an individual are most important. Ancestors are concerned about how well their offspring live up to the role or roles expected of all members of the clan. Furthermore, their offspring are fated to join them and must therefore be worthy, so to speak, of their role as ancestors. They are the guardians of the tribe and of wisdom. Wisdom is the universal virtue of early societies. It provides a guide for everyday living and allows every person to make some kind of sense out of the world. To mix a metaphor, traditional wisdom is the cement that keeps early societies together and the oil that enables them to function smoothly. It helps the individual with what would be called, in modern societies, 'neuroses' and enables him to transcend the nasty, brutish, and short qualities of life which have always assailed mankind. It supports order and upholds rulerships and, at the same time, ultimately makes all persons equal in a rather special but valuable sense.

The rise of the Enlightenment and the psychologistic morality of Kant, which emphasizes self-development, began to kill the idea of wisdom in intellectual circles. The notion that the past had anything to teach us, or that there was a body of commonsense knowledge which would be of use to us, began to seem ridiculous. Although the appreciation of wisdom survives in a somewhat minimal form in modern Western societies, it has, in the past two centuries, lost its hold on leaders of opinion and intellectuals.

Early societies likewise believed in the power of magic, even long after Christianity came to the West. In most traditional and semi-traditional societies magic is a normal part of life. With the continued influence of astrology, dowsing, and divination over the centuries and the new wave of interest among urban Westerners in such arts within the past twenty years, we can say that to some considerable extent societies, even now, are under the domination of magic. The belief in the efficacy and power of language is at the heart of the primal magic view of the world, and along with the notion that imitative action can have real effects, it makes credible the basis of all magical activity, including that knowledge of the future commonly called prophecy.

---

[10] See below especially chap. 2 for a general discussion, and chapters 3–6 (under Category 5) for specific examples.

In a culture dominated by wisdom, in which people believe that there is a proper time and place for everything, the idea that names carry innate correctness is deeply imbedded. Not only are things as they are, but true names are as they are. Nothing is arbitrary about naming, and this belief in Biblical times is manifested in Adam's giving names to everything in the early days of creation. All things and beings are properly named unless they deliberately mask themselves in false or misleading names. The possession of one's true name by others gives others power over one. Panegyrists use praise names as the proper naming epithets when they award public praise, and satirists apply blame names to their victims.

Today, we substitute numbers for names, and even a knowledge of these numbers (social security, credit cards, and telephone) gives one power over others. An enemy can make use of a name to do harm, and a friend can use it to heap blessings. The notion of magic rests on the idea of a rational universe in which words and language play a very important part. The wise man who can effect magic and, by his knowledge of the rationale of things, can control events for his own benefit, or that of a client or the whole community, can determine in some sense what is to follow. These controls, of course, may be used for either evil or good ends. Part of one's troubles are due to witches and wizards against whom one can sometimes be protected by diviners and by witch doctors.

Ruth Finnegan, in her valuable book *Oral Literature in Africa*,[11] discusses the importance of names in African culture and literature. Some names are variant names for a single person used by his neighbors in divergent circumstances. Praise names, to which we have already referred, abound. Many of these are suggestive of epithets such as we find in folk epics and in Homer.[12] Variant names can be used to make comments on one's neighbors: conveying greeting, friendship, praise, criticism, and, sometimes, oblique comments. The Karanga, for instance, give their dogs names that embody criticism of others.[13] Events, proverbs, and characteristics are all used in names. Metaphoric understatement abounds and is sometimes linked to well-known proverbs. Sometimes the names are chosen by their bearers, and sometimes by the friends or neighbors of the bearers. The origin and meaning of personal names fascinate a community in as much as they are assumed to provide the rationale, one might say, or one of the rationales of the persons who bear them.

The root of the belief in the inherent power of words and names lies, no doubt, in the fact that words are, in a very strong sense, magical.[14] They

---

[11] (Oxford, 1970), pp. 152ff and pp. 470ff.
[12] See below, chap. 2, note 39.
[13] Finnegan, p. 471.
[14] See Toshihiko Izatsu, *Language and Magic*, Keio University, Studies in the Humanities and Social Relations 1 (Tokyo, 1955).

enable one to recall the past and call up distant places and scenes. The oral signals we call language bring us help in various forms and make possible the relief of hunger, desire, and thirst. A child in his crib is soon aware that, by making certain noises, he can affect things at a distance and produce results. By crying or, when he is able, by uttering 'mama', he can get comfort, food, or drink. Words are surely magical and proper to their form. They work.

Our gift of language is a magical gift, and because it can cause or lead to certain miracles of action, we assume that, if we know the proper words, we can ourselves produce or effect almost anything. In fact, some scholars have argued that the notion of verbal therapy, which we find in Greece, is closely linked to the idea that words, especially those applying to psychic disturbances, can cure diseases. Thus, in Homeric epic, words in the form of prayer, magic charm, and suggestive or fascinating speech are used to heal.[15]

Reading the early books of the Bible, we find again and again the etymologies of place and personal names given to us. In early societies, many stories or poems are devoted to explaining the why of names. In Old Irish literature, for instance, we find in *dindshenchas* (place-name lore) and in *Cóir Anmann* (*The Fitness of Names*) the lore of famous places and their etymologies. In other cultures, comparable poems or stories are found, even if they are not given a generic name.

Just as a man's words can bring things into being, so God's word can make non-being into being. 'In the beginning was the Word' (*en arché én ho logos*) is much more than a metaphoric statement; it is, to believers, and indeed to most human beings in the world, literally true. The larynx is a weaver and out of air weaves rationality and meaning. Many words referring to poetry and language have etymological links with the notion of weaving.[16]

Language, we know or at least assume, was invented; but to each one of us, as we enter a linguistic community at birth, language is there just as bread, furniture, or the sun are there. It seems to be part of nature, and we discover it as we discover nature. Hence it creates a deep-seated notion in us that language, in particular our language, is as natural as faces, hills, or trees. It is often difficult for young children to believe that foreigners do not understand their language, because their own language seems to belong to the nature of things.

As exemplified by the assumption of accuracy in naming, the value of truth is a major factor in the life of early societies. Praise and blame will not work if they are not just and true to things as they are.[17] Magic will not be effective if it is not truly and correctly performed. Because early literature was closely

---

[15] See Pedro Lain Entralgo, *The Therapy of the Word in Classical Antiquity*, ed. and trans. L. J. Rather and John M. Sharp (New Haven and London, 1970), especially p. 240.
[16] See H. Wagner, 'Studies in the Origins of Early Celtic Civilization II', *ZCP* 31 (1970), pp. 46–57. The word *fath*, however, probably meaning 'covering garment' is not readily to be related to *fáth* 'subject-matter' or to *fáith*, 'poet, prophet.'
[17] See above note 8.

associated with magic and was oral and hence evanescent, truth was a very important criterion. Early art had to be authenticated, or when deliberately fictitious (that is, made up) it had to be clearly fictitious.[18] Wisdom literature always had to be true.[19] Hence the ubiquitous claim of literature, down almost to today, that it is true.[20] If early literature was not true, its magic would not work. The continuing dispute between history and poetry is based on the claim, unacceptable to the historians, that what the poets write is true.[21] One of the most important functions of bringing the teller into the poem or tale was to help authenticate it. 'I was there; I saw it.' Authenticating is a major element in the Bible, whose claim to truth rests upon historical veracity. The evangelists claim to have seen Jesus and his resurrection. Towards the end of Deuteronomy, the Deuteronomist writes, 'Moses therefore wrote this song the same day and taught it to the children of Israel' and 'Moses . . . made an end of writing the words of this law in a book until they were finished' (31:22 and 24). Both Moses and Jesus were also concerned with how to distinguish false from true prophets. Early poetry served a religious function, and truth was not a matter of high-mindedness but one of practicality.

The battle between history and poetry alluded to above could be amply illustrated. Perhaps two quotations will suffice. Polybius in his great history (XII: 12) writes: 'If you take away the truth from history, what is left is a tale without any utility,' and in the nineteenth century we find Carlyle thundering:

> It is reasonable to prophesy that this exceeding great multitude of
> Novel-writers and such like, must, in a new generation, gradually do
> one of two things: either retire into nurseries, and work for children,
> minors and semi-fatuous persons of both sexes; or else, what were far
> better, sweep their Novel-fabric into the dust-cart, and betake them
> with such faculty as they have to understand and record what is
> true, – of which, surely, there is, and will forever be, a whole

[18] See Morton W. Bloomfield, *Studies and Ideas, Language and Literature* (Cambridge, MA., 1970), pp. 177–183.

[19] See Mircea Eliade, 'Littérature Orale', *Histoire des Littératures*, ed. Raymond Queneau (Paris, 1956), I p. 4, argues that true stories had perhaps to be recited at special times.

The fictitious could be indicated by the very extravagance of the tale or poem. See Wm. Nelson, 'The Boundaries of Fiction in the Renaissance: A Treaty between Truth and Falsehood', *ELH* 36 (1969).

[20] *Ibid.*, p. 1.

[21] See G. Giovannini, 'The Connection Between Tragedy and History in Ancient Criticism', *PQ* 22 (1943), pp. 308–314; Wm. Nelson and Moses Hadas, *Ancilla to Classical Reading*, Columbia Bicentennial Editions and Studies (New York, 1954), pp. 42ff.

Two representative philosophical discussions of the cognitive status of fiction may be found in Margaret MacDonald, 'The Language of Fiction', *Proceedings of the Aristotelian Society*, Supp. 38 (1954), pp. 166–184, reprinted in Cyril Barret, *Collected Papers on Aesthetics* (New York, 1966), pp. 107–124, and J. O. Urmson, 'Fiction', *American Philosophical Quarterly* 13 (1976), pp. 153–157.

infinitude unknown to us, of infinite importance to us. Poetry, it will more and more come to be understood, is nothing but higher knowledge; and the only genuine Romance (for grown persons) reality.[22]

This dispute goes right back into the beginning of literature. The problem of fiction versus reality, or poetry versus history, is intimately bound up with the notion of truth and its magical power, and it still concerns the philosophers and logicians.[23]

The test of truth is of great importance in the oldest Irish and Sanskrit literature, and Myles Dillon suggests it goes back to a common Indo-European origin.[24] It is probable that similar tests go back to a very early stage in human societies when language, with its possibility of lying available to everyone, was developed. We find a similar emphasis on truth all over the world.

Traditional Irish story tellers, even to this day, round off their stories with comments like, 'That is my story! If there be a lie in it, be it so! It is not I who made or invented it' or 'I know this tale to be true because I was present.'[25] By 'true' in these cases, we must not take a scientific definition of the adjective, but rather construe it to mean 'approximately or more-or-less true' and certainly not a deliberate lie. One must also say that to be true in some cases is to correspond to the underlying structure of events or even people, or as Eliade puts it, the archetype.[26] The advice to princes which we find in older literatures such as Irish emphasizes again and again the importance of the virtue of truth to the ruler upon whom the prosperity of his realm hangs.[27]

---

[22] In his essay 'Diderot' first published in the *Foreign Quarterly Review* (1833) and reprinted in *Critical and Miscellaneous Essays* (1839).

[23] See above note 21. Kantorowicz in 'The Sovereignty of the Artist . . .', *De artibus opusculis XL, Essays in Honor of Erwin Panofsky*, ed. Millard Meiss (New York, 1961), points out that St. Thomas defended fiction only as used by the Bible because it is *figura veritatis* in ST III 9.55 art 4 ad 1.

[24] See Myles Dillon, 'The Archaism of Irish Tradition', *Proceedings of the British Academy* 33 (1947), esp. pp. 245–264, and D. Dubuisson, 'L'équipement de l'inauguration royale dans l'Inde védique et en Irelande', *RHR* 193 (1978), pp. 153–164.

The test of truth is a term used to determine whether a person (often a ruler or less frequently a story or phrase) is true (tells or reflects the truth, that is, what really is).

[25] For the first, see Alwyn Rees and Brinley Rees, *Celtic Heritage, Ancient Tradition in Ireland and Wales* (London, 1961), p. 15. For the second, W. J. Gruffydd, *Rhiannon, An Inquiry into the Origins of the First and Third Branches of the Mabinogi* (Cardiff, 1953), pp. 2–3.

[26] The various guslari of Yugoslavia Professor Lord writes about in his *Singer of Tales* (Cambridge, 1964) must be thinking of the deep structure or the archetype (see Mircea Eliade, *Cosmos and History*, trans. W. Trask [New York, 1954] p. 34) when they insist that their variant versions of a saga, clearly somewhat different, are the same.

[27] See for example *Audacht Morainn*, ed. and transl. Fergus Kelly (Dublin, 1976), pp. 5–9.

Truth, adherence to and action based upon things as they are, is the highest royal virtue.

3. ORAL LITERATURE

The difference between oral and written literature has been widely discussed. Eduard Fraenkel remarks, 'In the modern world it is a familiar idea that a poem has its normal place in a book and that it is primarily to the potential reader of the book that the poem addresses itself.'[28] But even with the advent of books, when few knew how to write, as Gilbert Murray has commented, 'literature was still oral, a thing to be performed and heard. A book was not a thing to be given to the public.'[29]

In recent years there has been great revival of interest in oral literature thanks to scholars like H. M. and Nora Chadwick, Stith Thompson, Milman Parry, and Albert Lord. In the late nineteenth and early twentieth centuries, a comparable interest existed, inspired by Romantic critics such as Herder, but, in the West at least, it gradually subsided until its more recent manifestation, which is based upon close study of extant texts and surviving oral societies. When we study early societies, we are dealing with oral literature, literature that by its very nature is transient, evanescent, but self-renewing. Although in decreasing number, societies still survive where oral literature flourishes, but almost all of them have been affected by book culture to the extent that they have been removed from anything that could be called their primal state.[30] The breaking-up of these societies by the process of urbanization, even more than the arrival of the book itself, threatens the survival of their unique culture.

Although Professor Lord has argued that a society's culture must be either oral or written, there is much evidence to the contrary,[31] even though it may be that there can be no transitional stage between formulaic composition as Professor Lord will have it and written composition. The answer depends

[28] Eduard Fraenkel, *Horace* (Oxford, 1957), p. 36.
[29] Gilbert Murray, 'Prolegomena to the Study of Greek Literature', *Greek Studies* (Oxford, 1946) (Lecture given at the Ashmolean Museum, Oxford, 1933), p. 24.
[30] See the useful and still not completely outdated Nora K. Chadwick, 'The Distribution of Oral Literature in the Old World', *Journal of the Royal Anthropological Institute* 69 (1936), pp. 77–94.
[31] See e.g. J. Opland, *Anglo-Saxon Oral Poetry* (New Haven, 1980), Chapter I; E. N. Obiechina, 'Transition from Oral to Literary Tradition I', *Présence Africaine* 63 (1967), pp. 145–1161; and Harold Scheub, 'Translation of African Oral Narrative – Performances to the Written Word', *Yearbook of Comparative and General Literature* 20 (1971), pp. 28–36.

partly on what is meant by transitional stage. There are Xhosa poets who compose orally and also write poetry down, even though it may not be the same kind of poetry. In any case, it is clear that we must know a great deal more about extant oral communities and poets, more than the Jugoslavian *guslari* and Xhosa *imbongi*, before we can confidently make generalizations.

Professor Lord is primarily interested in the process of oral composition: what are the themes and formulas of oral narrative poetry and how does the poet use them? In particular he is concerned with the problem of how poems the length of the Homeric epics could have been composed orally. Our concern here is different. We are interested in the social function of oral poetry in early societies and the conditions of its performance. We wish to ask: What kinds of poems are oral poems? How do the poets operate within their society? In what relation do they stand to their chiefs, their fellow poets, and their audiences? When do they recite poems? What roles do the poets and poems play in their societies?

Marshall McLuhan and Father Ong, each in his own way, have in recent years called attention to the rebirth, in some form, of orality in our Western society. Inasmuch as they believe that the forms of communication determine in large measure what is communicated ('The medium is the message' as McLuhan put it), they attribute the new rise of orality to the invention and increasing use of radio and TV, especially the latter, which they argue is not merely the substitution of one medium for another (the book). A new dominant mode of communication demands and creates a new view of the world. According to McLuhan, the mosaic replaced the linear view of the world, and what McLuhan called tribal culture reappears in a higher form (a kind of Hegelian synthesis, perhaps). The rise of TV means the increase of tribalism (the breaking down of large communities into smaller ones and all that that process implies). A tribal person thinks differently from a non-tribal person. What is now happening, McLuhan urged, is the coming of a new kind of tribal, mosaic society with many centers rather than one, with an abundance of sub-societies (ethnic groups in the USA perhaps), and with a new old way of thinking because of the new orality which is somewhat like the old.

This view of the modern Western world, if correct, changes our way of looking at early and traditional societies. Our book is not the place to define and explore the cultural revisionism that this change implies, but if Western society is becoming more tribal and oral (and there is some evidence to support this notion), there is much that older oral societies can teach us. It is also true, however, that an oral society founded on TV and modern recording techniques is not, nor will be, the same as a traditionally oral society.

Oral poetry is composed by improvisation, and often preserved by memory, frequently with the help of formulaic expressions, and it circulates by means of performance. Plays and pieces of music may still circulate by performance, but their existence is not dependent on performance since we have an alphabet, musical notation, and technology to record them in a standard form. True oral literature can only live by performance. It has no standard text. In a truly oral society, each performance is the only means of circulation. The performers of an oral work all differ in some degree, but they all think that they are performing the same work.[32] They think of the work in terms of what we may call its 'deep structure' or its archetype.

We may, of course, believe, as Gerard Manley Hopkins argues, that the reading of a literary work is equivalent to its performance, but even he felt that until poetry 'is spoken it is not performed', because the eye does not give the effects that the ear demands, and the ear is primary in poetry.[33] The performance of poetry, music, and dance in early societies is, at once, the creation, the text, and the circulation.

Nor all oral poetry is traditional, for initially, new poems are composed for particular occasions, and traditional poetry does change with the passage of time. Just as history, as a descriptive body of knowledge, is always open to reinterpretation, so the body of traditional oral poetry slowly but surely undergoes changes of emphasis and elaboration. It must be emphasized that certain episodes are basically untouched over the years. The story of a hero that ignored his well-known exploits would be an insult to his memory. Yet these exploits can be modified and embroidered. Instead of slaying a hundred men, a hero may slay a thousand. The versions of a story or poem are held together by an underlying structure, which is the final test of its truth. This deep structure cannot be violated. The 8:40 train J71 fulfills the same function every day in spite of the fact that no two journeys are exactly the same.

There is also the problem, as Ruth Finnegan points out,[34] of determining what is literature in an oral culture. Is a speech literature? Is a serious address literature, say an address of welcome? This problem we shall not concern ourselves with. All conscious verbal art except ordinary conversation can be regarded as literature in our sense. Hence our definition includes even speeches and proverbs as well as praise poems and tales.

As we have mentioned above, it is impossible to deny the status of oral literature to cultures which practice it, even during the period of their transition to book cultures. Memorial transmission is active in oral cultures and cannot be ignored. It is just as oral as improvisation with formulas. Our purpose is not, in this book, to explain the Homeric epic,[35] and we shall not

---

[32] See above, note 26.

[33] See the interesting quotation from his letter to his brother Everard Nov. 5, 1885 printed in part in *TLS* Dec. 8, 1972 (p. 1511).

[34] See Finnegan, pp. 15–25. One may of course define oral culture in such a way that only *purely* oral culture can be called oral culture.

[35] We would not rule out for any particular formulaic work, even the Homeric poems, the possibility that memory as well as improvisation were active in its composition or

neglect memorial transmission when it is clearly indicated.[36]

An oral culture is a different culture from a book culture. We shall not here be concerned with the many ways the step from ear to mouth to eye affected life, but we are concerned with its impact on verbal art in its social setting. What we have to work with is basically hypothetical, for orality leaves no artifacts. But the evidence of modern oral, or largely oral, societies, and with the reflexes of early societies still extant in our minds and world, we hope to get a grasp of the nature of early oral literature so that we can reexamine written literature, especially early written literature, in a new and more accurate light. This process is somewhat like the famed philological circle to which Leo Spitzer has called our attention in our century – a movement back and forth which can illuminate texts even if the emphasis here is not on the philological. This circular process can, however, give us clues that, when reinterpreted in the light of our reconstruction of early societies, may lead to a new understanding of early literature and, in turn, will cast new light even on philological matters.

transmission. Formulas may very well have been invented to make improvisation easier, but a genetic explanation does not necessarily explain what is present any more than the etymology of a word indicates its present meaning.
[36] See Alan Jabbour, 'Memorial Transmission in Old English Poetry', *Chaucer Review* 3 (1969), pp. 174–190, and James A. Notopoulos, 'Homer, Hesiod and the Achaean Heritage of Oral Poetry', *Hesperia* 29 (1960), p. 192.

CHAPTER 2

THE PRIMAL SITUATION: POETRY AND PATRONAGE

The history of poetry in the broadest sense is irretrievably lost, as is the history of human utterance. The Paleolithic peoples who first, perhaps some 750,000 years ago, developed the art of making chipped stone tools may also have developed some system of elevating their normal speech into poetic utterances for special occasions. Not until 5,000 years ago, however, did human beings develop various writing techniques for recording their utterances. The earliest poetry that has been preserved in writing is mostly poetry composed for patrons, kings, chiefs, and religious leaders, and is made to their taste and cast in traditional molds.[1] The voices of the aboriginal singers and the tunes of the instruments which must often have accompanied them are evanescent, and any songs that may be said to be of a primal nature have been preserved in recent times only through the writings and field recordings of antiquarians, scholars, and folklorists.

Because early poetry as we have it is largely the product of 'courts', rulers, and occasionally priests, we are here chiefly concerned with the social scene out of which that poetry grew and which nourished it. By analogy with modern survivors, these milieux can with some confidence be reconstructed. We shall present in the immediately following chapters[2] a series of convenient charts which undertake to relate the categories of early and pre-modern 'poetry' to their various social functions. We are most interested in the poetry of priests and kings, or poetry written by retainers for them, because they exist in considerable number and their ambience can be deduced with some confidence.

Whatever the origin of the state or rulership may be, it certainly goes back to very early times.[3] We know of no society which does not have some central

---

[1] In contemporary traditional societies, information about popular literature can, of course, be obtained. See for example Emmanual Obiechina, *An African Popular Literature: A Study of Onitsha Market Pamphlets* (Cambridge, Eng., 1973).

[2] Chapter 3 presents three diagrams, which cover different cultural periods; Chapter 4 presents a fourth; Chapters 5 and 6 dispense with diagrams but discuss the relevant categories.

[3] Historically this topic has been a fruitful and indeed fateful subject for speculation going back to Maimonides, Aquinas, Ibn Khaldun, Hobbes, Montesquieu, Rousseau,

organization or authority, even if it be a rather rudimentary one. To understand the immediate social circumstances of much early poetry, we must begin by recreating what we call, borrowing a term from Freud, the primal situation. This is an ideal construct and does not necessarily correspond to any actual arrangement. It enables us, however, to see how verbal art could have been woven into the fabric of governance in early societies. We can use it as a kind of template upon which to locate specific 'courts' as we know them or can reconstruct them.

It is important first to identify the ideal functions of governance in early societies. They may be enumerated under broad rubrics such as ruling, guarding, and controlling the tradition and past; defending against and attacking enemies; and making possible working, hunting, and producing goods and children. The role of ruling is embodied in the chief or king; guarding and controlling the tradition are embodied in the priest, or occasionally in female specialists;[4] defending and attacking are embodied in the warrior; and the actual working, hunting, and producing are embodied in the worker or ordinary man and woman. Reflections of this division appear in various forms. Sometimes the ruler must serve both as priest and as warrior. Producing may actually be the work of the lower classes, but its success may, at least in the cosmological framework, depend upon the king, priest, and warrior. The lower classes may in some cases be organized as little 'states' with the elder parent, usually though not always male, representing the king, priest, warrior, and producer within his extended family. Other combinations are possible.[5]

Although some poets may double as chiefs, priest-prophets, or even as warriors,[6] the role of the poet is not so readily classified. All men, and in some societies, women, are potential poets and on occasion have been poets. The poets we are primarily concerned with serve as partial or, on occasion, full functionaries. As Kenneth Jackson puts it, writing of the Celtic poet and sage, he 'was a functionary in society, and was an essential part of the aristocratic

---

Marx, and many others. With the increasing emphasis on genetic explanations from the eighteenth century on in the West, theories of societal origin have been of great importance in analyzing contemporary societies – when the genetic explanation becomes a normative explanation. Our own sympathies go to the theory proposed (rather badly, alas) in A. M. Hocart's *Kings and Councillors*, recently reedited by Rodney Needham (Chicago, 1970), which supports a ritual and religious origin of the state.

[4] See David K. Rycroft, 'Southern Bantu Clan-praises: A Neglected Genre', *Bulletin of the School of Oriental and African Studies*, University of London 39 (1976), pp. 155–159.

[5] Georges Dumézil has written at length on the 'class' and corresponding myth structure of early Indo-European culture and has focussed much interest on the governance of early society.

[6] See e.g. James A. Notopoulos, 'The Warrior as an Oral Poet: A Case History', *The Classical Weekly* 46 (Nov. 17, 1952), pp. 17–19 who refers to Achilles (Iliad 9:186–189) and General Makriyiannis during the nineteenth-century Greek War of Independence.

structure of that society'.[7] Such poets enjoyed special favors and received gifts. In certain societies the 'dynastic' poets were part-time functionaries, as among modern southern Bantu peoples, and in others, as the Rwanda and ancient Celtic societies show, they are full-time functionaries.

These poets, of course, often performed other functions besides manipulating the verbal art in support of the ruler – sometimes bolstering weak claims to the throne, sometimes increasing popularity, sometimes bringing prosperity to, or warding off evil from the clan and the ruler. They might sing in support of hunters[8] or warriors. they might operate as historians of the clan (not just propagandizing the claims of the ruler).[9] These poets also controlled the official record of the past. The totality of the past no doubt eluded their grasp, for popular poetry preserved religious and heroic stories of the past, but much lay within their province. The 'use of the past for social purposes', as J. H. Plumb has remarked, 'occurs in all early civilizations for which we have written record. In this the past legitimizes authority and status'.[10] They also flattered and criticized the king and in some cases participated in religious rites. We know that among some peoples, like the ancient Germanic tribes, the poets sang in battle the praises of their ancestors.[11] They were also a conduit whereby the feelings of the people could be conveyed to the ruler, a task for which they had a privileged position.[12] They, in some cases along with the women, acted as archivists and record-keepers. Some of them were prophets and diviners. Although Shamanism as such is not a special feature of most African societies as it is of Siberian and North American,[13] a poet as seer,

---

[7] See also A. Coupez and Th. Kamanzi, *Littérature de Cour au Rwanda* (Oxford, 1970), who discuss in their introduction the two sorts of literature and poets in Rwanda: the popular and the dynastic (of the Tutsi, no longer dominant).

[8] See *The Songs of Seydou Camara*, trans. Charles Bird with Mamadou Korta and Bourama Soumaouro (African Studies Center, Indiana University Bloomington, 1974), vol. I pp. vff.

[9] See G. L. Huxley's remark about Tyrtaios, the Spartan poet who was 'an able propagandist and a successful exponent of the despicable craft of rewriting the past: The Spartiates made good use of him in the emergency' (after their defeat by the Argives at Hysiai in 669 BC). See his *Early Sparta* (Cambridge, 1962), pp. 53–55.

[10] See his *The Death of the Past* (Boston, 1970), p. 28 (and on the whole topic pp. 26ff). See also Jack Goody and Ian Watt, 'The Consequences of Literacy' reprinted in Jack Goody ed., *Literacy in Traditional Societies* (Cambridge, Eng., 1968), pp. 31ff; and Robert C. Denton, *The Knowledge of God in Ancient Israel* (New York, 1968), p. 86.

[11] See E. A. Thompson, *The Visigoths in the Time of Ulfila* (Oxford, 1966) p. 59 and the references there.

[12] See Archie Mafeje, 'The Role of the Bard in a Contemporary African Community', *Journal of African Languages* 6 (1967), p. 221. This whole article is enlightening (pp. 193–223).

[13] On Siberia, see V. Dioszegi, ed., *Popular Beliefs and Folklore Tradition in Siberia* (Indiana University Publications, Uralic and Altaic, Series 57)(Bloomington and the Hague, 1968) (original: Budapest, 1968) and on North America, the Dec. 73/Jan. 74 Thirteenth anniversary issue of *Arts Canada* numbers 184, 185, 186 and 187 called 'Stones, Bones and Skin: Ritual and Shamanic Art'.

prophet, and visionary is fairly common.[14] The poets are repositories of wisdom; they remember laws; and they heal by their knowledge of charms, medicines, and herbs. They also entertain (as reflected later in the role of the court fools) and encourage the people to celebrate. When writing came in, some of them became scribes and heralds and continued their memorial role with the help of tablets or books.[15]

Let us, however, return to our ideal construct, the primal situation. We can reduce the variety and differences to the four roles – king, priest, warrior, and common man. Each has his court or assistants. The king has councillors, recorders, praisers, satirists, rememberers, and entertainers. The priest has his subordinate acolytes, prophets, and magicians. The warrior has his troops or spear-bearers. The common man has his wife (or wives) and children. As we have pointed out above, the number of these assistants varies considerably, and even the primary group of functionaries may be reduced to three when the king also takes the priest's role. The poet is usually under the control of the king, but his role can be to carry out any one or a group of these tasks for any one of the four 'classes'. He can sing popular songs and tales for the common man as he works or relaxes. He can encourage the warriors by singing their praises, or the praises of their ancestors, and by hurling curses and satires at the enemy. For the priests, he can sing charms and incantations, help them in their rites, or aid them if they perform ecstatic dances or visions. He can encourage the king, sing his praises, act as a conduit of criticism (usually muted but clear) from his subjects; he can recite the names of the tribal ancestors, remember the praise-names of neighboring chieftains; he can entertain the people with riddles and stories, console them with proverbs and gnomes, protect them with words, move them with history, and provide them with practical knowledge.

More than all this, the poet finally makes possible the *success* of various people and activities. He blesses them as the priest blesses the fishing boats before they set out on their tasks. He brings supernatural powers to the support of the king and the activities of his people. Without his help, success is impossible. Unless the powers of the universe are on the side of man or the activity, both will fail. The poets and wise men are able to control these powers as no one else can.

The 'court' poet is supported by his patron. His status may vary. In some cases, he draws a regular stipend with occasional additional rewards. In

---

[14] See N. Kerhsaw Chadwick, *Poetry and Prophecy* (Cambridge, 1947) (although somewhat out of date). On the relation between priests and prophets, see T. O. Beidelman, 'Nuer Priests and Prophets: Charisma, Authority and Power among the Nuer', *The Translation of Culture: Essays to E. E. Evans-Pritchard*, ed. T. O. Beidelman (London, 1971), pp. 375–415.

[15] On the early scribes as bureaucrat, poet, and scholar, see A. Leo Oppenheim, 'The Position of the Intellectual in Mesopotamian Society', *Daedalus* 104, No. 2 (Spring, 1975), pp. 37–46

others, he works at a regular job and gets special hand-outs from his patron. He sometimes has to compete with fellow poets. Such poets often have a recognized status, as in the kingdom of Rwanda, or they may have to depend on their own skill to receive honors. There are also, among the Hausa in Nigeria, free-lance specialists who move from place to place.[16] *Griots*, the free-lance poets of Senegambia, are regarded as belonging to an especially low caste. Others bring news from community to community like a kind of 'gazette chantante', as they have been called. Certain men or women are regarded as specialists for certain occasions and may be called upon, as the Luo *nyatiti* singer is, to lament. Some are not specialists at all and just break out into song on special occasions or when they feel like it.

The king's role varies from society to society, but he is obviously a key figure. Yet curiously enough, at least in tales and romances, his subordinate sometimes takes over, and the *dux* becomes in effect the *rex*, and the *rex* becomes otiose,[17] somewhat similar to the otiose great god many of these societies have inherited. The Arthurian romancers lose their interest in Arthur after a while, and Gawain, Lancelot, Percival, or Galahad take over as heroes of the romances. Tacitus (*Germania* 7) refers to two kinds of leadership among the Germanic peoples – *reges ex nobilitate* and *duces ex virtute*. The Germanic *rex* seemed to have inherited some sacral power[18] which the *dux* could only rival by personal prowess.

The king, as Frazer has shown, stands in many societies in a religious role – on him depends the fertility and prosperity of his people. In ancient Mesopotamian cultures he annually reenacts his enthronement at the New Year. In some societies, when he loses his vigor, he may be replaced. Furthermore, he may be, as Virgil points out (*Aeneid* 9:327), both *rex* and *augur* so that he can foresee the future and intercede with gods or ancestors. He can determine through omens what is *fas* or *nefas*.[19]

In other societies, the roles of priest and king are kept separate. The priest often appears as a shaman-figure[20] who can divine the past, present, and

---

[16] See Ruth Finnegan, *Oral Poetry* pp. 92ff to which we are deeply indebted. See also M. G. Smith, 'The Social Functions and Meaning of Hausa Praise-Singing', *Africa* 27 (1957), pp. 26–43.

[17] See Georges Dumézil, *The Destiny of a King*, trans. Alf Hiltebeitel (Chicago, 1973).

[18] See Jan de Vries, 'Das Königtum bei den Germanen', *Saeculum* 7 (1956), pp. 289–310.

[19] See Bertrand de Jouvenel, 'The Mover and the Adjuster', *Diogenes* 9 (1955), pp. 28–42.

[20] This name, ultimately from Sanskrit, taken from the Tungusic *shaman* through the Russian into Western European languages, applies in its narrow sense to the diviners of Siberia and North America. We are using it here in its broadest sense to cover all kinds of diviners, magicians, and medicine men as well as shamans in the narrower sense of the word.

For the phenomenon, see Mircea Eliade, *Shamanism: Archaic Techniques of Ecstasy*, trans. from the French by Willard R. Trask, Bollingen Series 76 (Princeton, 1964). The

future. He may use ecstatic techniques, or he may divine from bones, livers, flying birds, stone configurations, and the like. In African societies, especially among the sourthern Bantu, the Shaman (who may be either male or female) may be a herbalist or, more frequently, work in conjunction with one. Shamanistic activity can be clearly traced in Western European traditions. According to Stefán Einarsson,[21] for instance, ample evidence for its importance comes from Old Norse Skaldic poetry, the *Eddas*, and the *Heimskringla*. Shamanism and magic here are closely connected with Odin and Vanr. Chant songs of various sorts effect magic and are a particularly important shamanistic activity.[22] Some priests or diviners interpret oracles, as is the case with the Voice of the Karanga, a people of sourthern Rhodesia and around Fort Victoria. The Voice is a kind of Delphic oracle.[23]

The priest and the diviner are considered, above all, to be wise men who understand the nature of things. A beautiful African example of their status is preserved in the Maninka word for sorcerer or magician, *Kunnyine-na*, which means literally 'reason-seeker', he who seeks the reason for things. The craftsman and poet are also regarded as possessing some magic power often as much as priests and diviners. They too are wise men.

The warrior is the hero *par excellence*. Often his weapons are charged with magic. Hatto has argued that the animal figures engraved on extant Germanic swords and shields and the references in early Icelandic and English literature convey the aggressive and defensive power of the designated animals to this armament.[24] He parallels this Germanic custom with the Ainu epic 'where the animals depicted on the sword sheaths leap off to join in the fray.'

The warrior hero is often the *dux* who replaces the *rex* we have written of

original appeared in 1951; the translation is enlarged and corrected. Eliade takes shamanism in the narrow sense of the word although he does make interesting and important comparative references to other cultures besides the Siberian-North American shaman. See also John Andrew Boyle, 'Turkish and Mongol Shamanism in the Middle Ages', *Folklore* 83 (1972), pp. 177–193. See above notes 17 & 12.

On divination, see the recent valuable collection of essays by diverse authors edited by J. P. Vernant *et al.*, *Divination et rationalité, Recherches anthropologiques* (Paris: Editions du Sevil, 1974) and Paul Vicaire, 'Platon et la divination', *Revue des études grecques* 83 (1970), pp. 333–350. See also Robert Flacelière, *Greek Oracles*, trans. Douglas German (London, 1965). (original: Paris, 1961).

[21] See his 'Harp Song, Heroic Poetry (Chadwicks), Greek and Germanic Alternate Singing: Mantic Song in Lapp Legend, Eddas, Sagas and Sturlunga', *Budkavlen* 42 (1963), pp. 13–28.

[22] See G. Kara, *Chants d'un barde mongol* (Bibliotheca orientalis hungarica 12)(Budapest: Akaddmiai Kiado, 1970) for the importance of singing in a Siberian bard's work

[23] See Michael Gelfand, *An African Religion, The Spirit of Nyajena, Case History of a Karanga People* (Cape Town: Wynburg and Johannesburg, 1966). Gelfand also speaks of secret societies in West Africa who are possessed by spirits and report information especially when the ancestors are irritated.

[24] See his 'Snake-swords and Boar-helms in *Beowulf*', *English Studies* 38 (1957), pp. 145–160. The quotation below in the main text is from p. 160.

above. His deeds afford the opportunity for hero-worship and for re-telling that a more quiescent kingly life does not allow. It is not surprising, therefore, that in legend and song he should often replace the more colorless king.[25]

The clothes and armament the warrior wears are often designed to be awesome and fearful. In some societies like those of the southern Bantu, the animal skins and assegais which the court poet in his official role wears seem to reflect the time when he accompanied the warrior into battle, although the present-day *imbongi* (as one of the authors has observed) no longer regards his outfit in this way. The robes which oral poets sometimes wear are also signs of their very special role, for in public societies such these, one's uniform indicates one's status and power, and is part of his public image and a guide to the proper honor to be paid to him.

The charisma of the warrior is manifested in some societies, formerly more common than at present, by the fact that if captured, he may be eaten by his enemies or even, on death, by his own comrades, either of whom wish to participate in and gain his numinous power, or, as we know from Celtic evidence, his head may be preserved for its apotropaic power. We even suspect that epic and heroic poetry, as one of its functions, serves to provide its hearers with an opportunity for participation in the *numen* of the hero or heroes, a step forward from eating him, which has also the advantage in that it may be repeated without difficulty.[26]

When we come to ascertaining the status of the common man, the situation is somewhat obscure because his life is hardly ever remembered in preserved verbal art, although there are vague clues here and there. We can only rely on common sense and on the evidence of present-day traditional societies to gain a picture of his existence. The lives of most people are often lives of toil and misery, but there were some compensations, particularly for the men. The women must have carried the greater burden of existence; still, we suspect even they had their moments of celebration and joy. The poetry of the ordinary people has tended to disappear and has only been recorded relatively recently – in the past two centuries.[27] Their poetic activity was almost certainly not carried on by professional poets but by improvising poets for particular occasions. Their songs and tales were preserved in the mouths of the people, and in some cases, although not without change, down to modern times.

The performance of ritual and semi-ritual poetry that is frequently the task

[25] We are, of course, assuming that the king and warrior are separate persons. This is not always the case. Sometimes the warrior wins his way to the throne and then becomes a fainéant king. His early life is exciting, but his later days are dull and sober.
[26] See Morton W. Bloomfield, 'Understanding Old English Poetry', (1968) reprinted in *Essays and Explorations: Studies in Ideas, Language and Literature* (Cambridge, 1970), p. 69.
[27] For a good example of modern oral collection – in this case of Scottish ballads, see Willa Muir, *Living with Ballads* (London, 1965). For African material, see Richard M. Dorson, ed. *African Folklore* (Bloomington, 1972).

of the court poet is, as we know from contemporary witnesses, complex and full of allure for eye and ear.[28] Both audience and performer share what Scheub calls *core-clichés* and the potential expansible image (which the performer expands). Repetition, as in most early 'poetical' art, is heavily utilized and helps to build up and control the tension which the story or lyric unfolds. As Scheub writes, 'All of the aesthetic tensions in the productions, the repeated images, the surface plot, the song, the dance, are calculated to attract and involve the audience in the developing image' (p. 30). An extraordinary solidarity builds up between narrator and audience.[29]

Although the actual speaking force of the delivery of these primitive poems can only be divined, we may be sure that much of the power and impact of the oral poet came from his eloquence. Eloquence is always prized in early societies, and later, in those societies, such as the Greek and Roman, in which public address was highly honored. Wisdom and eloquence joined together were frequently praised as the ideal combination. Perhaps the best reference to this matter is Cicero's remark at the beginning of his *De inventione*:

> As for me after long thought, I have been led by reason itself to support this opinion first and foremost, that wisdom without eloquence does very little for the good of states, and that eloquence without wisdom is generally very disadvantageous and is never helpful. (our translation)

One of the authors has himself seen an audience struck into a kind of wonder by the elocutionary force of a praise poem. Wisdom must not be hidden in a corner but must persuade and win over. Wisdom must stir people to action and move into the busy streets of life.

Our best information on the primal situation in the Western world comes from early written literatures and, for our purposes here, Old Irish, early Welsh, Old English, and Old Norse. From elsewhere there is massive evidence, too, particularly in the Islamic World, India, Siberia and the Far East; and a relatively recent study[30] has dealt with the late (pre-Islamic) Egyptian scene (especially for wandering poets who lived on patrons and were feared by many). We shall, however, pass over these areas.

Professor Opland in recent years has been pointing to the parallels between Bantu and Old English oral poets (and poetry); and it is to him[31] that we are

---

[28] I am drawing here on Harold Scheub's 'Translation of African Oral Narrative Performances to the Written Word', *Yearbook of Comparative and General Literature* 20 (1971), pp. 28–36. See also his valuable 'The Technique of the Expansible Image in Xhosa *Ntsomi* Performances', *Research on African Literature* 1 (1970), pp. 119–146.

[29] See E. N. Obiechina, 'Transition from oral to literary tradition', *Présence africaine* 63 (1967), p. 148.

[30] See Alan Cameron, 'Wandering Poets: A Literary Movement in Byzantine Egypt', *Historia* 14 (1965), pp. 470–509.

[31] See his '*Scop* and *Imbongi* – Anglo-Saxon and Bantu Oral Poets', *English Studies in*

largely indebted for the picture of the Anglo-Saxon poet, the *scop*, which we shall briefly present here. Throughout the 600 odd years of the Anglo-Saxon rule in England, things no doubt changed. Our main sources, as collected by Opland, are from the earlier poetry. The *scop* was a professional figure who sang for his king or thane and who could on occasion, as *Deor* testifies, lose his position. The oldest preserved English poetry is of an aristocratic and courtly nature, highly structured and most certainly artificial in vocabulary. Opland believes that the harper and the *scop* performed, as Xhosa poets do, without music, although possibly like them in a chanting and characteristically loud voice. There is considerable evidence from councils, poetry (*Béowulf*, *Widsith*, and *Deor*, for instance), and letters that the primal situation of king and bard obtained in pagan English times and continued, modified in varying degrees, down to the Norman Conquest. From Tacitus onwards there is evidence for such a situation among all the Germanic peoples, and in some ways Old Norse preserves more of this Germanic arrangement than Old English. Unferth, the thyle who counselled Hrothgar in *Béowulf*, and the poets who treat of Béowulf's victories over Grendel and Grendel's mother are described vividly in the poem and bear witness to the persistence of early Germanic poetic customs in the seventh or eighth centuries in England, or if recent scholarship is right, down to the late ninth and early tenth centuries. Christianity, when it became dominant, attempted with some success to transmute the role of the pagan tradition, and the details of the surviving features have been obscured. Further back, however, there is much Indo-European evidence, especially among the Celtic and Indian peoples of Indo-European descent, that court poets who sang songs of praise and dispraise and engaged in poetic contests flourished.[32]

The famous Caedmon story in Bede emphasizes the improvisational powers of the inspired poet and implies that such poetry was frequently composed as entertainment at dinner. In the monasteries, of course, the poems were praises of God. The notion here is that God inspires the poet to sing in His honor. In the famous passage at the end of the saint's life *Elene*, Cynewulf speaks of the

Africa 14 (1971), pp. 161–178; '*Beowulf* on the Poet', *Medieval Studies* 38 (1976), pp. 442–467; and *Anglo-Saxon Oral Poetry* (New Haven, 1980). In his *Beowulf* piece note 1, Opland gives a brief bibliography of the earlier work done on the *scop* in English. There are a number of items in German which should also be included, such as Egon Wehrlich, *Des westgermanische Skop, Der Aufbau seiner Dichtung und sein Vortrag*, Inaugural Dissertation ... der Westfälischen Wilhelms-Universität zu Münster (Westf.) (Münster, 1964) (to be used with caution); Piet Wareman, *Spielmandichtung, Versuch einer Begriffsbestimmung*, Academisch Proefschrift ... aan de Universität van Amsterdam ... (Amsterdam, 1951).

[32] See Calvert Watkins, 'The Etymology of Irish *Dúan*', *Celtica* 11 (1976), pp. 270–277. In this article Watkins links this social arrangement with the Irish word *dán* which means 'gift, talent, poetic faculty, craft, possession' and also 'poem'. A poem was a gift in exchange for a more tangible gift, and he links it with the ancient exchange of gifts in early societies, with negative as well as positive implications. See below Chapter 5.

mighty king (*mægencyning*) bestowing on him wisdom, the gift of song-craft (*leodcraeft*, ll. 1241–51). He wove with wordcraft (*wordcraeftum woef*, l. 1237) and composed in his mind poetry.[33] Alcuin (MGH 4 124), in a famous passage repudiating the relation between Ingeld and Christ, speaks of the value of hearing the words of the Fathers at banquets rather than the songs and poems of the pagans (*sermones patrium, non carmina gentilium*).

The imagery of kingship applied to God and Christ is pervasive in the Bible and the writings of the Fathers. To transfer the role of the court poet to that of divine poet was an easy matter. Instead of praising the local chief or king, the poet was to transfer his allegiance to God and Christ, the King of kings.

In Chapter 8 we shall discuss how much of extant Anglo-Saxon literature is illuminated by looking at it in terms of the magical universe of early societies with its great emphasis on wisdom. Anglo-Saxon poetry, like the early poetry of other societies, reflects in some measure, more or less depending upon the particular works dealt with, the functions and social goals it was aimed at fulfilling.

The older Irish and Welsh poetry reflects even more obviously the society from which it arose. Irish court poets, especially the earlier *filid*, were highly trained in 'history' and performed under rigid language restraints. The poet was under the patronage of a chief or king. 'The two are', as Calvert Watkins has remarked, 'in an exchange or reciprocity relation: the poet gives poems of praise to the patron, who in turn bestows largesse upon the poet. The institution is of Indo-European antiquity; exact parallels exist in Indic and Germanic.' A king needed the poets for his fame and honor.[34]

In the first century BC, Diodorus Siculus (5, 31, 2) speaks of Gaulish bards who compose panegyrics and satires. As usual, with Gaulish matters we have little direct evidence, although there is no reason to doubt the truth of his remark, especially since both encomia and satires are plentiful in other Celtic (Irish and Welsh) sources. James Carney[35] describes Eochy O'Hussey of the

---

[33] On the image of weaving for poetic composition, see above Chapter I.

[34] Watkins, *op. cit.*, p. 271. See also E. C. Quiggin, 'Prolegomena to the Study of Later Irish Bards, 1200–1500', *Proceedings of the British Academy* 5 (1911); J. Lloyd-Jones, 'The Court Poets of the Welsh Princes', *Proceedings of the British Academy* 34 (1948); John J. Parry, 'The Court Poets of the Welsh Princes', *PMLA* 67 (1952), pp. 511–520; James Carney, *The Irish Bardic Poet, A Study in the Relationship of Poet and Patron* (Dublin Institute for Advanced Studies) (Dublin, 1967); Brian O Cuív, 'Literary Creation and Irish Historical Tradition', *Proceedings of the British Academy* 49 (1963), pp. 233–262 (on a broader topic but makes a contribution to the understanding of the patronage situation in Ireland); and J. E. Caerwyn Williams, 'The Court Poet in Medieval Ireland', *Proceedings of the British Academy* 57 (1971). Still also valuable is J. Vendryes, *La Poésie de cour en Irlande et en Galles* (Paris, 1932).

Satiric poetry is discussed by F. N. Robinson in his 'Satirists and Enchanters in Early Irish Literature', in *Studies in the History of Religions Presented to Cramford H. Toy*, ed. O. G. Lyon and G. F. Moore (New York, 1912).

[35] See above, note 34.

sixteenth century as an *ollav*, a kind of 'Christianized druid' as he puts it, who would satirize and praise his prince and maintained with him a kind of symbolic wife and husband relationship.

The picture for Wales is similar to that of Ireland.[36] In a late Welsh tale, *Taliesin*, based on early tradition, we find that Elphin, the patron of the bard Taliesin, boasts before Maelgwn Gwynedd of the superiority of his own wife and his own bard. After a comic scene, Taliesin proves his superiority. The story-teller emphasizes in his telling of the tale the importance in his days of bards and heralds.[37]

The medieval Welsh grammatical treatise of Einion the Priest discusses praise–poetry at some length. We also find numerous examples of this important genre,[38] some of which survive from a period perhaps as early as the sixth century.

A similar picture emerges from our information about Old Norse poetry. Here there is emphasis on secret names which the poets know, also found in the *Rig-veda* and early Irish tradition. Watkins in his article on the language of gods and of men[39] refers to the Old Norse *Alvíssmol*. Only the poets know the language of the gods. The notion survives in early Sanskrit and Hittite literature, as well as in the Homeric hymns. Secret names are sources of power, especially for poets. The praise name is the opposite – it is the open name. The secret name is never bandied about.

It is skaldic poetry that preserves most of our Old Norse eulogies, but other information about court poets is available from the *Prose Edda* and from some of the sagas. One thinks of the *Heidreks Saga*,[40] which, in somewhat of a mishmash, combines narrative and wise sayings, and of the Eddic poem *Vafthrudnismal*, with the riddling contest between Odin and the giant Vafthrudnir.[41]

---

[36] See Patrick Ford's 'The Poet as Cyfarwydd in Early Welsh Tradition', in *Studia Celtica* 10/11 (1975/76), pp. 152–162; 'A Fragment of the Hanes Taliesin by Llywelyn Siôn', *Études Celtiques* 14 (1974); 'Welsh *asswynaw* and Celtic Legal Idiom', *The Bulletin of the Board of Celtic Studies* 16 (1975), pp. 147ff; and above all his *Poetry of Llywarch Hen* (Berkeley and Los Angeles, 1974).

[37] See *The Mabinogion*, trans. Lady Charlotte Guest (London: Everyman's Library, 1906), p. 269. For a reliable modern translation, see Ford's *Mabinogi and Other Welsh Tales* (Berkeley and Los Angeles, 1977). See further, below, chap. 5.

[38] An early fifteenth-century grammatical treatise presents a hierarchy of things to be praised (printed along with Einion's treatise in G. J. Williams and E. J. Jones edition of *Gramadegau Penceirddiaid* [Cardiff, 1934] and discussed in the Foreword, p. xli). For a translation, see *A Book of Wales*, ed. D. M. and E. M. Lloyd (London and Glasgow, 1953), pp. 102–104.

[39] See his 'Language of Gods and Language of Men: Remarks on Some Indo-European Metalinguistic Traditions', in *Myth and Law Among the Indo-Europeans*, ed. Jaan Puhvel (Berkeley, 1970).

[40] Christopher Tolkien ed. and trans., *The Saga of King Heidrek the Wise* (London, 1960).

[41] Available in English in Patricia Terry trans., *Poems of the Vikings: The Elder Edda* (Indianapolis and New York, 1969), pp. 39–48.

The *Hávamál*, another wisdom poem from the *Poetic Edda*, which is a repository of gnomic sayings, remarks:

> Cattle die, kinsmen die,
> one day you die yourself;
> but the words of praise will not perish
> when a man wins fair fame.[42]

The survival of patronage continues in modified form in the West well beyond the early Middle Ages. Its survival in the most primitive form is to be found, as already indicated, among the Celtic peoples, certainly until the seventeenth and eighteenth centuries and even perhaps down to today. This form was a basic kind of patronage based upon personal relations between the bard and his chieftain, with each giving fair exchange. This personal element continued in England until the late Middle Ages.[43]

Later, the relation between patron and poet lost its magic, and patronage tended to become more impersonal, even if the patron did gain some praise for supporting letters and culture. Patronage of this latter sort was common in England down into the early nineteenth century. Governments on the Continent and even, to a mild degree, in Great Britain (with the giving of a small pension to superannuated writers) continue this practice down to today. In the United States, the government until quite recently stood resolute against patronage of the arts, but private foundations such as the Carnegie Endowment, which supported medieval publications until the late 1920s, often helped to publish expensive but valuable editions of older literary and other works.

In 1967, however, the establishment of the National Endowment for the Arts and Humanities brought the American government into the active role of patron. In Canada, the Canada Council had been active since the end of the second World War in supporting similar projects.

It should be noted that painting and sculpture have, since the eighteenth century, been able to obtain much more support than the literary arts, probably because until recently inexpensive reproductions were difficult to make, a situation which reduced popular support. Patrons liked to have their appearance in paint. In the nineteenth century, however, the development of a large literate public made a potential market for books possible. Music, even down to today, has also had to struggle for patronage. The nineteenth-century taste for large orchestras made musical support expensive, and symphony orchestras and opera still struggle for support.

The counterpart to the patron with its publishers and expert readers is the

---

[42] *Ibid.*, p. 24.
[43] See Karl Julius Holzknecht, *Literary Patronage in the Middle Ages* (Philadelphia, 1923), mainly confined to Great Britain.

profession of literature.[44] In early societies, as we have seen, there were semi-professional men of letters as well as amateurs, but with the gradual decline of patronage, any kind of professional *littérateurs* found support difficult. The rise of journalism helped a little, but it also created Grub Street.

The professional writers today, especially poets, like their *imbongi* and bardic ancestors, are dependent either on patronage (usually from the government or the Guggenheim Foundation) or on an appreciative audience which will buy their books. The poets of the Romantic movement tended to look down on patronage, seemingly unaware of its necessity in one form or another. In any case, unlike their praise-singing prototypes, modern writers need not sing too loudly for their supper. A quiet acknowledgement in a preface and an adequate number of buyers are enough. Although the practice of patronage has changed, it still continues to this very day, now in a less humiliating form but also in a somewhat less tightly knit social relationship.

---

[44] See J. W. Saunders, *The Profession of English Letters* (London and Toronto, 1964). For more limited treatments of the subject, see Phoebe Sheavyn, *The Literary Profession in the Elizabethan Age* (Manchester, 1909); Edwin Haviland Miller, *The Professional Writer in England, A Study of Nondramatic Literature* (Cambridge, 1959); and Alexandre Beljame, *Men of Letters and the English Public in the Eighteenth Century, 1660–1744, Dryden, Addison, Pope*, ed. Bonamy Dobrée and trans. E. O. Lorimer (London, 1948) (French original 1881, second edition, 1897).

CHAPTER 3

EARLY IRISH LITERATURE

1. ANCIENT IRELAND

The earliest and most extensive surviving remains of a native vernacular literature in Western Europe are those recorded in Ireland. Some features of this early literature and of early Irish society in general are indeed so archaic that they clearly reflect peripheral survivals of Indo-European culture which are actually paralleled by similar archaic survivals in the most ancient Vedic and later Sanskrit traditions of India.[1]

Early Irish literature is the product of an ancient culture, and, at its most archaic, it mirrors a once coherent Celtic way of life less affected than one might expect by the introduction into Ireland of Christianity (in the fifth century), by the Viking invasions (from 825 on), and even by the Anglo-Norman Conquest of Ireland (in the twelfth century). Inevitably the new religion, the new invaders, and the new conquerors all wrought profound changes upon Ireland; and the actual manuscript records of the native literature are for the most part comparatively late in date of compilation (usually not earlier than the twelfth century), and their contents have been subjected to considerable revision. Yet the native custodians of the oral tradition were loath to discard their lore, which earlier they had transmitted orally and which at last they – somewhat anxiously perhaps – set down in writing lest it be lost. Hence, Irish manuscripts provide an unrivaled source of information about an early Western culture that reflects what we have reconstructed as the 'primal situation'.

The tribes of Ireland were – at least, ideally speaking – ruled by tribal kings and guided by tribal priests, historians, lawyers, and soothsayers, all of whom were accepted as masters of word-craft and word-magic. The welfare of the tribe was dependent upon the king's ability to maintain *fír*, 'the truth' – a word cognate with the Latin *verum* that gave us the English word 'veracity' and implied a sense of rightfulness and a capacity to render justice. If the king

---

[1] See Myles Dillon, *Celts and Aryans: survivals of Indo-European Speech and Society* (Simla: Indian Institute of Advanced Study, 1975), where earlier cross-cultural references may be found. See above chap. 1, note 24.

committed a 'lie' (*gáu*), he lost 'face' (*enech*), his tribe and territory suffered, and he had to be replaced, for he was expected to be the living embodiment of wisdom and tradition.[2]

The officers of state were tied to the welfare of the tribe by binding legal privileges and obligations, for the king himself rewarded them with 'treasures and wealth', and they in return applied their knowledge of the past, present, and future to the support of the king and thus to the protection of the tribe.

All members of the tribe were bound by the requirements of a behavior that was arbitrarily prescribed by their traditional understanding of what was 'proper' (*cóir*). Thus, for instance, unless the story-tellers are fabricating a tradition, it was tabu for the men of Ulster to speak before their king had spoken, and for their king to speak before his druids,[3] just as even today in Britain, protocol requires that the Queen must initiate every conversation in which she engages. The picture which we gain from early Irish legends of pre-Christian times reflects a highly ceremonious, regulated, and archaistic tribal life, dependent for its stability just as much upon the might of the word as upon the might of the sword.

There is much that we do not know about early Irish rituals and ceremonies, but we do at least know something about the range of the verbal utterances associated with them. How to interpret these is often a question, and in that attempt we may well turn to a schematic categorization of the principal functions of the verbal artificers who as custodians of wisdom served the tribe in traditional capacities and sustained society by the magical power of their words.

In order to sift the evidence, we have in Diagrams A, B, and C separated the functions of the various kinds of verbal utterances, discussed generally in our previous and ensuing chapters, according to whether they pertain chiefly to (a) the past, (b) the present, or (c) the future. Hence, for instance, laws are here classified as pertaining to the present, although they are built on the customs and the authority of the past and in fact pertain to the future of those for whom they are adduced.

In function, generally speaking, utterances pertaining to the past are exemplary, utterances pertaining to the present are regulative, and utterances pertaining to the future are projective. Cumulatively they serve to transform the inchoate experiences of life into some kind of pattern. They place the tribe within the cosmos; they establish norms; and they suggest certain ways of controlling events. They represent society's method of sharing and trans-mitting experience by means of stereotypical applications of tribal wisdom uttered by those appointed authorities whose status endorses their validity.

[2] See Philip T. O'Leary, Jr., *Honor and Ethics in the Ulster Cycle* (Harvard doctoral thesis, Cambridge, Mass., 1978), typescript, chap. 6, and footnote references.
[3] For references see Tom P. Cross, *Motif-Index of Early Irish Literature* (Indiana Univ. Folklore Series no. 7)(Bloomington, Ind., 1952), motif C402.1.

Applications of Wisdom

Sphere	Past	Present	Future
sacral	1 myths, origins	4 invocations	.7 prophecies
regal	2 genealogies, annals, legends, lays	5 laws, poems of praise and dispraise, counsels	8 spells, oaths, blessings, curses
tribal	3 [tales]	6 gnomic lore, [work-songs]	9 charms

Diagram A: Pre-Christian Ireland

In the diagrams, utterances have been stratified according to whether they apply primarily to the sphere of the sacral (that is, the realm of the gods and other supernatural beings), or to the sphere of the regal (that is, the sphere of the ruler along with his regal ancestors and successors, whose ancestry may reach back to the gods), or to the sphere of the tribal (which includes: the ruler at the human level; other high ranking members of society such as warriors; professionals such as poets, priests, and doctors; and artisans, farmers, serfs, and even slaves).[4]

Because of the fragmentary nature of the sources, we must add that this inventory cannot pretend to be exhaustive, and square brackets have been used to indicate categories for which the evidence is merely presumptive.

Myths and Origins (1)   As an example of the kinds of materials that survive, under Category 1, myth is well represented by *The Book of Invasions* and *The Second Battle of Moytura*.[5] Despite the fact that the earliest version of *The Book of Invasions* was not recorded until the twelfth century, the work contains not only a mass of antiquarian inventions but also a remarkable mythological core that presumably reflects what must once have been part of a coherent concept of a Celtic pantheon. Typical is the following description of the war between the Fir Bolg and the Túatha Dé Danann:

> Now Nuadu of the Silver Hand was the king of the Túatha Dé Danann for seven years before they came to Ireland, and his arm was cut off in the first battle of Moytura. . . . Bres the son of Elada then took the kingship of Ireland for seven years until Nuadu's arm was

---

[4] For a concise summary of the social structure see D. A. Binchy, 'Secular Institutions', in *Early Irish Society*, ed. Myles Dillon (Dublin, 1954), pp. 52–65.

[5] For convenient excerpts of the mythological material and for further bibliography, see Tom P. Cross and C. H. Slover, *Ancient Irish Tales*, rev. Charles W. Dunn (New York, 1969) [hereafter *AIT*], pp. 3–27, 28–48, 602.

healed. Then Nuadu of the Silver Hand ruled for twenty years. He had an arm of silver, with the full strength of either hand in each finger and each joint, provided for him by Dían Cécht the physician and Creidne the artisan.[6]

The stark, terse, and almost offhand style of the written record obviously reflects the attitude of a Christian scribe who feels obliged to preserve his ancestors' pagan traditions but does not wish to endorse them; in the pre-Christian period, however, such myths were doubtlessly recited as matters of belief and were probably reinforced by ritual dramas and by a processional display of carved or sculptured representations of the gods. In fact, with regard to this particular passage, archaeology does provide some evidences of an actual cult associated with the god Nuadu, corroborating the written evidence; but what is significant is the fact that the myths imbedded in *The Book of Invasions* and in *The Second Battle* still reveal in their structure, as might be expected, the pre-Christian Irish conception of human origins and the value-system of the society which created them.

Genealogies, Annals, Legends, Lays (2)   Custodians of sacral lore understandably also served as custodians of royal genealogies and of legends and their related lays (Category 2). The functions of the *senchaid* (in modernized anglicized form 'shenachie') were numerous. He was held responsible for knowing about all things that were old (*sen*, cognate with Latin *senex*, 'one who is old'), and his responsibilities included even serving as a witness in disputes about real-estate, since presumably he would know the history of the transmission of the property.

Buttressed by such traditional authority, even as late as in a twelfth-century manuscript, several genealogies of the leading families in Ireland still claim the god Nuadu of the Silver Hand as an ancestor,[7] despite the fact that such genealogies were subsumed within the Christian antiquarians' all-embracing Biblical schematizations of the origin of the Gaels. The annals that recorded passing events also became, as they reached back into history, the repository of the legendary lore of the story-tellers.

At some unidentifiable period, the role of the 'shenachie' was supplemented by that of the *scélaige*, the 'news-bringer', the 'story-teller', and, perhaps because of this additional support, pre-Christian legends of superhuman

[6] *Lebor Gabála Érenn*, ed. trans. R. A. S. MacAlister (Irish Texts Society 41)(Dublin, 1941), IV, 112–115. (The mythical material is interwoven into an invented antiquarian account of the origin, wanderings, and arrival of the Gaels in Ireland.) For the traditions attached to Nuadu, see *Cath Maige Tuired: The Second Battle of Mag Tuired*, ed. trans. Elizabeth A. Gray (Irish Texts Society 52)(Dublin, 1982), pp. 135–1131.
[7] *Corpus Genealogiarum Hiberniae*, ed. M. A. O'Brien (Dublin, 1976) [hereafter *CGH*], pp. 714 (index) and, for instance, p. 137 (line 140 b 1). On Nuadu-Nodons, see Anne Ross, *Everyday Life of the Pagan Celts* (London, 1970), pp. 32, 120, 172.

heroes and of dynastic founders, fictitious in origin, have survived in profusion not only among the earliest remains of Irish recorded literature but also in late renditions. Among the heroes of these narratives, the most celebrated are Cú Chulainn and Finn mac Cumhail. Cú Chulainn is represented as the human incarnation of Sétanta, the son of the god Lug, and his exploits are celebrated in a whole cycle of legends glorifying Ulster, and these legends in turn have been spliced into the annals that were compiled in the Christian period.[8] Finn, who was also once regarded as a god, similarly became the hero of the vast Fenian cycle of tales which were once respected as 'pre-history' and were later cherished as adventure tales.[9]

Many of the tales which became attached to popular narrative cycles were probably invented long after the coming of Christianity to Ireland, but some of the surviving legends concerning Irish kings presumably reflect the activities of pre-Christian story-tellers who were rewarded by their patrons for their ability in collecting, arranging, and even inventing traditions concerning regal ancestors.[10] Indeed, so enthusiastically did the professional legend-makers perform their services that they also composed heroic lays related to their legends and invented stories concerning innumerable Irish place-names associated with gods, kings, queens, heroes, and heroines.[11] Since the past was so intimately related to the present, they saw to it that nothing should be left arbitrary or unexplained.

A brief excerpt may suffice to illustrate their approach to their traditions. A strange tale known as *The Adventures of Art Son of Conn* tells us, among other things, how Conn of the Hundred Battles (Conn Cétchathach) tried to maintain his sovereignty by finding a second wife after his first wife had died. The reporting of the tale is confused, but the story-tellers had important reasons for telling it. Conn was the eponymous founder of the Connaught dynasty; his name appears in many distinguished genealogies, as does that of his son Art mac Cuinn. The following passage, in which the story-teller comments on the death of Conn's first wife, is typical of the circumstantial and almost matter-of-fact style of such narratives:

> After their living a long time together, Ethne died and was buried with honor in Tailltiu, for Tailltiu was one of the three chief burial-places of Ireland, which were the Fair of Tailltiu [Teltown in Ulster], and the Brug [in Meath] beside the Boyne, and the cemetery of Cruachu [Rathcroghan in Connaught].
> And he was dejected on account of his wife Ethne's death, and it weighed so heavily on him that he was unable any longer to rule or

[8] John V. Kelleher, 'The Táin and the Annals', *Ériu* 22 (1971), 107–127.
[9] See *Duanaire Finn*, ed. Gerard Murphy (Irish Texts Society, 43)(Dublin, 1953), III, pp. xi-lxxxvii
[10] See Myles Dillon, *The Cycles of the Kings* (Oxford, 1946).
[11] See, for instance, *AIT*, pp. 596–599, 606.

govern the kingdom. And there was lacking to Ireland at that time one thing only, that the king of Ireland should find a helpmate worthy of him in her stead.[12]

The story-teller may seem to lack a sense of drama, but he does understand his audience's deeply rooted concern that a king must be whole and complete. He knows their interest in the pre-Christian traditions of the sacred places of Ireland, and he adds authority to his narrative by mentioning the names of the three eminent sites located in Ulster, Meath, and Connaught that are celebrated elsewhere in surviving place-name poems and prose accounts. Then in the ensuing narrative he records the incidents associated with the legend of Art, not so much for the sake of their bizarre flavor as for their tribal significance.

Tales (3) Under Category 3, the diagram for pre-Christian Ireland also allows a place for tales such as have always circulated orally throughout the world – the popular folk-tales that deal with heroes and heroines living in a never-never-land. In early Ireland, such tales presumably seemed too unimportant to be worthy of being recorded in writing, despite the fact that they served the exemplary and even magical function implicit in story-telling. Nevertheless, it may be assumed that story-tellers in early days narrated them with the same enthusiasm that the modern Irish and Scottish Gaelic 'shenachies' bestow upon similar tales today.

Invocations (4) To exemplify the categories of verbal utterance that pertain to the pre-Christian invocations addressed by Irish druids to their gods is tantalizingly difficult. Classical Greek and Roman writers have recorded their own extensive observations of the Celtic rituals, ceremonies, and customs that were characteristically associated with verbal magic, but they have not preserved the actual utterances of the participants.

Writing in Rome on the basis of hearsay, Pliny the Elder reports that the Celts in Britain are 'fascinated by magic', adding that Britain 'performs her rites with so much ceremony that it almost seems as though it was she who had imparted the cult [of magic] to the Persians'.[13] And no doubt he would have said something to the same effect concerning the Celts in Ireland if he had visited them. Other classical ethnographers have commented in detail, for instance, on such matters as human and animal sacrifices and on the ceremonies connected with the inauguration of kings. The ritual invocations associated with such occasions, however, have for the most part been lost for ever.

[12] *AIT*, p. 491.
[13] Pliny, *Natural History*, 30:13.

At least one early Irish pagan invocation, though recorded after the Christianization of Ireland, does, however, preserve some lines that exemplify what such appeals to the supernatural powers probably sounded like:

> I call on the seven daughters of the sea
> Who shape the threads of long life.
> May three-fold deaths be taken from me,
> May three-fold lives be given to me,
> May seven waves of plenty be poured for me. . . .
>
> I call on Senach of the Seven Lives
> Whom fairy women suckled on propitious breasts.
> May my seven candles not be quenched'.[14]

This mysterious invocation has been in part christianized, but the surviving text still reflects pagan belief. The three-fold death referred to is an international motif associated with the prophecy, well-known in Irish legend, that a hero will die as the result of a fatal sequence of three improbable events.[15] The three-fold lives could possibly be equivalent to the miraculous process of three-fold birth, described in the Old Irish tale entitled *The Birth of Cú Chulainn*, through which Cú Chulainn was eventually ushered into the court of Ulster.[16]

The seven candles, though reminiscent of the symbolic seven-branched candlestick referred to both in the Old and in the New Testaments, may, in fact, be in some way connected with the Irish attributes of regal power.[17] And the deity invoked by the name of Senach bears a name that is presumably derived from the Old Irish root *sen*, meaning 'aged', which thus implies the notion of a divine protector of age-old lineages.[18]

Laws, Poems of Praise and Dispraise, Counsels (5) Despite their archaism, copious materials pertaining to this wide-ranging Category 5 are remarkably well preserved, especially within the sub-category of the laws. Some of the surviving early Irish laws perpetuate traditions that presumably were shared

---

[14] *A Golden Treasury of Irish Poetry*, ed. David Greene and Frank O'Connor (London, 1967), p. 35.
[15] References in T. P. Cross, *Motif-Index of Early Irish Literature*, M 341.2.4.2.*
[16] Cross, *Motif-Index*, A 511.9.*
[17] Reference to the seven-branched candlestick occur in Ex.25:31–40 and Rev. 1:12. One of the references under *caindel* in the Royal Irish Academy, *Dictionary of the Irish Language* [hereafter *RIAD*], is obviously Christian (Blathm. 222), but another citation (Laws IV, 52.9) is possibly archaic; compare Kathleen Hughes, *Early Christian Ireland* (Ithaca, N. Y., 1972), p. 56.
[18] See Patrick K. Ford, 'Llywarch', *Speculum* 45 (1970), 442–450, for a discussion of the significance of the word *hen* in Welsh and *sen* in Irish in genealogies. See also below, chap. 4, footnote 13.

in common by Indo-European peoples even before the migration of the Celts to Ireland. At an early stage such legal lore was customarily cast in metrical form and was handed down orally. The anonymous author of the preface to the collection of Irish legal traditions known as 'The Major Tradition', the *Senchas Mór*, asserts that Fergus the Poet-seer (*fili*) and Dubthach Maccu Lugair 'put a thread of poetry' around this corpus, and there are indeed passages of an archaic metrical type within the *Senchas*, as there are in other early Irish law tracts. And a later commentator unwittingly emphasizes the antiquity of the contents of this material when he writes concerning the traditional custodians of the oral tradition:

> It was only necessary for them to exhibit from memory what their predecessors had chanted, and then it was corrected in the presence of Patrick according to the written Law which Patrick brought with him.[19]

Whatever corrections the introduction of Patrick's 'written' Christian Law may have wrought, the kinship between the surviving early Irish recorded material and other Indo-European codes is unmistakable.

The judges or 'brehons' (Irish *breithem*, pl. *breithemain*) who had memorized the ancient lore were respected for their possession of esoteric knowledge, and at the same time because of their importance they were socially constrained, just as the poet-seers were, to tell the truth. If a brehon rendered a false judgment, blotches would appear on his face, just as would happen to a poet if he recited an unjustified satire. Some notion of their status is suggested by the early poem concerning Judges[20] which begins with a praise of their function:

> Hail to the judge's judgment,
> mighty and doubly secured.

At this same high level of importance, court poets were expected to produce eulogies of kings and rulers, laments for their deaths coupled with congratulations to their successors, and satires against their enemies.

Of all the survivals of Celtic verbal utterance, the poetry of praise and dispraise is the most fully and extensively documented. One Greek traveler, for example (writing around 50 BC), notes that the bards of Gaul 'compose praises for some and satires on others and chant them to the accompaniment of a kind of lyre.' Another Greek commentator provides an illustrative story. Once when a king threw a bag of gold as a reward to a Gaulish bard, the poet replied extemporaneously:

[19] *Ancient Laws of Ireland*, ed. W. N. Hancock (Dublin, 1865), I, 22–25; see D. A. Binchy, 'The Pseudo-historical Prologue to the *Senchas Már*', *Studia Celtica* 10/11 (1975/76), 14–28.

[20] Calvert Watkins, 'Indo-European Metrics', *Celtica* 6 (1963), 242; Charles W. Dunn, 'Celtic', in *Versification: Major Language Types*, ed. W. K. Wimsatt (New York, 1972), p. 137.

> The tracks of your chariot on the ground
> Bring gold and benefits to men.

This reply, so characteristic of later impromptu Celtic versifying and of Celtic panegyrics in particular, is recorded in Greek prose translation, but the original was presumably composed in the metrical form appropriate to Gaulish encomiastic verse, all trace of which has otherwise been lost.[21]

Many such praise and dispraise poems survive in Ireland, where they comprise a major literary genre, as they probably once did in Gaul.[22] As an example one may quote a poem celebrating the first thirty-five kings of Leinster (attributed to a poet who flourished around 400 AD, though it is recorded in language which cannot belong to a period earlier than the seventh century):

> It behooves me not to forget
> The destinies of every famous king,
> The reigns of the kings of Tara,
> Innumerable hosts on the march.

> A noble battle-hero, fair and tall,
> Was Labraid Loingseach Maín,
> A battle-ready lion, a praise-worthy companion,
> A powerful helper in time of combat.

The poet continues in similar vein for a total of twenty-two stanzas, concluding:

> They were blood-red battle-victors
> Over neighboring hosts most powerful;
> Unscathed they hurled their spears from Tara's slopes,
> Those radiant heroes.[23]

Another early example of an Irish praise poem, non-Christian in its conventional reference to the 'gods and non-gods', is in its form and language typical of the same immutable bardic tradition. Its eight stanzas are addressed to Aed son of Diarmait (presumably a claimant to the throne of Leinster early in the ninth century):

---

[21] The references are to Diodorus Siculus (5, 31.2) and to Athenaeus (4, 37); they are discussed in a wider context in J. J. Tierney, 'The Celtic Ethnography of Posidonius', *Proceedings of the Royal Irish Academy*, 60 (1960), 203, 248; 206, 251, respectively. For the name *Louvernios* or *Louerios*, see Strabo (4.2.3).

[22] For the role of the Irish poet, see J. E. Caerwyn Williams, 'The Court Poet in Medieval Ireland', *Proc. of the British Academy* 57 (1972).

[23] Kuno Meyer, ed. trans., 'Über die älteste irische Dichtung', *Abhandlungen der königl. preuss. Akademie der Wissenschaften*, Phil.-hist. Classe, 6 (Berlin, 1913), 14–25. Also in *CGH*, pp. 8–9. For 'Maín', see *RIAD*, M 35.86–36.6.

The son of Diarmait, dear to me, –
  If it were asked, not hard to tell –
The praise of him, more beauteous than treasures,
  Will be exalted in lays by me. . . .

The sovereignty is his heritage,
  Every favor from gods and non-gods. . . .

At the ale-drinking, odes are chanted;
  The fine steps of genealogy are scaled;
Sweet poems extol,
  Over pools of liquor, the name of Aed.[24]

Eulogy such as this served a serious purpose, especially at a solemn occasion such as an inauguration. It was not primarily intended to be flattering, for its function was, as is so often the case in praise poetry, not so much personal as social. It not only related a ruler to his ancestors but also related the entire tribe to those ancestors. It could magically create a metaphorical image of the ruler as one who was potentially more impressive and supportive than the real hero himself. To call Labraid Loinseach a lion was to make him a lion, and to provide the members of the tribe with a lion in time of need was to guarantee their invincibility.[25]

Conversely, to satirize an enemy was to destroy him and thus, again, to save the tribe. In early Irish tradition, a satire could cause a king to waste away; it could cause a victim to melt; it could raise blotches on his face; it could cause human deformities; it could kill animals; and it could make the land sterile. Equitably, also, it could recoil on the satirist himself, if he uttered an undeserved satire, and at the least raise blotches on his face or even cause his death.[26]

We may reasonably assume that Irish poets frequently resorted to the dangerous art of satire, although relatively few examples of their poems, whether early or late, have been recorded. The reason for their scarcity is clear. To preserve a satire in written form would be somewhat like recording for all time the unpublished evidence relating to a political murder, for the satirist possessed a verbal weapon which could kill his victim, not by spilling his blood but by destroying his acceptability within the tribe. An analogous

[24] *Thesaurus Palaeohibernicus*, ed. Whitley Stokes and John Strachan (reprint, Dublin, 1975), II, 295; see Eleanor Knott, *Irish Classical Poetry* (Dublin, 1957), pp. 53–54. The subject of the poem might be the 'Aed m. Diarmata m. Tuidgcc' of the Uí Maine, listed in *CGH*, p. 172.

[25] On primitive metaphor, see James W. Fernandez, 'Persuasions and Performances', *Daedalus*, no. 101 (1972), pp. 53–54.

[26] For instances and bibliography, see Cross, *Motif-Index*, motif M 400.1; F. N. Robinson, 'Satirists and Enchanters in Early Irish Literature', in *Studies in the History of Religions Presented to Crawford Howell Toy*, ed. D. G. Lyon and G. F. Moore (New York, 1912), and reprinted as *Reprints in Irish Studies* 1 (American Committee for Irish Studies, n.p., n.d.); and R. C. Elliott, *The Power of Satire* (Princeton, 1960).

political process of this sort is, after all, still familiar. A compromising tape is discovered; an editor publishes the contents; and the villain, unmasked, looses his credibility.

The antiquarian author of *The Second Battle of Moytura* provides us with a paradigm of Celtic satire. He claims that the first satire composed in Ireland was based on a complaint directed against the mythological king of the Fomorians, named Bres. The king, ignoring the obligations of his royal status, was notoriously and unforgivably inhospitable. His guests 'found no grease on their dinner-knives', and 'their breath never carried away from his banquets the smell of ale'.[27] A poet named Coirpre belonging to another mythological tribe, the Tuatha De Danann, visited Bres. He was insulted by the niggardly treatment he received, for a poet would lose face if he were not publicly rewarded. Indignantly he resorted to his permitted remedy and hurled a brief but sufficient satire against Bres. Here it stands, freely translated:

> Lacking food that's promptly served,
> Lacking milk to feed the calves,
> Lacking shelter while darkness lingers,
> Lacking the support of chroniclers,
>   May that be the fate of Bres!'

Coirpre then declared – to translate his words literally – 'The prosperity of Bres now no longer is'; that is to say, 'it no longer exists; it has ceased to be.' And, the storyteller adds, from that time on there was nothing but blight upon Bres.

Technically, the words of the satire here recorded should perhaps be classified as a curse, but the relationship between the king who does not maintain the *fír*, the truth, and the justified poet who uses the truth against him is classic. The myth reflects precisely the major function of the many real-life satires which must have constantly reverberated in the honor-conscious, face-saving world of the Celts.[28]

A secondary aspect of satire, not, as it happens, represented in Coirpre's verse, is that it frequently contains extensive passages of unqualified vituperation directed against an enemy of the poet's patron or even, at a lower level, against an enemy of the poet. Typical is the blast directed by an unknown satirist against a victim named Dallan:

> Oh Dallan, you undistinguished, luckless man,
> You warped, wither-handed, shaggy-dog-haired, twisted one!'[29]

Rulers were not only praised and dispraised by the poets; they were also counseled by sages. In the Mirror for Princes attributed to Morann, for

---

[27] *AIT*, p. 33; *Cath Maige Tuired*, ed. trans. E. A. Gray, §§ 36–39, and note on line 172.
[28] See O'Leary, *Honor*, pp. 148–151.
[29] Vivian Mercier, *The Irish Comic Tradition* (Oxford, 1962), p. 114.

instance, the ruler is warned that he must preserve the truth, for nature itself depends upon his integrity. This text was probably compiled around 700 AD, but the following archaic passage is even earlier and is quite untouched by Christian tradition:

> It is through the justice (*fír*) of the ruler that plagues and great lightnings are kept from the people, ... that he secures peace, tranquillity, joy, ease, and comfort, ... that every heir plants his house-post in his fair inheritance, ... that abundance of fish swim in the streams.[30]

Here the poet asserts the universally held belief that the ruler who is totally just can maintain a perfect balance within the whole realm of nature.

Gnomic Lore, Work-Songs (6)   At the tribal level (6), wisdom pertaining to the present is represented particularly by proverbs and other gnomic lore such as that contained in riddles (which are, in a functional sense, proverbs couched in the interrogative mode) and presumably also by work-songs. Gnomic lore states what is customary (Irish *gnáth*, that is, 'well known', hence 'natural') and, by implication, what is therefore appropriate and even socially requisite. A clear and characteristic example of the proverb (or 'old saying', *sen-fhocul*, as it is called in Old Irish) occurs in *The Cattle-Raid of Cooley* when the wounded hero Cú Chulainn, alone in battle, laments his lack of support:

> This is a proverb for many generations:
> 'A single log does not catch fire.'
> If there were two or three of them,
> The firebrands would blaze.[31]

Some proverbs were arranged in the triads that are common to 'list science', as were items of legal and other kinds of information. Typical is the triadic gnome:

> Three slender things that best support the world: the slenderness of a jet of milk in the milking pail, the slenderness of a blade of corn on the face of the land, the slenderness of a thread over the fist of a good wife.[32]

At the non-heroic level, and sometimes even at the heroic level, the Irish also indulged extensively in the curious proverbial trick equivalent to the

---

[30] *Audacht Morainnn*, ed. trans. Fergus Kelley (Dublin, 1976), pp. 6–7 (§§ 12, 14, 16, 20).
[31] *Táin Bó Cúalngne from the Book of Leinster*, ed. trans. Cecile O'Rahilly (Dublin, 1967), pp. 55, 195 (lines 2040–2043).
[32] Kuno Meyer, *The Triads of Ireland* (Royal Irish Academy: Todd Lecture Series, 13)(Dublin, 1906).

English use of phrases referring to self-defeating activities such as 'bringing coals to Newcastle'. These metaphors of fatuity, as they might be called, were used playfully, for instance, in the twelfth-century parody *The Vision of Mac Con Glinne*, a phantom who appears before the hero of the tale says that the futile warning he has given the hero was merely equivalent to:

> Mocking a beggar,
> Dropping a stone on a tree,
> Whispering to the deaf,
> A legacy to a glum man.[33]

Such an example, of course, does not serve to illustrate the more serious applications of the gnomic tradition, but undoubtedly in ancient Ireland proverbs contributed to the sum of everyman's wisdom just as they still do in many parts of the world today.

At a more ingenious level, the gnomic tradition is also illustrated by the Irish triads, as for example in the epigram, also characteristic of 'list science':

> Three smiles that are worse than grief: the smile of snow as it melts, your wife's smile at you after she's slept with somebody else, and the smile of a dog as it leaps.[34]

Riddles may also be found in early Irish texts, such as in *The Wooing of Emer* at the point when the incomparable Cú Chulainn first meets the aristocratic young lady whom he seeks as his wife. In their brisk conversation, Emer, as is appropriate for a well-instructed heroine, immediately understands all the hidden meanings of his references and is able to answer him with correspondingly esoteric phrases. When, for instance, Emer asks what was cooked for him during his journey, he replies, 'The violation of a chariot', referring – as best modern scholars can guess – to a 'foal', which of course could not effectively be harnessed to a war-chariot. When Emer replies to Cú Chulainn's questions, her responses are equally enigmatic, as when she states that she is 'a Tara of women, a fairness of girls, a paragon (?) of chastity'.[35]

Riddling of this aristocratic sort was an Indo-European art cultivated among the Irish as seriously as in other cognate cultures such as that of India, and Emer's training is strikingly reminiscent of that specified in the *Kama Sutra*, which requires that a girl should study 'solutions of riddles, enigmas, covert speeches, verbal puzzles, and enigmatical questions'.[36]

In the perspective of later tradition it seems justifiable also to assume that

---

[33] *Aislinge Meic Conglinne*, ed. trans. Kuno Meyer (London, 1892; rpt. New York, 1974), pp. 70–71.

[34] Meyer, *Triads*, no. 91.

[35] *Compert Con Culainn and Other Stories*, ed. A. G. van Hamel (Mediaeval and Modern Irish Series 3)(Dublin, 1933), p. 26 (chap. 17), p. 27 (chap. 18).

[36] *The Kama Sutra of Vatsyayana*, trans. Sir Richard Burton (London, 1963), p. 109.

sowing and reaping, rowing and fishing, milking and churning, and such basic activities were lightened by the accompaniment of work-songs. As might be expected, no early popular examples of these mundane folksongs seem to have been recorded, but Mider's poem in *The Wooing of Étaín*, addressed as it is to supernatural helpers, can be thought of as a magical counterpart. When the reluctant creatures of the elf-mounds are forced to labor over the making of a road, they recite:

> Put in hand, throw in hand,
> Excellent oxen, in the hours after sunset.
> Unduly hard is this exaction.
> No one knows whose is the gain and whose the loss
> From the roadway over Móin Lamraige.[37]

Prophecies (7) To acquire a knowledge of the future and thus benefit from it is surely a most human and universal desire, and, not surprisingly, early Irish literature provides many instances of prophecies and hopeful interpretation of coming events. In pre-Christian Ireland, the poets exercised a special art of divination similar to that practiced by shamans elsewhere in the world. Cormac mac Cuilennáin reports in his *Glossary* that the poet-seer (*fili*) would chew the raw flesh of a pig or a dog or a cat (any one of which if eaten raw would presumably be tabu for human consumption) and would sing an incantation over it and would offer it, along with another invocation, to the gods, who in turn would reveal the future to the poet while he slept.[38]

A particularly dramatic manifestation of this prophetic art appears in the Irish epic *The Cattle-Raid of Cooley*, though the story-teller does not describe the preliminary process. The imperious queen Medb of Connaught asks Fedelm, the *ban-fháith*, the prophetess, for an augury concerning the welfare of her army. Fedelm replies, 'I see crimson, I see red,' and then recites a lay portending the destruction of Medb's army by Cú Chulainn of Ulster.[39] *The Cattle-Raid of Cooley* is not extant in any manuscript earlier than the twelfth century, and its lost source probably dates back no earlier than the ninth century, but the function of the prophetess as portrayed by the narrator is clearly ancient. Indeed, the very term used for her, *fáith*, is derived from the same Indo-European source that provided the Latin word for 'prophet', *vates*, and the associated word *vaticinatio*, 'vaticination' ('the chanting of the

---

[37] Osborn Bergin and R. I. Best, ed. trans., 'Tochmarc Étaíne', *Ériu* 12 (1938), 178, 179 (chap. 8).

[38] For instances, see T. P. Cross, *Motif-Index*, motifs V 12.4.1, V 12.4.2, V 12.4.3; for discussion, see Thomas F. O'Rahilly, *Early Irish History and Mythology* (Dublin, 1964), pp. 323, 339–340.

[39] *Táin Bó Cúalngne from the Book of Leinster*, ed. trans. Cecile O'Rahilly (Dublin, 1967), pp. 6–8, 143–145.

prophecy'), and the place-name *Vaticanus mons*, 'the hill of prophecy', later Christianized as 'the Vatican'.

Spells and Oaths (8)   In the regal sphere of verbal utterances pertaining to the future we find a wide range of manifestations associated in particular with the concept of what the Irish called *geis*. The noun *geis* (plural *geisi*, later *geasa*) is related to the verb *guidid*, 'he prays', and might be briefly defined as meaning 'a binding prayer'. In Diagram A for the sake of brevity we have used the word 'spell', but there is no one word in English which can convey the Irish notion. Unlike a law which states in general terms how people should behave, a *geis* is an utterance aimed at a particular individual, permanently constraining his future behavior in some specific and peculiar way. Sometimes these constraints, emanating inexplicably from the past, were considered to be inherent in a particular rank or office. So, for instance, according to *The Book of Rights*, there are *geasa* on the King of Ulster which arbitrarily prohibit him from approaching the lair of a boar, from listening to the birds of Loch Swilly, and from bathing in Loch Foyle during the month of May. If he does these things, he will never succeed to Tara and thus, symbolically, to the High Kingship of Ireland.[40]

On other occasions story-tellers recount the particular occasions that have elicited the binding spell, which often functions as the major resource for constraint available to women. So, for instance, in the tragic legend *The Pursuit of Diarmaid and Gráinne*, when Diarmaid refuses to accept the advances of Gráinne, the forth-putting heroine casts him under spells (*geasa*) of strife and destruction involving 'the pain of a woman in childbirth, and the vision of a dead man over water, and the life of Niall Caille [a king who died by drowning]', and thus compels Diarmid to abduct her from the court of Finn.[41]

In some legends the hero is destroyed because he unavoidably breaks one, or even all, of the arbitrary prohibitions that he has inherited, as for instance in *The Destruction of Da Derga's Hostel* when King Conaire is tragically compelled to break eight *geasa*, one after another, in order to preserve his honor.[42]

Similarly, a warrior may impose a binding oath upon himself. So, for instance, Cu Chulainn in the oldest recorded version of *The Cattle-Raid of Cooley*, having determined to take revenge on Fóill as an enemy of his tribe, proclaims, 'I swear by the god by whom my people swear that he shall not

---

[40] *Lebor na Cert*, ed. trans. Myles Dillon (Irish Texts Society 46)(Dublin, 1962), pp. 135–1131. For concept, see *RIAD*, under *geis*; T. P. Cross, *Motif-Index*, motif C and following.

[41] *Tóruigheacht Dhiarmada agus Gráinne*, ed. trans. Nessa Ní Shéaghdha (Irish Texts Society 48)(Dublin, 1967), pp. 10–11. Professor John V. Kelleher reminds us that in fact Niall Caille died in 846, some five centuries after the era to which the story-tellers assigned the Fenians.

[42] *AIT*, p. 98.

play his deception again on the Ulstermen if once the broad spear of my master Conchobar may reach him from my hand.'[43]

Parallel in form and function is the oath that binds a king or warrior because of the sureties he has named, as when King Loegaire swears by 'the sun and moon, water and air, day and night, seas and land' that he will not exact any tribute from the Leinstermen and is subsequently destroyed by those very elements when he breaks his oath.[44]

Geasa and oaths, however personal in function, obviously constituted an important part of the repertoire of verbal utterances available to early Irish society, and they deserve mention here because they belong to the very core of the Irish social system. They are strikingly parallel to the Irish non-verbal practice of constraint by means of fasting, such as employed, for instance, by the legendary poet Amairgen when he fasted for three days and three nights against Finntan in order to win from him a knowledge of the past.[45] Hence, like any human expedient designed to effect constraint short of bodily aggression, they can very properly be classified as a part of the verbal devices that pertain to social wisdom.

Charms (9) At the tribal level, verbal utterances designed to reveal and even to control the future are represented in a wide range of what are generally called charms and curses, the former designed to effect beneficial change, the latter to produce malign results. Both charms and curses are akin to *geasa*, except that generally they express a constraint aimed defensively against a threat, often supernatural or intangible rather than human.

One of the earliest extant Irish charms is so primitive that it is hard to understand its details, but it seems to say:

> I save the living dead
> From belching, from spear-thong, from sudden swelling. . . .
> May that become whole whereon this spell goes.
>
> I put my trust in the remedy
> That Dían Cécht left for his family,
> So that whatever it touches may become whole.[46]

---

[43] *Táin Bó Cúailnge: Recension I*, ed. trans. Cecile O'Rahilly (Dublin, 1976), lines 736–738, trans. p. 145. See T. P. Cross, *Motif-Index*, motif M 119.2.

[44] *Lebor na hUidhre*, ed. R. I. Best and Osborn Bergin (Dublin, 1929), lines 5135–37, 5183, 5195. See James F. Kenney, *The Sources for the Early History of Ireland* (New York, 1929; rpt. 1966), item 138, pp. 346–347; T. P. Cross, *Motif-Index*, motif M 119.1.

[45] See F. N. Robinson, 'Notes on the Irish Practice of Fasting as a Means of Distraint', in *Putnam Anniversary Volume* (Cedar Rapids, Iowa, 1909), p. 572; for references, see T. P. Cross, *Motif-Index*, motif P 623. For Amairgen's fasting, see ed. trans. in *Zeitschrift für celtische Philologie* 15, p. 278.

[46] *Thesaurus Palaeohibernicus*, ed. trans. Whitley Stokes and John Strachan (rpt., Dublin, 1975), 2, p. 249.

Here, obviously, an Irish scribe has preserved fragments of an ancient pre-Christian tradition, for Dían Cécht belonged to the Celtic pantheon and was the divine physician who cured the arm of Nuada of the Silver Hand (referred to above).[47]

Curses, likewise expressed in rhythmical form, are also recorded in archaic texts. Athirne the Importunate, for instance, while still in his mother's womb was excited by the aroma of the ale that was being brewed for a feast. His mother asked the brewer for a drink to satisfy the thirst of her unborn son but was refused, and Athirne therefore cursed the brewer and his barrels:

> May your ale be a flood
> of the earth . . . ,
> seas fast encircling the earth . . . ,
> suddenly breaking forth . . . ,
> the staves bursting like a nut-shell.

Needless to say, the barrels burst, and ale ran ankle-deep throughout the hall.[48]

Function

To turn now from examples of verbal utterance to the basic question of their function, we may remark that all of the samples of our nine categories quoted in this chapter can be said to pertain to the 'poetic arts' and that they all incorporate traditional wisdom.

The Irish recognized that all the verbal crafts served a common social function, and they assigned a special place within society to all craftsmen whether their crafts were verbal or non-verbal. The Irish word for 'craft' is *dán* (a word of Indo-European origin, meaning basically 'gift', cognate with Latin *dónum* and Greek *dóron*), and craftsmen were known as *áes dána*, 'people of crafts', with the implication that each was endowed with the 'gift' for a particular craft.[49] These 'people of crafts' varied, however, in rank and emolument. Within the general category of *áes dána* the laws recognize wood-workers, metal workers, bronze-workers, gold-smiths, doctors, judges, and priest (druids), as well as lesser artisans such as leather-workers, comb-workers, chain-makers, and the like; but the poet-seer (*fili*, later *file*, plural *filid*) occupied a specially exalted status. Farmers, in contrast, were excluded from any such classification, presumably on the ground that in their routine and

---

[47] See note 6 above, and *RIAD, Dían Cécht.*

[48] E. J. Gwynn, 'Athirne's Mother', *Zeitschrift für celtische Philologie* 17 (1927), pp. 153–156.

[49] See *RIAD, dán*, especially section iv (col. 73.13–73.61).

diverse work they did not produce professionally unique and enduring artifacts.

The deeply rooted belief that poetry, above all other crafts, in particular is divinely inspired is reflected in the most ancient survivals of Irish mythology. In somewhat the same way that Plato refers to the musical arts as 'a gift (*dóron*) of the muses and of Apollo',[50] Irish mythographers refer to three gods who preside over craftsmanship and are the begetters of esoteric Wisdom (*ecna*) and whose mother is the goddess Brigit the poet-seer.[51] Despite the fact that the surviving Irish evidence has none of the neatness of Greek mythology, the parallel is striking, especially since Brigit is said to be the daughter of the Good God (*Dagda*), otherwise known as Eochu the Father of All (*Ollathir*), just as Apollo is the son of Zeus.

Other Irish mythological patterns further support the concept of an all-embracing wisdom that inspires the various crafts inherent in the social order. When the Irish, for instance, adopted a system of writing, they called their alphabet *ogum* (now anglicized as 'ogham'), presumably in reference to a culture god, in Ireland named Ogma and in Celtic Gaul named Ogmios, the god of eloquence who controlled the magical binding power of the word.[52] Similarly, the wise judge Morann, already referred to, may well have been regarded as the god of law, and it is presumably significant that he as a master of word-craft is associated with the invention of certain names of the letters of the *ogum* alphabet.[53]

The Irish expressed their admiration for the verbal crafts not only through their mythological constructs but also abstractly in such sophisticated works as the odes addressed to Poetic Inspiration and to Judgment. The former of these, which we have quoted as a frontispiece for this book, begins:

> Hail poetry,
> Daughter of true wisdom,
> Sister of reason,
> Daughter of prudence,
> Noble, revered.

The other ode, which has been mentioned already, in as much as it pays equally remarkable respect to the kindred process of enunciating legal judgments, closely resembles the ode to poetry; and both compositions reflect the dependence of early Irish society upon verbal artificers.[54]

---

[50] Plato, *Laws*, 796E. Plato is referring to the musical arts in the broadest sense. See *The Dialogues of Plato*, 3rd ed., trans. B. Jowett (London, 1892), V, 474–475.
[51] See T. F. O'Rahilly, *Early Irish History*, p. 315, n. 5; and *RIAD*, *Brigit*.
[52] See *RIAD*, *Ogma* and *ogum*.
[53] *Auricept na n-Éces*, ed. trans. George Calder (Edinburgh, 1917), pp. 276–285 (lines 5528–5614). For Morann, see note 30 above.
[54] For both odes, see Watkins, note 20 above.

47

Stylistically, the surviving literary monuments of early Irish poetry tend to be most curiously wrought and, verbally, most intricately decorated, very much in the manner of early Irish sculptures and jewelry and manuscripts; but this fact does not mean that the verbal artificers, as we have for convenience called them, were primarily concerned with craft for craft's sake. Rather it means that they were concerned with their function in society for the sake of their society's survival.

Extant Irish treatises on poetics – more ancient in form and content than anything similar that is known in other Western European literary traditions – prescribe extraordinarily elaborate regulations for those who were entitled to accept the privileges and responsibilities of becoming poets.[55] Indeed, the training of the chief poet-seer (*fili*) is, in its rigor, reminiscent of the ancient training of the Brahman scholar in Hindu society. The *fili* belonged to a privileged hereditary class, and in preparation for his primary service to his tribal ruler, he had to spend twelve years in mastering the intricacies of meters and in memorizing myths, legends, and genealogies, and he had to understand the traditions of law. In the most archaic descriptions, the function of the *fili* ('the one who sees', 'the poet-seer') is not in fact distinguished from that of the *breithem* ('the one who bears judgment') or of the *senchaid* ('the one who knows past history').[56]

The poet's duties were awesome. He had to learn not only how to manipulate the artificial language of poetry according to the exacting rules of metrics and linguistic conventions. He also had to be able to recall the past, interpret the present, and predict the future; and he was at all times required to preserve 'the truth'. The reward paid to a poet for a poem was 'conveyed absolutely', to quote the phrase of an early Irish legalist, but – he adds ominously – the poem must be 'truthful and correct'.[57] Even poets of lower rank than a *fili*, such as 'bards',[58] enjoyed important privileges, but probably for a long period in pre-Christian society the poet-seer, the *fili*, played a central role.

2. CHRISTIAN IRELAND

Eventually the introduction of Christianity by St Patrick and other Christian missionaries in the fifth century changed Irish culture dramatically. Some of

[55] See Gerard Murphy, *Early Irish Metrics* (Dublin, 1961), pp. v-vi; Charles W. Dunn, 'Celtic', in *Versification*, ed. W. K. Wimsatt (New York, 1972), p. 146, n. 16
[56] See *RIAD*, *fili*, *breithem*, and *senchaid*.
[57] Kuno Meyer, 'Mitteilungen', *Zeitschrift für celtische Philologie* 13 (1919), p. 20 [*Bretha airechta*, line 19].
[58] See *RIAD*, *bard*.

the new sources of utterances, exemplary, regulative, and projective, associated with this innovative phase are suggested in Diagram B.

Christian Wisdom

Sphere	Past	Present	Future
sacral	1 Bible and Apocrypha	4 liturgy, sermons	7 prophecies
regal	2 saints' lives	5 monastic rules	8 excommunications
tribal	3 exempla	6 meditative lyrics	9 prayers

Diagram B: Christian Innovations in Ireland
[partly replacing some categories listed in Diagram A]

The missionaries not only introduced a new religion but also established a whole new social organization of hermits, male and female monastics, missionaries, scribes, and clerics. The belief in the old gods diminished; the role of the druid evaporated; and even the authority of the king and poet-seer declined.

Monasteries were founded by, or in memory of, native 'saints', who themselves were frequently of aristocratic origin. The saint's devotees considered themselves to be members of the saint's family, just as in secular life the members of a tribe considered themselves to be members of the king's family. Saints' lives were composed to add sanctity to the tradition of the saint and to reinforce the monastery's claim to the land upon which the saint's disciples were settled.[59] Hence it seems entirely appropriate to list 'Saints' lives' by analogy in Category 2.

It must be remarked, however, that these innovations did not completely erase the old patterns of Irish culture, for, if Christianity changed Ireland, it is also true to say that the Irish molded Christianity in their own way. The Christian art of the decorated Irish crosses and of the monastic illuminated manuscripts is uniquely Irish; the lives of the Irish saints are adorned with motifs borrowed from pagan myth and legends; and the peculiarly fervent devotion of the hermits and monks to their new rules seems somehow to reflect an ancient druidical passion for obedience to an esoteric code.

---

[59] See Stefan Zygmunt Czarnowski, *Le culte des héros et ses conditions sociales: Saint Patrick* (Paris, 1919).

3. NORMAN IRELAND

The establishment of continental monastic orders, the introduction of a diocesan system, and the invasion of Norman knights and ecclesiastics into Ireland in the twelfth century wrought a different kind of change. A Norman Governor was superimposed on Ireland; papal authority was extended over the Irish church; and the newly founded international monasteries (particularly Cistercian) provided new cultural centers throughout the land. The conquest thus introduced many attendant new forms of utterance, the most significant of which are listed in Diagram C.

Norman Wisdom

Sphere	Past	Present	Future
sacral	1	4	7
regal	2 chronicles	5 feudal law, church canons	8
tribal	3 memoirs	6 letters, personal lyrics	9

Diagram C: Norman Innovations in Ireland
[partly replacing some categories in Diagrams A and B]

At the sacral level, the coming of the Anglo-Normans supplied nothing essentially new, but at the regal level the Norman overlords did, in particular, further displace the authority of the Irish kings; and the Norman lawyers introduced a rival code of law devised to protect the feudal rights of the invaders – a code that eventually left the roles of the native poet and native lawyer more decorative than functional.

Thus, by the end of the twelfth century, the schematic primal state which we have here attempted to reconstruct was altered, but it was not obliterated beyond all recognition. In the records, the survival of native Early Irish culture can still be discerned despite the successive superimpositions first of Christianity and then of Norman culture.

4. INTERPRETING THE TRADITION

What should concern the cultural historian and literary critic is, then, the interpretation and assessment of the surviving early Irish records, representing as they do three antithetical and diverse cultural streams. Here a functional approach seems well suited to dispel the romantic mists that have accumulated over the Irish past.

When, for instance, an Irish-born poet, Enoch O'Gillan, composed at some late date a poem which he entitled *The Graves of Clonmacnois*,[60] he did so because he felt that it was his duty to exalt the sanctity of his ancient cemetery and his religious community over all other Irish cemeteries and religious communities. He understood his poem's function and his own task. Like previous Irish poets, he was composing a poem within the expectations of our Category 2, concerning the regal past of the tribe, in this case linking the site with the genealogies of the royal patrons and of the abbots of Clonmacnois.

Other Irish monastic poets had composed similar pious panegyrics by at least the end of the tenth century, and the underlying genre was presumably traditional, perhaps even from early Celtic times. Certainly an anonymous Welsh bard had composed in his own language a more primitive non-Christian poem, *Englynion y Beddau* (*Stanzas of the Graves*) linking heroic traditions to certain sites in Wales that were singularized by standing stones and other mysterious mementoes of the past. This Welsh poem probably dates back at least as early as the ninth century, and in its attitude towards the regal past it suggests a derivation from an ancient Celtic poetic function.[61]

What, however, has been the fate of such poems? O'Gillan's *Graves of Clonmacnois* was turned into a poem by T. W. Rolleston (born 1857, educated at Trinity College and in Germany, secretary of the Irish Literary Society in London). Only the first five of the nineteen stanzas were translated in Rolleston's version, which was first published in 1888 by W. B. Yeats and has been frequently acclaimed and anthologized.[62] A literal translation of the original Irish of the first and fifth stanzas runs as follows:

> Clonmacnois is the seat of Ciarán,
> A place dew-bright and red-rosed. . . .
>
> Many are the offspring of Conn of the Hundred Battles
> Covered with red clay and turf,
> Many a blue eye and white limb
> Under the earth of the tomb of Clann Colmáin.

Rolleston turns these six lines into the following memorable transformation:

> In a quiet-water'd land, a land of roses,
>   Stands Saint Kieran's city fair. . . .
>
> Many and many a son of Conn the Hundred-Fighter
>   In the red earth lies at rest;

[60] For bibliography, see J. F. Kenney, *Sources*, item 172, p. 383.

[61] See Thomas Jones, 'The Black Book of Carmarthen "Stanzas of the Graves",' *Proc. of the British Acad.* 53 (1967), pp. 97–137.

[62] *Poems and Ballads of Young Ireland*, ed. W. B. Yeats (Dublin, 1888), p. 61; T. W. Rolleston, *Sea Spray* (Dublin, 1909), p. 47.

> Many a blue eye of Clan Colman the turf covers,
> Many a swan-white breast.

Harsh though it be to say so, Rolleston's charming lines inevitably miss the function of the original. Rolleston has, for instance, gratuitously supplied a 'swan-white breast' in this all-male monastic cemetery, and – more grievously from the point of view of the original diligent composer – he has also omitted the names of more than a dozen important families celebrated by the poet.

Deservedly perhaps, at a later date, when the ancient burial sanctuary had been desecrated by modern tomb-stones, that instinctive critic of the sentimental, Frank O'Connor, composed a devastating parody of Rolleston's version.[63] It begins:

> In a smelly, weedy place,
> A place of mourning,
> Stand some heaps of ruined stones,
> Where the Irish middle classes
> Under massive heaps of granite
> Rest their bones.

The Welsh *Graves of Heroes* (seventy-three stanzas in length) which has been mentioned as a primitive parallel to O'Gillan's poem was accorded comparable acclaim when W. B. Yeats included Ernest Rhys's free and sometimes inaccurate translation of the original in his anthology, *The Oxford Book of Modern Verse 1892–1935*, but it has escaped later parody.

In the terse Welsh original, the first stanza, which typically contains no main verb, reads in a somewhat more expanded English version:

> The graves which the rain wets –
> Men who had not been used to being provoked,
> Cerwyd and Cywryd and Caw.

Rhys, however, gratuitously interposes himself as the suffering poet:

> In graves where drips the winter rain
> Lie those that loved me most of men:
> Cerwyd, Cywrid, Caw lie slain.

In short, the poetic function of the Irish and of the Welsh traditional poets has been totally transformed to suit an audience whose point of view is utterly alien to that of the original composers. For the purpose of enlivening the poetry of the ancients, translators and anthologists have with the best of intentions worked through early Irish literature in search of the moving voices

---

[63] Frank O'Connor, *Leinster, Munster, and Connaught* (London, 1950), p. 96. We are indebted to Professor John V. Kelleher for this irreverent reference.

of ancient poets and story-tellers, and in their quest they have often been aided and encouraged by literary historians and literary critics. In this blameless process, Yeats and Lady Gregory created a whole new and magnificent Anglo-Irish literature, but they were concerned not so much with discovering the meaning of the past as with transmitting the symbolic value of the ancient Irish heroic spirit to their own contemporaries in 'Young Ireland'.

A less romantic task still remains, however, for the literary critic and literary historian to interpret ancient utterances functionally within their original contexts. Concerning the early Irish materials exemplified here, our functional analysis suggests a number of generalizations which may be relevant to any over-all investigation of the poet's function as a custodian of wisdom.

The early Irish poets, along with their audiences, did not, we would argue, draw any sharp division between what are often called 'literary' and 'non-literary' utterances. All of their poetic utterances were in some sense designed to promulgate tribal wisdom. All of these utterances fulfilled appropriate social purposes, some more practical than others. Generally, they were pronounced by official, trained practitioners and were cast in appropriate traditional forms, and their efficacy was associated with the 'verbal magic' attributed to the utterances of the poets.

The traditionalism of early Irish society encouraged all that was customary, or what we would now call 'archaic', and discouraged any departure from approved norms, or what we would now call 'innovative'. Thus, having written his official version of the Ulster epic *The Cattle Raid of Cooley*, the scribe adds a significant message addressed to all readers and story-tellers: 'A blessing on everyone . . . who does not impose any other form upon this.'[64] Within such constraints, poets understandably were not tempted to introduce any novelty in their verse.

At any of the levels of poetics here examined, utterances, though limited by traditionalism, tended to be intricately wrought. Thus the language of poets and story-tellers seldom resembled that which is attributed to simple, rural, untutored people. Rather, their linguistic style corresponds to what art historians have called the 'barbaric' and 'non-classical' features so clearly evident in early Irish art. The reasons for the use of such ornate diction are various. In part, set conventions provide considerable aid to composition, just as, in an oral culture, they assist the process of memorization. In part also, they serve to elevate poetic utterances above the level of common speech.

In the Irish tradition, poetry is used for certain purposes, and prose is used for other and different purposes; sometimes, as in the epic, prose and poetry are intermingled; and the use of poetry did not distinguish 'literary' matter from prose 'non-literary' matter.

The early Irish poets do not seem to have left behind them any trace of what

[64] *Táin Bó Cúalngne from the Book of Leinster*, ed. trans. Cecile O'Rahilly (Dublin, 1967), pp. 136, 272.

might be called personal, self-expressive, or self-directed utterances. If they had done so, we might usefully have included in Diagram A a fourth level labelled PERSONAL. Some meditative lyrics listed in Diagram B could perhaps be assigned to such a level; and certainly the memoirs, letters, and personal lyrics listed in Diagram C could be so labelled; but the personal level seems to be irrelevant to any reconstruction of the primal state, in which the expression of the poet's personal views and individual experiences was neither expected nor desired.

To be sure, certain apparent exceptions to this last generalization may be found if we search for examples of the meditative lyrics listed in Category 6 of Diagram B. Examples of such items would include the intellectual poems of scholars and the meditative reflections of monks and hermits.

One famous and remarkably academic example of the first type is provided by *Pangur Bán* – a poem addressed by a scholar to his cat. The poem was composed privately and impromptu in the ninth century by an Irish monastic living in pious exile at the monastery of Reichenau. Pangur Bán rejoices, says the scholar, 'when a mouse is caught in his sharp claws. *I* rejoice when I grasp an outstanding knotty problem.'[65] This rare poem is reminiscent of the occasional verse written in Latin on the Continent by other Irish monastic exiles such as Colmán and Sedulius Scottus,[66] and it shares the obvious inspiration of the epigrammatic and dialectic traditions of monasticism, differing from the Latin poems only in the fact that it is written in the Irish language.

The meditative tradition of native Irish hermit poetry is less sophisticated. Generally the hermit reflects upon the perfection of God's creation and upon the imperfections of man. Typical is the anonymous, restrained, *haiku*-like poem composed in praise of a blackbird that sings in the gorse:

> The little bird
> who whistles
> from the tip
>   of his bright-yellow bill
>
> has sung his note
> over Loch Laig,
> the blackbird, from his branch
>   heaped in yellow.

Another poem, somewhat more doctrinaire, is composed by a pious hermit who praises his monastic bell as it sound the canonical hours:

---

[65] *Golden Treasury*, ed. D. Greene and F. O'Connor, pp. 81–83; see J. F. Kenney, *Sources*, item 535, pp. 677–678.

[66] See, for instance, Helen Waddell, *Medieval Latin Lyrics* (New York, 1933), pp. 74–77, 118–125; Sedulius Scottus, *On Christian Rulers and The Poems*, trans. Edward G. Doyle (Binghamton, New York, 1983).

> O bell of sweet tone
> That rings in the windy night,
> I would sooner tryst with it
> Than tryst with a wanton woman.[67]

Because of their perceptivity and expressiveness such poems appear in all the best anthologies, and properly so. But these apparently personal *jeux d'esprit* were in fact composed by anonymous devotees in honor of their hermit life. The hermits celebrated the joys of solitude, purity, piety, frugal diet, simple living, and the companionship of nature. As poets they were in a sense serving an official poetic function on behalf of God just as their secular brethren served a king or chieftain in a similar role.

Another apparent exception to the usually impersonal role of the poet lies in the compositions of the secular bards of the twelfth century and later, who produced poetry which seems at times almost crassly autobiographical. Typical is the following stanza (ca 1213):

> Little, I suppose, do you know
> Who *I*, among Irishmen, am.
> Respect to my verses you owe,
> For *I* am O'Daly of Meath.[68]

One might, of course, expect at this period that a poet would feel free to express his individuality as a result of the emancipating effects of the renaissance of the twelfth century; but, in this particular case at least, the highly egocentric tone of the poem is the result of the bard's attempt to present an *apologia* for misdemeanors to his offended patron. Such compositions are common in Irish and Scottish Gaelic tradition; and the Welsh bards, who also at time found it expedient to compose them, even had a word for the genre: *dadolwch*, 'appeasement'. The apology was, in short, part of the official Celtic bardic system, and the purpose of O'Daly's self-emphasis was chiefly defensive.

Thus the conclusion seems compelling that in cultures close to the primal state, even at a late date, the forms in which wisdom is dispensed and the genres through which verbal utterances are deployed are virtually fore-ordained by their social function, although, as the later manifestations of Gaelic culture in Scotland seem to suggest, the function of the genres may descend from a serious level of instruction to a simpler level of entertainment.

---

[67] *Early Irish Lyrics*, ed. trans. Gerard Murphy (Oxford, 1956), pp. 7 and 5 respectively.
[68] *Irish Bardic Poetry*, ed. trans. Osborn Bergin (Dublin, 1970), pp. 90, 253 (stz. 17); see Charles W. Dunn, 'Ireland and the Twelfth-Century Renaissance', *University of Toronto Quarterly* 24 (1954), pp. 85–86.

CHAPTER 4

SCOTTISH GAELIC CULTURE

1. THE TRADITIONS

We have in the previous chapter argued that the earliest remains of Irish literature may usefully be examined in the light of the poetic function theoretically attributable to the primal state. To a remarkable degree, a reconstruction of the primal state is also applicable to the Gaelic folk-culture of much later periods. Thus, if we draw up an inventory of the latter-day Scottish Gaelic culture in the Highlands and Western Islands, we find that many ancient Celtic features still survive. To be sure, the Gaelic-speaking culture that St Columba and his monks brought to Scotland in the sixth century had already been Christianized in Ireland; but in many respects the underlying Scottish-Gaelic culture, as in Ireland, remained pagan, and even the practices associated with Christianity retained many peculiarly Celtic features.

The diligent nineteenth-century folklorists who lovingly recovered Gaelic traditions in the Highlands and Islands considered these to be mere 'waifs and strays' or 'flotsam and jetsam' that reflected an ancient and once coherent Indo-European past, yet many of the traditions which they recorded belie such metaphors, for they have remained functional within the native culture.

Diagram D sketches the nature of the surviving culture as it is represented in the copious records of the eighteenth and nineteenth centuries and can still be observed even in the living Scottish-Gaelic tradition. Modern Irish Gaelic survivals might equally well be examined, and the continuity from Diagrams A, B, and C, as outlined in the previous chapter, would be self-evident, but – as often happens in the outermost periphery of a culture – the Scottish traditions seem to have conserved particularly archaic yet functional features of the early Celtic culture.

Scottish-Gaelic Wisdom

Sphere	Past	Present	Future
sacral	1 Otherworld (O.T., N.T.)	4 invocations incantations (hymns)	7 prophecies divinations
regal	2 legends, lays genealogies	5 clan customs poems of praise and dispraise (charters)	8 spells oaths
tribal	3 folk-tales	6 gnomic lore work-songs dance-songs	9 charms blessings (prayers)

Diagram D: Scottish-Gaelic tradition
[Christian and feudal accretions in parentheses]

Myths (1) Christianized as they were from the very beginning of their settlement in Scotland, the Gaels lost the key to their older mythology. The later medieval bards still, it is true, do refer to the old gods such as Balar and Lug, but their learned references are drawn perfunctorily from the remote recesses of their bardic training.[1] Thus the specific deities who are to be mentioned in section 4 below survive only in name rather than in anything like active belief and are detached from the larger, lost Celtic pantheon except in the preservation of traditional cult rituals.[2]

Scottish Gaels have retained some sense of the ancient cosmology, however. They still to some extent maintain a living belief in the existence of an Otherworld separate from the everyday world – an Otherworld where potent ancestors still lurk, and from which fairy inhabitants can cross into this world, especially at the time of certain calendrical festivals, and into which rash mortals can occasionally venture. Supernatural events otherwise inexplicable are attributed to Otherworld forces, and many of the tales, songs, and charms discussed below are connected with human attempts to control the malignant forces of the Otherworld.

As in early Irish legend, Gaels still believed that marriages might occur between mortals and Otherworld beings and that mortal children might be carried away to this Otherworld. As one of the most remarkable survivals of such belief, there is a long-standing tradition that forebears of the

[1] See, for instance, *Scottish Verse from the Book of the Dean of Lismore*, ed. trans. William J. Watson (Scottish Gaelic Texts 1)(Edinburgh, 1937), lines 1505, 377, 1503; *Heroic Poetry from the Book of the Dean of Lismore*, ed. trans. Neil Ross (Scottish Gaelic Texts 3)(Edinburgh, 1939), lines 932, 1202.
[2] For a summary of survivals, see Anne Ross, 'Sanctuaries, temples, shrines', in *The Companion to Gaelic Scotland*, ed. Derick S. Thomson (Oxford, 1983), pp. 255–257.

MacCodrum family, from which the celebrated bard John MacCodrum was descended, had intermarried with the seals who abound on the shores of North Uist, and as a result members of the clan used to avoid joining in the annual seal-hunt – an avoidance easily understandable by anyone who has looked into the extraordinarily human eyes of a seal.[3] Thus the mythology of the Otherworld, though indistinctly conceived, can still add a special dimension to the Hebridean view of the world.

Legends (2)   The concept of the past, real or fictitious, that characterized the older tradition also, in general, lost its coherence. Memories of the legends of the Ulster Cycle still survived but only hazily. In Scotland the glorification of Ulster was irrelevant, so that the erstwhile Irish-based legends tended to drop to the level of folktales, as in the versions of *The Cattle-Raid of Cooley* which have been collected from oral tradition in the Hebrides in the nineteenth and twentieth centuries and in the remarkably long-lived legend of *The Death of Cú Chulainn* collected as recently as 1977 in Cape Breton Island, Nova Scotia.[4] In one of the nineteenth-century adaptations Cú Chulainn is portrayed not as a tribal, semi-divine hero but as an exceptional crofter's son who wins the support of the local Highland laird, and the hero's close friend is the laird's own son, who, we are told, has attended college in England! The miraculous events in the tale are more or less equivalent to those in the early Irish epic versions, but the tone of the folk version is non-heroic, and, apart from the story-teller's anachronistic reference to the aristocrat's English education, the setting is the kind of non-specific Never-Never-Land typically found in most folktales.

The tale of Deirdre has followed a somewhat different course, yet one that is still associated with a descent from legend to folktale. In the Ulster cycle, it is intimately connected with the fate of the lecherous King Conchobhar, from whom Deirdre and her lover Naoise seek refuge in Scotland. For the early Irish story-tellers, Conchobhar's treacherous betrayal of the *femme fatale* and her lover is central to the tragic theme of tribal destiny. In killing Naoise and seizing Deirdre, the King breaks the obligatory code of honor. For the story-tellers in the Highlands of Scotland, on the other hand, this issue is less interesting. For them, Deirdre becomes a romantic heroine associated with Alba (Scotland), the beloved country in which for a while she finds refuge. When trapped into returning to Ulster, she sings:

---

[3] *The Songs of John MacCodrum*, ed trans William Matheson (Scottish Gaelic Texts 2)(Edinburgh, 1938), pp. xxxiv–xliv. Professor John V. Kelleher points out that a comparable Irish tradition is associated with the O'Driscolls in South Cork.
[4] For bibliography, see Calum I. Maclean, 'A Folk-Variant of the Táin', *Arv* 15 (1959), pp. 165–1181. For a Cape Breton version of the Death of Cù Chulainn, see Joe Neil MacNeil, *Tales until Dawn*, ed. trans. John Shaw (Kingston and Montreal, 1987), item 13.

> Beloved is the land, this land
>   Of Alba, full of woods and lakes.
> Sore is my heart to leave you,
>   But I must go with Naoise.

Early Irish story-tellers found Deirdre fascinating because she was fated to become the nemesis of Ulster. Scottish story-tellers were charmed by the legend which they had inherited from Ireland. They treated her as a pathetic and romantic heroine who had found her only happiness in Scotland, and they enthusiastically bestowed Gaelic place-names upon the sites which they associated with her stay in the Highlands. Deirdre and Naoise, they claimed, lived for a while at Castle Urquhart on the shores of Loch Ness – 'Naoise's loch'. Deirdre's favorite *grìanan*, her 'sunny bower', was situated at Dalness in Glen Etive, and – as they still used to say in the nineteenth century – 'it was thatched on the outside with royal fern from the dells and with red clay from the pools and was lined on the inside with pine from the mountains and down feathers from birds.'[5]

Tales of Finn mac Coul and the members of his Fenian band were also readily adopted from Ireland by the Scottish story-tellers, just as the tale of Deirdre had been. These, again, all tended to sink to the popular level of folk-tales, even though they produced as a by-product the popular 'heroic lays', which consisted of terse, ballad-like chants centering upon the heroic deeds of the Fenians.

The tone and attitude of the story-tellers also tended to drop from the high style of legend, so that we find in their narrations numerous evidences of epic degeneration. So, for instance, in *Finn in the Kingdom of the Big Men*, the usually brave hound Bran repeatedly saves his master Finn from horrendous opponents, but finally even he is daunted by a particularly menacing opponent. 'Are you going to let him murder me?' Finn cries. But, says the story-teller, 'Bran let out a yowl and ran off and sat down at the sea-shore.'[6] In earlier serious legends, of course, such unheroic behavior would never have been attributed to any hero or even to his dog.

In the Gaelic past, as we have seen, the genealogies of chieftains were frequently attached to familiar legends. So too in Scotland, although some chieftains can lay claim to verifiable human genealogies, folk-historians have not hesitated to amplify and aggrandize the early stages of a clan's development by ingeniously splicing on a legendary background. Thus, for example, genealogists have traced the chieftains of the Campbell clan plausibly enough back to an obscure leader named Duibhne, but to dramatize this otherwise shadowy ancestor they have claimed that he was the son of Diarmaid and Gràinne – the hero and heroine of one of the well-known tales of the Fenian

---

[5] See *Deirdire*, ed. trans. Alexander Carmichael (Paisley, 1914), pp. 74–75, 139, and generally 135–155.
[6] *The Fians*, ed. trans. John Gregorson Campbell (London, 1891), pp. 181, 189.

cycle. Then, even more preposterously, they have traced the Campbell genealogy farther back to King Arthur, despite the fact that the equally shadowy Arthur belongs – if anywhere – not to Gaelic Celts but to South British Celts. And in a final test of human credulity they have added a claim that the line of the Campbell chieftains can be traced back to Nemed – one of the mythical settlers of Ireland, whose deeds are recorded in the pseudo-historical Irish *Book of Invasions*.[7]

In general, however, apart from these ingenious historical inventions, Gaelic story-tellers seem to have been satisfied with presenting their legendary materials on a par with folktales whose function was merely to entertain, and so the traditional wisdom of the old legends was not abandoned but rather was adapted to suit a simpler need.

Tales (3)   During the nineteenth and twentieth centuries innumerable Gaelic tales have been recovered from oral tradition in the Highlands and Islands. In addition to the traditional narratives that had become detached from the earlier 'official' legends, such as those concerning Cú Chulainn or Finn mac Cumhail already discussed, story-tellers delighted in reciting tales of a varying range that might range in length from compositions of epic proportions requiring five hour to recite through medium-length international folktales and native tales, both serious and comic, and down to short tales concerning the place-names, the fauna, and the flora of the Highlands and Islands, and anecdotes concerning local characters.

Until a compulsory national educational system brought English to the rural areas where Gaelic had been the only language spoken, this broad repertoire provided the mainstay of Gaelic culture. Young and old used to gather nightly to hear the best story-tellers exercise their art. But what, then, was the cultural function of the tales? For the most part, if we are not to beg the question by replying that their purpose was merely to entertain, we may say that they were felt to be basically edifying and reassuring. They provided satisfying scenarios for those who wished to dream of becoming heroes and heroines and they provided a reassuring view of a world in which the menaces of the supernatural and the threats of the natural environment could be overcome by a mingling of magic and bravery.

For an outsider to Gaelic culture, it is perhaps difficult to understand how, for instance, the *Tale of Conall Gulban* could have become so popular in the Gaelic-speaking world. Remarkably, fifty-four manuscript versions of the tale survive, including one recorded in Ireland as early as 1684 and another recorded in Scotland in 1691. According to the oral version recited by Angus MacLellan, M.B.E., of South Uist in 1960, the hero is the magically begotten

---

[7] See William F. Skene, *Celtic Scotland*, 2nd ed (Edinburgh, 1891), III, 339–340, 458–460.

son of an Otherworld woman and of the King of Ireland. He is reared by his Otherworld grandmother, but when his father goes off to war, Conall somewhat reluctantly but successfully protects his father's kingdom. Later he sets off in search of the beautiful Anna, daughter of the King of Leinster. He rescues her from a monster, brings her back to Ireland as his bride, and gains the province of Leinster as her dowry.[8]

Historically, Conall Gulban of Ulster, the son of Niall of the Nine Hostages, was a real person, distinguished in particular by the fact that he was the great-grandfather of St Columba. No doubt some of the earlier story-tellers were aware of this important connection, but for them and for their later successors and their folk-audiences the real interest of the tale lay in its wonder-elements. The unpromising but well-descended hero vindicates himself in love and in war. His heroic determination has a reassuring appeal for the audience, especially for those Gaels, whether in Ireland or in Scotland, who long to maintain their ethnic identity in the face of alien landlords; and the story-tellers have added the encouraging suggestion that a truly fortunate hero may hope for some kind of supernatural aid from the Otherworld such as Conall himself received.

Whatever its historic origins, the narrative has come to contain the basic core of the wide-spread and immensely popular international folktale concerning the unpromising hero who by the aid of magical helpers overcomes monsters and wins the hand of a king's daughter. The various Gaelic reciters in deploying their adaptations of the inherited scenario were able to develop particular incidents at will to suit their own taste, and the more skillful story-tellers decorated their recitals with vivid conversations, lurid descriptions, and traditional 'runs'.

So, for instance, Angus MacLellan in 1960 still knew how to vivify the arming of Conall for battle by introducing an alliterative run of some three hundred words, many of them archaic, and recited at full speed, the effect of which is difficult to imitate accurately in translation:

> 'Tis then that the hero engaged in counter-charge and cruel combat; and a counter-charge and cruel combat it was when he cloaked himself, slipping and slithering, in a smooth surcoat of golden silk and sparkling iron armor and a glittering golden head-piece to protect his neck and fair-skinned throat.[9]

Such then was the latter end of the Gaelic tales that may once have dealt with historic legend.

[8] See, for instance, J. L. Campbell, 'The Story of Conall Gulbann', *Trans. of the Gaelic Soc. of Inverness* 44 (1967), pp. 153–192.

[9] See references in Campbell, 'Story of Conall', p. 183.

Invocations, Incantations (4) For the Gaels, almost every action of the daily round of life from morning to night was preceded by an appropriate invocation to some divine power or supernatural intercessor. The spirits whom they invoked might be the old mythic deities or Christian saints and divinities. The invocations, expressed in time-tested formulas, ranged in content from expressions of veneration, to supplications for prosperity, to personal petitions for future benefits, which were akin to the blessings mentioned below (Category 9); but no matter what the content was, the function was entirely clear.

The most frequently invoked of all the saints in the Highlands and Islands was St Brigit (or St Bride), whose cult was celebrated by traditional rituals that had once been associated with the Celtic goddess Brigit (already referred to).[10] The ancient pagan quarter-day called *Imbolc* in Old Irish that marked the beginning of Spring (*Earrach* in Gaelic) became blended with the Feast of St Brigit, and until recent times the occasion was enthusiastically commemorated in Gaelic-speaking areas by Catholics and Protestants alike. Rhymes hailed the reassuring control that Brigit was believed to exercise over the mysterious changes wrought by Nature.

> Bride put her finger in the river
> On the Feast Day of Bride,
> And the Mother that breeds the cold departed.

As in Early Irish pagan tradition, she was still conceived of as presiding over art and was associated with fire; and, as a Christian saint, she was turned into the legendary foster-mother of Christ and was consequently invoked at times of child-birth:

> Bride, Bride, come in.
> Welcome, in truth, you are.
> Give aid to this woman
> And present her child to the Trinity.

So also, at an even more basic level, the Gaels like their ancestors still heartily greeted the sun, the moon, and the stars in various conventional greetings, finding – we may assume – reassurance at their daily rotations.[11]

Sometimes the derivation of an invocation may be tantalizingly obscure. So, for instance, Martin Martin of Skye, the well-educated author of *A Description of the Western Islands of Scotland* (written ca 1695), tells his readers that the natives of Lewis used to gather at the Church of St Mulvay (Eorapie, Ness) on Hallowe'en (October 31, the Eve of the Gaelic quarter-day of Samhain),

---

[10] For a summary of the tradition, see *Carmina Gadelica*, ed. trans. Alexander Carmichael (Edinburgh, 1928), I, 164–173, where the Gaelic originals of the invocations translated here can be found; see also references in *Carmina*, VI, Index (1971), pp. 179–180.

[11] See *Carmina*, III (1940), pp. 274–311, and further references in *Carmina*, VI, Index.

where they would brew ale, and one of their number would wade out into the sea at night-time, and would cry out 'Shony, I give you this cup of ale hoping that you'll be so kind as to send us plenty of sea-ware for enriching our ground the ensuing year.' The group would then return to the church and would extinguish a candle which they had left burning, and then they would withdraw to the fields where they drank the remainder of their ale and, somewhat predictably, prolonged the festivity by dancing and singing.

Martin Martin reports that the local ministers had 'persuaded the local natives to abandon this ridiculous piece of superstition thirty-two years past', but it is perhaps significant that almost a century later the minister of the parish in returning his local commentary for the *Statistical Account of Scotland* (1791–1799) remarks that the people living around the remains of the 'Popish chapel' of St Mulvay 'pay it as yet a great deal of superstitious veneration'.[12]

Furthermore, even in the nineteenth century Alexander Carmichael recorded a rhyme recited in the Hebrides on the eve of 'Gruel Thursday', associated with St Columba (April 16), which obviously reflects the same tradition. At midnight a member of the community would walk out into the sea up to his waist and would pour out an offering of gruel or mead or ale and would recite:

> O god of the sea,
> Send weed on the incoming wave
> To enrich the land
> And to shower food upon us.

It seems highly probable that this 'god of the sea' is the same personage as Martin Martin's 'Shony', and it is also possible that this mysterious deity 'Shony', nowhere else recorded in Scotland, reflects a memory of the god 'Senach' (pronounced *Shawnach*) who is addressed in the Old Irish invocation quoted in Chapter 3.[13]

The incantations frequently recorded in Gaelic-speaking areas, unlike invocations, may be said to be directed towards obtaining magical support for a human request without resort to a specific supernatural helper, but the technical differentiation is somewhat academic, for in fact invocations, incantations, blessings, and charms tend to flow into one another within the course of a folk ritual.

A striking example is afforded by the series of interconnected rituals and utterances associated with the annual celebration of St Michael's Festival in the Hebrides. This festival was still fully observed as late as 1820 by the Catholic population of South Uist. The people may have lost any memory of

[12] M. Martin, *A Description of the Western Islands*, 2nd ed, (London, 1716; rpt. 1976), pp. 28–29.
[13] *Carmina*, I, 162–163. Martin's reference to 'Shony' is listed as unique in *The Scottish National Dictionary* (Edinburgh, 1971), VIII, 202.

what the various parts of the ceremony may one have meant, but each part still contributed to a significant totality in the people's communal life.

Three clearly interrelated themes seem to be involved in the rituals: ancestor-worship, human fertility, and crop-and-livestock fertility. Such primordial themes have tended to coalesce in the harvest-home festival that had been transferred by Christian tradition to the feast-day of St Michael (September 29), and St Michael the Archangel, the 'captain of the heavenly host', has thus become the patron of the entire cluster of ceremonies.[14]

At the sub-heavenly level, on the first day of the festival, the girls of the island collected wild carrots on the afternoon of what was called 'Carrot Sunday', the Sunday immediately prior to St Michael's Day. In digging up the carrots they first cut a three-sided cleft in the soil around it, and they rejoiced particularly in finding a forked carrot. Clearly their incantations involving these carrots were designed as supplications for fertility:

> Fruitful, fruitful, fruitful cleft,
> The good fortune of choice carrots for me,
> Michael the brave to support my fruitfulness,
> Fair Brigit to be aiding me.

They kept their carrots in storage until St Michael's Day, at which time they presented them to their lovers:

> 'Tis I myself who have the carrots,
> Whosoever might win them from me.

On St Michael's Eve, women and girls baked a special cake, a *strùan*, made from all the cereals grown throughout the year (specifically, in South Uist, oats, barley, and rye).

> Each grain-meal underneath my roof
> Shall all be mixed together, . . .
> Milk, and eggs, and butter,
> The good produce of our portion.

Each prosperous family would slaughter a male lamb, and on St Michael's Day this was cooked and shared by all, and the remainder was distributed along with some *strùan* to the poor as a harvest-home oblation.

Subsequently 'all ranks of both sexes' would ride in what Martin Martin describes as a 'cavalcade' to the cemetery.[15] Here they would offer up private prayers at the oratory, and then they would circle on horse-back sunwise around the graves of their ancestors:

[14] *Carmina*, I, 198–215; see also *Carmina*, VI, Index, p. 160.
[15] Martin, *Description*, pp. 79, 89, 100, 213, 270.

Michael of the graces,
I make my circuit under your protection. . . .
Be at my back,
Ranger of the heavens,
Warrior of the King of the Elements.

Then they would compete in bare-back horse racing along the sea-shore, riding on horses that had sometimes by communal sanction been stolen on St Michael's Eve and were to be returned after the races.

Finally on St Michael's Night the entire community gathered together at the largest available house in order to dance the night away. Significantly, on this occasion they not only danced the usual popular dances but also watched seasonal ritual dances. One of these, *Cailleach an dudain*, 'The Old Woman of the Mill-dust', now forgotten and never adequately recorded, represented a wizard who with druidic wand kills and then revives his female partner. Thereafter, the young women would proffer their choicest carrots to their lovers; lovers would exchange *struàn* and other gifts; all would dance; and some would consummate the harvest-home by making love. Thus, in a complex intermingling of traditions, under the aegis of a venerable archangel who perhaps in early days had been substituted for some pre-Christian Celtic deity, the people found an appropriate occasion to revere their ancestors and to secure fertility for field, flock, and family. And herein, year after year, the appropriate time-honored formulas devised by the tribal poets served to ratify the process.

Praise, Dispraise (5) The professional Gaelic poet was, as has been noted, expected to extol his patrons and to vilify their enemies, and for this service he was entitled to an appropriate reward. This legal relationship, firmly established in Ireland, survived in Scotland until the power and wealth of the chieftains declined to such an extent that the rewards became optional, although perhaps they could still be subtly extorted by the covert threat implicit in the poet's power of satire.

In terms of public relations and image-building, the earlier arrangement had been very convenient. As late as 1249, Alexander III, a Norman in origin, saw fit to include a Highland shenachie in his ceremony of inauguration as King of Scotland. This genealogical expert was able to hail the new king in Gaelic as the *Rìgh Albainn*, the 'King of Scotland', and to recite Alexander's ancestry all the way back to the entirely apocryphal Gaidheal Glas, founder of the royal line of Gaels in Ireland.[16]

At a less regal level, Highland bards regularly performed similar services at

---

[16] See M. D. Legge, 'The Inauguration of Alexander III', *Proc. of the Society of Antiquaries of Scotland* 80 (1945–46), pp. 73–82.

the installation of new chieftains and also provided appropriate praise-poems for them.[17] Indeed, their official participation was deemed absolutely essential as is clear from the fact that poems in praise of rulers and in dispraise of enemies are preponderant over any other types in the surviving repertoire of Scottish Gaelic poetry.

Both in Ireland and in Scotland the pattern of such songs had become stereotyped at an early stage. In fact, to quote Eleanor Knott, bardic poetry 'shows . . . no epochs or tendencies. It is a flat table-land stretching from the thirteenth to the seventeenth century.'[18] Whether the song was composed to serve as a eulogy or as a lament, the Gaelic bard followed a clear-cut pattern, the argument of which may be paraphrased as follows:

	Eulogy	*Lament*
A	Hail to the Chief!	Alas, our Chief is dead!
B	His pedigree legitimizes/legitimized his rule.	
C	His brave ancestors established their rightful claims.	
D	He is/was valiant in war.	
E	He is/was generous in peace.	
F	His wife/widow is/was of good pedigree.	
G	His heir is worthy to succeed.	Hail to his successor!
H	I as bard exhort him/his successor to assert his territorial claims.	
I	I as bard satirize the enemies of the clan.	

The arrangement of these nine convenient items was entirely optional, and bards felt free to amplify or contract their treatment of any one particular item in the light of circumstances or even of plausibility. Understandably enough, not all the chieftains whom they found themselves required to praise were notable paragons of virtue, but Items H and I in particular allowed the bards opportunity to editorialize if they so desired.

Though their sentiments may thus at times seem somewhat evasive, they displayed considerable ingenuity in decorating and individualizing their songs. They used strict and intricate metrical forms, and they expanded the raw materials of their poems by drawing ingenious analogies from their traditional bardic lore, sometimes compounding it with references to the Bible and the classics. So, for instance, they might praise a chief by claiming his descent from some mythical or legendary hero such as Milesius of Spain or might exhort him to conquer his enemies just as Cù Chulainn had done.

[17] Martin, *Description*, pp. 102, 241.
[18] *The Bardic Poems of Tadhg Dall Ó hUiginn*, ed. trans. Eleanor Hull (Irish Texts Society 22)(London, 1922), I, li.

No matter how much they decorated their compositions, however, they never felt any need to deviate from the traditional pattern which they had learned in the process of memorizing the praise-songs composed by their forebears. That model served them ideally to fulfill their function within society, allowing them, as it were, a wide flight between authoritative assertions, recondite allusions, subtle innuendo, and outright satire, yet all confined within the tight compass of the respected genre of praise-poetry.

Thus, for instance, of the forty-one recoverable songs attributed to John Lom MacDonald (composed between 1640 and 1707),[19] fifteen are eulogies of clan leaders, thirteen are laments for leaders, and two are satires of enemies of the clan. Apart from these thirty songs, the remaining eleven might be called personal, but even these are not in any sense introspective lyrics; rather they are all impassioned exhortations addressed at large or in particular to the bard's own clansmen and allies, and they actually represent a special form of the bardic editorial mode listed as Item H above.

As elesewhere in the Celtic bardic tradition, in Scotland the pattern of poetic praise and dispraise was applied not only to chieftains and clans but also to territory. Many of the songs that might in a different cultural tradition be classified as nature poetry are in fact intended to exalt the bard's native setting above that of all rivals. So, for instance, even in innumerable recently composed songs the bards in one way or another claim, 'There's nowhere more beautiful under the sun than here', whether the 'here' be in Mull, or Lewis, or Skye, or Cape Breton. Ultimately – no doubt – behind such praise lies the atavistic hope that the land, the chieftain, and the clan may for ever be bound together in a magical symbiosis.

The human experiences of the Gaels can be traced in the instinctive, inveterate, and spontaneous compositions of the bards. Even when their status has diminished, and patrons no longer reward them, they react to every major event affecting the lives of their community, and their songs mirror their folk-history. So, in particular, the painful experiences of the people who emigrated from the Highlands and Islands during the eighteenth and nineteenth centuries are minutely recorded in song.

Prior to emigration, bards had always praised their own native land, but they had begun to dispraise their landlords; then after emigration bards praised their new places of settlement abroad but lamented the absence of the friends they had left behind them. Later, bards praised the places to which the descendants of the first settlers had more recently moved and bemoaned the decay of the first homesteads built by the settlers in the New World. Thus, even at this late remove, those bards who still retained their own mother

[19] *Orain Iain Luim: Songs of John MacDonald*, ed. trans. Annie M. MacKenzie (Scottish Gaelic Texts 8)(Edinburgh, 1964).

tongue instinctively continued to compose new songs of praise and dispraise cast in the old pattern and set to the old tunes.[20]

Gnomic Lore, Work-songs, Dance-songs (6)   Proverbs, as has been remarked, are everyman's wisdom, and as such they reflect the culture of a people. It is not surprising that the conversation of the Gaelic-speaking people is still enlivened with witty and pungent examples of the genre, for proverbs are still a part of the everyday thought-process of any eloquent Gael. Frequently they reinforce the traditional ideals of honor, clanship, and hospitality and satirize those wretches who fail to measure up to the ancient codes.

Some proverbs refer specifically to native traditions, as in the byword concerning the generous Finn mac Cumhail: 'Finn never fought a fight without offering terms.'[21] Sometimes they perpetuate the droll Gaelic habit of supplying bizarre comparisons, which have been referred to earlier as 'proverbial fatuities':

That would be lulling an ant into sleeping on a frying-pan.

That would be entrusting a sausage to the black dog.

That would be seizing the eel by the tail.[22]

Sometimes they are profoundly sardonic:

'Two will find peace tonight – myself and the white horse', as the wife said when her husband died.[23]

Sometimes the Gaelic proverbs are cryptic and obscure. More often they belong to the universally known and internationally distributed repertoire, and some times their content is comparatively commonplace; but the people trust their wisdom, for as the Gaelic saying goes, 'Although a proverb can be strained, it cannot be belied.'[24]

Riddles, which are – so to speak – proverbs in the interrogative form, also abound in the Gaelic tradition. They frequently play a part in tales, especially as tests of a heroine. So, for instance, Gràinne is said to have gained the attention of Fionn not only by her beauty but also by her wisdom when she answered such questions as: Fionn: 'What is a ship for every cargo?' Gràinne: 'The tongs of a smith, for they can hold hot or cold.'[25]

---

[20] See Charles W. Dunn, *Highland Settler* (Toronto, 1953), pp. 58–73; Margaret MacDonell, *The Emigrant Experience: Songs of Highland Emigrants in North America* (Toronto, 1982).

[21] Alexander Nicolson, *A Collection of Gaelic Proverbs* (Edinburgh, 1881), p. 100.

[22] Nicolson, *Collection*, pp. 48, 51, 40.

[23] Nicolson, *Collection*, p. xxxii.

[24] Dunn, *Highland Settler*, p. 52.

[25] *Popular Tales of the West Highlands*, new ed (Paisley, 1892), ed. trans. J. F. Campbell, III, 47

Riddles, at least in pre-modern societies, appeal not only to children but also to grown-ups, who are enchanted by their ingenuity, by their picturesqueness, and often by their metrical perfection and who relish the mental challenge to match verbal utterances to external realities:

> I saw a wonder today
> As I sailed on the sea:
> An ox with no hair or flesh
> Tearing grass from the black earth.[26]

> [Looking shoreward, the riddler saw a harrow removing old grass from rich soil.]

Work-songs, it may be assumed, once circulated in Early Irish society even though no one saw fit to record them, and their more recent counterparts are fully represented in the living, oral Scottish Gaelic tradition. So, for instance, in 1911 when Frances Tolmie published the songs which she and her friends in the Island of Skye carried in their memories, she recorded a repertoire of one hundred and five songs that demonstrate the unquestionable pre-eminence of the work-song as a genre. The *contents* and the *melodies* of her songs are extremely varied, but their *functions* are remarkably clear-cut. Three quarters of her songs pertain to the tribal present (our Category 6) and were specifically sung as an accompaniment to the activities of child-rearing, cloth preparation (waulking), grinding oats, reaping, milking, and rowing. And if we add to this enumeration the songs which provided the tempo for dancing – a ritual intimately related to the welfare of the folk-communities – the total accounted for is four-fifths of all the songs she recorded.[27] The remaining fifth of her collection – it may be added – are all, though not work-songs, also functional in their own way within the categories that have been suggested here, some serving as heroic lays for night-time entertainment (regal past, Category 2) and some as songs of praise and dispraise connected with clan loyalties (regal present, Category 5). By way of contrast, only one song, composed by a local bard, could be described as autobiographical, and it had already been adopted by the bard's neighbors as a work-song and was soon, no doubt, to become anonymous.[28]

Other more recent and even more comprehensive collections of Gaelic folk-songs[29] reveal approximately the same pattern of functions within their samples of what the people sing. It seems evident that, just as chieftains

---

[26] Dunn, *Highland Settler*, p. 52.
[27] Frances Tolmie, *Collection* (*Journal of the Folk-Song Society*, vol. 4, no 16)(London, 1911). Songs nos. 38–40 can be called dance-songs, nos. 85–105 are associated with legends and clanship, and the remaining 81 songs are essentially work-songs.
[28] Tolmie, *Collection*, no. 105.
[29] See, for instance, in particular, Margaret Fay Shaw, *Folksongs and Folklore of South Uist*, (London, 1955).

required praise songs, so also the people required work-songs to support them in the labors allotted to them in life. As in other realms of society, the social function determined the repertoire.

Divination (7) Like the heroes and heroines of their native legends, the Gaels resorted to various magical practices in order to learn what the future held for them, although such arcane knowledge sometimes came to those who possessed 'second-sight' unsought and often unwanted without any formulaic appeal.

Those who read the future were acutely aware of omens:

> Early on Monday morning
> I heard the bleating of a lamb,
> And the cry of a snipe, . . .
> And I knew then
> That the year would not go well with me.[30]

Some seers knew how to perform an augury (Gaelic *frìth*, 'discovery') in order to obtain a vision of the whereabouts of an absent person or a lost object:

> Knowledge of truth with no knowledge of a lie,
> May I myself see
> A semblance happy and gentle of what I am seeking.[31]

What the seer then saw before his eyes would reveal some specific omen connected with the quest.

Prophecies on a larger scale are less fully documented, even though the ancient Indo-European words for 'prophet' (*fàidh*) and for 'prophecy' (*fàistinn*) still survive in Gaelic. Presumably, with the decline of the clan system, bards no longer felt obliged or even willing to serve in the perilous role of political forecaster.[32] Significantly, in the seventeenth and eighteenth century the Gaelic bards such as John Lom MacDonald, Sìleas MacDonald, and John MacCodrum chose to father their own prophecies on the legendary Lowland Scottish prophet Thomas the Rhymer.[33]

---

[30] *Carmina Gadelica*, ed. Carmichael (1928), II, 178–179.

[31] *Carmina* (1954), V, 296–297.

[32] Alexander MacKenzie, *The Prophecies of the Brahan Seer*, ed. Elizabeth Sutherland (London, 1977) – the latest edition of a work first published in 1877 – contains an account and bibliography of the most famous of the Highland seers. For a highly skeptical reexamination of the oral evidence concerning the Brahan Seer, see William Matheson, 'The Historical Coinneach Odhar', *Trans. of the Gaelic Society of Inverness*, 46 (1971), 66–88.

[33] See *Orain Iain Luim*, ed MacKenzie, lines 316, 634, 2727, and notes; *Poems and Songs by Sileas MacDonald*, ed trans Colm O. Baoil (Scottish Gaelic Texts Soc. 13)(Edinburgh, 1972), line 520 and note; *Songs of John MacCodrum*, ed Matheson, line 1934 and note.

Spells, Oaths (8) The concept of a binding spell (*geas*) described in the previous chapter is still familiar to Gaelic tradition-carriers but only as a narrative element in legends and folktales. As an actual practice in recent times, people did in fact resort to the casting of spells which they still called *geasa*, especially at Beltane (May 1) and Samhain (November 1), in order to protect their cattle from evil influences,[34] but at that level a *geas* was no longer a binding verbal sanction specifically directed at some human being, as it had been in Early Ireland, but merely served as an apotropaic charm cast over livestock to ward off disease and mishap.

Another kind of spell of similar antiquity is the one known in Gaelic variously as *fàth-fìth* or *fìth-fàth*, which can be traced back to the Old Irish *féth fiadha* (or *fía féth*), a spell capable of producing invisibility or metamorphosis. The gods of Irish mythology resorted to it, as did St Patrick when, according to Christian legend, he transformed himself into a stag in order to escape from the pagan King Loegaire. In the nineteenth century, Gaelic story-tellers in Scotland still explained that Ossian had received his name *Oisìn*, ('fawn', diminutive of *os* 'deer') because his mother had been transformed by *fàth-fìth* into a doe before his birth.[35]

Stylized self-binding oaths could also be sworn, for instance, 'by the hand of MacDonald', thus involving the honor of the clan, and these were also perhaps frequently resorted to, just as they may have been in Early Irish society, but understandably few examples have been recorded of what may once have been a common usage. Metrical oaths sworn upon the Bible are more fully preserved:

> I pledge my oath upon the Bible
> That it is the truth that is in my mouth.[36]

Blessings, Protective and Curative Charms, and Curses (9) Evidences for the types of verbal magic that may be included in this subdivision are rich indeed compared to those available for the earlier Irish stages of Celtic society, largely because utterances that were normally private were committed to writing only when inquisitive folklore collectors began to interrogate their Gaelic informants.

Gaelic offers a rich vocabulary for subtle varieties of these functions that English cannot readily match. As an equivalent, for instance, to the familiar

[34] Carmichael, *Carmina*, II, 300.

[35] *Carmina*, II, 22–26; V, 174, 175 n. The Old and Middle Irish *féth fiada* (see *RIAD*, '1 *féth*') seems to have been thought of as a magical performance rather than a verbal spell. The so-called *fáeth fiada* 'deer's cry', wrongly ascribed to St Patrick, was a Christian spell uttered before a journey (see Greene and O'Connor, *Golden Treasury*, p. 27).

[36] See *Carmina*, VI, 107–108 (*mionn*); George Henderson, *Survivals in Belief among the Celts* (Glasgow, 1911), p. 78; Angus Matheson, 'Swearing by Hands', *Eigse* 8 (1956–57), 247–248.

English self-blessing at night-time, 'Now I lay me down to sleep', Alexander Carmichael names everyday Gaelic forms that can be translated only awkwardly into English approximations such as 'bench-blessing', 'bolster-blessing', 'pillow-blessing', 'couch-blessing', 'couch-shrining', and 'sleep-prayer', and these represent a mere sample of the total repertoire of the specific formulaic utterances that pertain to Category 9.[37]

Blessings, charms, and curses, as has already been remarked, overlap with the invocations and incantations assigned to Category 4, but a distinction can be drawn. At the religious level (Category 4) the people might, for instance, have praised St Brigit in an invocation because of her importance to the preservation of the eternal scheme of things. When, however, travelers sought reassurance before a projected journey, they would bless themselves in the name of a variety of potential protectors without specifically extolling them.

> Passing through dells, passing through forests,
> Passing through valleys long and wild,
> Uphold me ever, fair-bright Mary.
> Shepherd Jesus, shield me in distress.[38]

Similarly hunters (as in many societies) and fishermen[39] also recited, or had recited for them, protective blessings before they set out on their quests. The beneficiaries of these blessings, charms, and counter-curses were, in fact, not so much concerned with the praise of their protectors as with the magical control of the future for their own sake.

Charms were directed against erysipelas, toothache, jaundice, sprain, the effects of the evil eye, and indigestion, to mention only some areas of human suffering.[40] These charms often followed the formula, 'As X did A, so may Y do B,' just as the bardic eulogists would say, 'As the god Lug did so and so, so may my chieftain do such and such.'

Thus we find in a Gaelic cure for sprain in a horse, which is ancient and international in its underlying formula, a specific attribution to St Brigit:

> She put bone to bone,
> She put flesh to flesh,
> She put sinew to sinew,
> She put vein to vein.
>
> As she healed that,
> So may I heal this.[41]

Curses must surely have been felt to be at least as potent as blessings, for the

[37] *Carmina*, I, p. 66.
[38] *Carmina*, I, pp. 316–317.
[39] *Carmina*, I, 310–313, 314–315.
[40] *Carmina*, II, 3–117.
[41] *Carmina* II, 18–19.

fury that evoked them produced a special kind of terrible eloquence. Because of their inflammatory nature, they have seldom been recorded, but we may sense something of their malevolence from their fictional counterparts. In the tragic lay – even more stark than any Lowland Scottish ballad – of the Laird of Brolas, one of the Laird's daughters directs the following curse against her pregnant sister, who, albeit unintentionally, has betrayed her:

> May never prosper that in which you put your love,
> Nor may dew ever fall on the soil of your garden,
> Nor may the lark ever sing above your dwelling,
> Nor may your eye behold the child that now lies beneath your
>   girdle.[42]

Even curses, spontaneous as one might expect them to have been, however, seem to have followed the formulaic patterns characteristic of other less aggressive forms of verbal utterance. It is difficult to imagine a more seamanly curse than that directed by a certain Macleod against a shipload of Macdonalds who were caught on a lee-shore storm off the savage rocks of Skye:

> The wind from the west toward Feiste Point,
> A dark night, fog, and rain,
> The Macdonalds on a boat with shattered strakes –
> *I* would feel none the worse for that!
> A cranky ship, narrow of beam,
> With tall, high-reaching sails,
> The crewmen cross and weary,
> Not one of them heeding another!'

Brilliantly original though this salty curse may seem, it belongs to a known type, a similar example being provided by a curse directed by a Macdonald against the Macleods.[43]

2. INTERPRETING THE TRADITIONS

The questions already raised in the previous chapter may now once again be raised: To what extent can the verbal utterances here illustrated be appropriately described as the product of 'poetic arts', and to what extent do they serve to transmit tribal wisdom? Obviously, the people have been Christianized; their chieftains have lost their traditional power; and the combined effects of

---

[42] *Carmina* V, 364–365.
[43] Nicolson, *Gaelic Proverbs*, p. 390.

radio, television, and tourism have superimposed a new culture on the Highlands and Islands, the results of which could easily be sketched in diagrams akin to those in Chapter 3.

Yet in fact much of the ancient culture has survived remarkably intact and coherent for over a thousand years. The reason for this durability, or 'archaism' as some might call it, lies clearly in the social utility of the component parts of that ancient culture, all of which together provide the Gaels with their own intelligible and acceptable mode of apprehending the universe.

At the very simplest level the Gaels relied upon the magical powers of the verbal arts. Thus Martin Martin describes the safeguards taken by the daring sailors who ventured out from Lewis in their tiny home-made vessels in order to collect fowl, eggs, down, feathers, and quills from the remote Flannan Islands. They would scrupulously deploy their equipment, as he says, according to their 'customs', 'rules', and 'punctilios', and they would protect their undertaking by using a secret language. So for 'rock' (*creag*) they would say 'hard' (*cruaidh*), and for 'shore' (*cladach*) they would say 'cave' (*uamh*), hoping to elude the omnipresent creatures of the malicious otherworld.[44]

At the higher level, the Gaels in Scotland also continued to rely upon those who were especially expert in the verbal arts to direct, control, and sustain the welfare of their communities. Inevitably the status of certain traditional experts declined along with a change in the importance and relevance of their function. Thus, though the Gaelic title of *breitheamh*, 'judge', would still be understood in a local Highland court, it would no longer carry the aura once associated with those traditional regulators of the present who were esteemed as experts in the rights of chieftains and in the accepted customs of the clan.

Similarly, the titles of those who were once regulators of the future tended to be degraded. The term *fili*, once applied to the poet-seer who advised his clan about the future, has now been reduced to the level of a *filidh*, 'a songster', or even 'a pop-singer'. Moreover, no one now would dare to proclaim himself a *fàidh*, a 'prophet', though that role is still vividly represented in Gaelic folktales. And, both in Scotland and in the New World, those who today possess the unwelcome gift of *dà-shealladh*, 'second sight', would shrink from being identified by the once well-known title of *taibhsear*, the 'perceiver of fore-runners'.[45] Two kinds of expertise, however, survive in full function: that of the *seanachaidh*, the 'shenachie, the custodian of that which is old', in his role as *sgeulaiche*, the 'story-teller', and that of the *bard*, the 'poetic commentator', the 'commentator on the present'.

In view of the complexity of these shifting functions, the relevant question

---

[44] Martin, *Description*, pp. 17–18.
[45] See Edward Dwelly, *Illustrated Gaelic-English Dictionary* (Glasgow, 1941), under *taibhsearachd*. On this much investigated subject, see *A Collection of Highland Rites and Customes* [by James Kirkwood, 1650–1709], ed J. L. Campbell (Cambridge, 1975)(The Folklore Society: Mistletoe Series), chap. 8 and accompanying notes and bibliography.

within the context of the present study is clear: How adequately has Scottish Gaelic culture been understood and interpreted outside its native confines?

For the English and even for Lowland Scots, the culture of the Highlands and Islands remained until the eighteenth century virtually unknown. In the sixteenth century, the scholarly historian John Major remarked that outsiders tended to classify the inhabitants of Scotland as belonging to two different divisions: the *domestici*, the Lowland householders, and the *silvestres*, which might be translated as the 'wild-wood' Highlanders.[46] Still later, Dr. Samuel Johnson, writing in 1773, remarked that, even to the southern inhabitants of Scotland, the state of the 'mountains and islands' was as unknown as that of Borneo or Sumatra.[47]

In the meantime, however, James Macpherson had cast a startlingly theatrical new spotlight on the Highlands. In 1760 he published his *Fragments of Ancient Poetry Collected in the Highlands* and then quickly followed up the venture in 1762 by publishing *Fingal: An Ancient Epic Poem Translated from the Gaelic Language*. Understandably, these curious forgeries, along with subsequent inventions, precipitated an international controversy as to whether his materials were 'genuine'.

In fact, the raw materials were of genuine Gaelic origin. James Macpherson was born and raised in Ruthven (in Invernessshire), where from the beginning he had some personal contact with Gaelic speakers, and here at an early stage he had attempted to collect Gaelic lays. But a college education in Aberdeen turned his ambition towards gaining literary fame by 'discovering' the kind of epics that would please a contemporary literary audience. For his purpose, he assumed that the critical canons set by the classics required that he discover an epic that was a narrative poem of considerable length, preferably divided into 'books', depicting heroic deeds, displaying noble gestures, composed in an exalted style, fraught with declamations and apostrophes, and decorated with metaphors, similes, and epic comparisons. Finding no such originals, since none such had ever existed in the Gaelic tradition, he created forgeries.

Adapting traces of narratives from the legends and lays that were still familiar to all Gaels, he blithely mingled two different cycles: the Ulster Cycle concerning Cù Chulainn and the Fenian Cycle concerning Finn (Fionn), whom he perversely called Fingal. He shifted the focus of his inventions away from Ireland to Scotland and created a chronology of events to suit his anachronistic purpose. Over his skeletal narratives, he cast a verbal mantle of strange texture, heavily shot with threads stolen from the King James translation of the Bible and from Milton. By Gaelic standards the resulting inventions were neither myth nor legend nor song nor history; nor by Neo-Classical standards were they epics.

---

[46] John Major, *A History of Greater Britain*, ed. trans. Archibald Constable (Publications of the Scottish History Soc. 10)(Edinburgh, 1829), book 1, chap. 8.
[47] Samuel Johnson, *A Journey to the Western Islands of Scotland*, ed. Mary Lascelles (Yale Edition of Johnson 9)(New Haven, 1971), p. 88.

Dr Johnson, of course, most sensibly refused to accept Macpherson's 'epics' as genuine, although he founded his objections upon a premise that – from a modern point-of-view – would no longer be considered tenable. As a good neo-classicist, he believed that an *oral* culture could not possess *any* literature. He declared summarily that 'in an unwritten speech, nothing that is not very short is transmitted from one generation to another'. Having searched in the Highland and Islands for Gaelic manuscripts which he did not expect to find, he found none. And so he peremptorily described the Gaelic bard as 'a barbarian among barbarians'.[48]

More than a generation later, the Highland Society of Scotland in its extensive *Report* (1805) published the testimony of qualified Gaelic-speaking native informants on 'the authenticity of the poems of Ossian'[49], but even at that date neo-classical preconceptions as to what constituted 'literature' precluded the possibility of acknowledging the existence of 'oral literature', as it has now come to be called for want of a better term.

Thus it was that Macpherson temporarily gained a back-door eminence for the name of 'the poet Ossian'. Yet living survivals of the ancient Gaelic tradition such as the orally circulated versions of *The Cattle-Raid of Cooley*[50] and of *Diarmaid and Gràinne*,[51] and the chanted lays derived from such folk-epics[52], and other favorites of the popular repertoire familiar to Macpherson's Highlanders still remained in the eighteenth century virtually unknown to the outside world except insofar as they were darkly perceived through Macpherson's mirror. Such exemplars of the verbal arts readily fulfilled a function within Gaelic society, but they could hardly be expected to arrest the attention of English-speaking *literati* except for a few inquisitive antiquarians.[53] In the nineteenth century the tradition reached a more sympathetic audience, particularly because of the activities of unbiased folklorists who not only collected oral traditions but also frequently became enamored interpreters of the folk whom they studied. Yet even in this favorable new climate, mis-representations of the tradition still appeared. The ultra-enthusiastic legatees of the Romantic Movement seized upon the songs of the Hebrides as

---

[48] Johnson, *Journey*, p. 116.
[49] Henry MacKenzie, *Report of the Committee of the Highland Society of Scotland Appointed to Inquire into . . . the Authenticity of the Poems of Ossian* (Edinburgh, 1805), Appendix, items II, VI, XVI, XVII, XIX.
[50] For discussion of three oral survivals of *The Cattle-Raid of Cooley*, se Calum I. Maclean, 'A Folk Variant of the Táin', *Arv* 15 (1959), 160–181.
[51] J. F. Campbell, ed. trans., *Popular Tales of the West Highlands* (Paisley, 1892) III, 45–160.
[52] See, for instance, *Heroic Poetry from the Book of the Dean of Lismore*, ed. trans. Neil Ross (Scottish Gaelic Texts 3)(Edinburgh, 1939), Ulster cycle items XVIII and XXIX, Fenian items VI, XI, XX, and XXV.
[53] Such as Jerome Stone and T. F. Hill; see MacKenzie, *Report of . . . the Highland Society*, Appendix, items VII and VIII; and J. F. Campbell, *Leabhar na Feinne* (London, 1872), pp. xvi and xxiii. Stone, in fact, probably inspired – quite unintentionally – Macpherson's original investigations.

expressions of a deeply pervasive eighteenth-century Macphersonian melancholy which, they fancied, hung over the sea-wrack and peat-reek of the Hebrides.

In particular, even in the twentieth century, Marjorie Kennedy-Fraser, a concert singer trained in opera, set the flowing, unaccompanied songs of the Hebrides to a strict metronome tempo and prepared accompaniments demanding adherence to the accepted scales of the pianoforte. She also selected her repertoire with an ear directed towards the nostalgic and the sentimental, so that the generations of English-speaking concert-enthusiasts who were caught by her interpretive spell were never offered any opportunity to appreciate the good humor, quick wit, jollity, and practicality of the typical Hebridean nor the subtlety of their music.[54] Once again the nature of Gaelic traditions and of their functions was misunderstood.

In the light of this summary, it is clear that the generalizations which were presented at the end of the previous chapter concerning the Early Irish tradition closely parallel those that can be adduced here, if allowance is made for economic and social change. The native Gaels still rely on the magical efficacy of the word, and they are not interested in differentiating between what others might consider to be 'literary' and 'non-literary' utterances. Traditionalism is still respected, and innovation is not considered to be a virtue. Utterances are now composed and transmitted by voluntary practitioners who find rewards in public approbation and a personal sense of utility. Utterances such as impromptu songs still follow the rules of Gaelic prosody, though somewhat relaxed, and tales are still told with histrionic skill, despite the fact that the repertoire is now dependent upon the standards of a folk-art rather than an aristocratic art.

Furthermore, members of the Gaelic-speaking communities at home and abroad still highly respect the verbal arts. Whether they will for long depend upon or accept the notion of their inherent verbal magic is an open question which is not relevant here, but even now the affection with which they regard the store of traditional wisdom transmitted by their bards and their story-tellers certainly suggests that, as in the past, they respect these custodians of tradition not just for their verbal virtuosity but also for their ability to transmit the treasured wisdom of the past.

[54] See Ethel Bassin, *The Old Songs of Skye* (London, 1977), especially pp. 116–143.

CHAPTER 5

OTHER EARLY WESTERN EUROPEAN CULTURES: WELSH

When we examine the written remains of other early cultures in Western Europe such as Welsh and Norse and Old English, we find the same predictable impediments to our understanding that we have already discussed with respect to the cultures of early Ireland and of Gaelic Scotland. As in Ireland and Scotland, the surviving evidence in Wales, Scandinavia, and England is late, ambiguous, and fragmentary; and ancient paganism has been cloaked by more recent Christianity.

Here we need hardly itemize in detail the contents of Welsh, Norse, and Old English literatures, for the discussion of a few specific aspects of the roles which were played by the poets in these three diverse yet similar cultural areas will suffice to round out a panoramic geographical picture of early Western European cultures, whether Celtic in Wales or North Germanic in Scandinavia or West Germanic in England.

1. THE TRADITIONS

The Welsh and other related British Celts, unlike the Irish Celts, had been Romanized soon after Julius Caesar had decided that 'Britannia' could be successfully and profitably invaded; and, shortly after Romanization, the Welsh – at least officially – were converted to Christianity even before Patrick made his famous missionary visit to Ireland.

Nonetheless, the native Celts in Wales possessed a sufficient resilience and cultural coherence that they retained their Celtic mother-tongue and, with it, the distinctive features of their own heritage. As converts to Christianity they repulsed the pagan Anglo-Saxon invaders who had conquered South Britain, and at a later date their descendants accepted the Norman invaders only to the extent that they intermarried with them.

In their native Celtic culture, poets had always played a dominant and respected role; and two Welsh traditional narratives have preserved an appropriately remarkable mythic narrative (Category 1) related to the origins of the gift of poetry, or rather – to be more precise – to the origins of the human possession of the *power* of poetry.

According to the first of the two narratives, *The Tale of Gwion Bach* (Little Gwion), the witch Ceridwen brewed a magic potion in order to endow her son with the three drops that would guarantee that he would acquire the gift of poetic wisdom. Little Gwion stoked the fire while a blind old man stirred the cauldron, and when three drops of poetic inspiration sprang from the cauldron, it was Gwion and not Ceridwen's son who contrived to swallow them.

In an ensuing struggle, during which the contestants repeatedly shifted from one form to another, Ceridwen swallowed Gwion, and was thus impregnated. She gave birth to a child, the reborn Gwion, and exposed her unwanted child in a boat.

The Tale of Taliesin provides a mythic sequel which has been attached to the name of the historical sixth-century bard Taliesin. A Welsh nobleman retrieved Gwion from the water and gave the foundling the human name of Taliesin. Taliesin became a poet and prophet who was able to travel through space and time and who excelled all others in wisdom.

Elis Gruffydd, who wrote down the earliest extant versions of the two stories in the sixteenth century, complained that they were 'contrary to faith and piety',[1] but whether he was reluctant or not to record these precious relics, he succeeded in preserving a rich body of motifs that echo many of the characteristics of the Indo-European traditions associated with the magical origins of poetry and of human wisdom.

Though the details are casually narrated in Gruffydd's late versions of these two tales, the details deserve close attention. Primarily they seem to reflect the ancient and wide-spread belief that human beings can only win divine gifts by outwitting the jealous gods. Just as in Greek tradition Prometheus stole fire from the gods for the sake of human beings, so Gwion stole poetic wisdom.

The magical process by which Gwion acquired the gift is also reminiscent of the mythic circumstances under which the Irish hero Finn mac Coul and the Norse hero Sigurd acquired wisdom.[2] The implication of all three instances is that an ordinary mortal cannot expect to acquire supernatural wisdom through the ordinary 'raw' materials of the universe but must feed upon ingredients that have been supernaturally prepared and 'cooked'.

While still in the otherworld, Gwion was dependent upon the mysterious blind person who, in an earlier understanding of the myth, may well have symbolized an otherworld divine counterpart of the human poets who, like Homer, are blind.

---

[1] For a recent translation, see *The Mabinogi*, trans Patrick K. Ford (Berkeley, 1977), pp. 263–285; for the scribe's complaint, see p. 163.
[2] See Robert D. Scott, *The Thumb of Knowledge* (New York, 1930).

Then, in his later career as Taliesin the human poet, the reborn avatar of Gwion is destined to fulfill his function at three predictable levels, sacral, regal, and tribal, in accord with the fact that he had swallowed the *three* drops of magic potion requisite for poetic inspiration, though the folkloristic use of the number 'three' is too much of a commonplace for this parallel to be argued.

Having acquired his original inspiration in the otherworld, Gwion is able to cross into the human world over a magical threshold between water and land, and the hour of his crossing is placed specifically at the magical moment of the night preceding the Welsh *Calan gaeaf* (literally, 'the first day of winter') – a calendrical festival identical in its magical associations with the Irish *Samhain* ('summer's end') and with the Christianized Hallowe'en.

As an avatar from the otherworld, the supernatural Gwion is reborn and becomes the superhuman Taliesin, who like Gwion can still shift shape and traverse time and space and possesses a universal knowledge of the past, present, and future. More particularly, he has carried with him the kind of knowledge that is requisite for all human poets and has become their ultimate exemplar. Predictably, a number of extant mythological poems are attributed to him.

Parallel in Welsh tradition to this myth is a persistent belief in the power of *awen*, which is associated with Taliesin and other poets as the supernatural source which they invoke for their inspiration (Category 4). Etymologically, *awen* means 'breath', 'breathing-in', and thus 'inspiration'. The archaic semi-pagan and later Christian references to this poetic process are copious. An early chronicler asserts that one of the contemporaries of Taliesin and Aneirin was called *'Talhaern tad awen*, 'Talhaern the father of poetic inspiration'.[3] As late as the twelfth century Gerald the Welshman commented on the power of *awen* among the Welsh *awenyddion*, 'the inspired poets'. In his day, they still perpetuated the old rituals. When consulted about future events, Gerald tells us, they would roar out and would seem to be possessed by spirits; some felt as if they had tasted sweet milk or honey; they would provide only indirect responses to the questions with which they dealt; and they would have to be shaken by others before they would emerge from their trance.[4]

The poet Aneirin, the sixth-century contemporary of the historical Taliesin, may possibly be alluding to this kind of poetic trance in *The Gododdin*, his lament for the British who were killed (ca 600) by Anglo-Saxon invaders at Catraeth. In a much debated passage, he seems to say that he himself 'sang' the lament (that is to say, composed it mentally for subsequent oral recital)

---

[3] For a discussion of this reference and of Taliesin's Welsh bardic heritage, see *The Poems of Taliesin*, ed. Sir Ifor Williams and J. E. Caerwyn Williams (Mediaeval and Modern Welsh Series 3) (Dublin Institute of Advanced Studies, 1968), p. xi and *passim*.
[4] Giraldus Cambrensis, *Description of Wales*, book 1, chap. 16; trans. in *The Historical Works of Giraldus*, ed. Thomas Wright (London, 1913), pp. 501–502.

before dawn – presumably a propitious time, as is suggested by the comment of the 'Holy Bard of Brecon' (see below). Aneirin seems to say that, when he composed his poem under the poetic inspiration of *awen*, he did so in such a detached state of consciousness that only his fellow poet Taliesin could understand the process:

> I, [and yet] not I, Aneirin –
> Taliesin powerful in spirit
> Will understand this –
> Sang *The Gododdin*
> Before dawn of day.[5]

Ironically, at a much less mystical and quite unambiguously materialistic level, the historical Taliesin (ca AD 600) boasts in one of his poems that his poetic inspiration, his *awen*, has served to win spoils for himself as a poet just as an ash-wood spear wins for a warrior the booties of war.[6] In this respect, if the poem was in fact actually composed by Taliesin, whatever his level of inspiration, he at least deserves credit for recognizing at an early stage that oral poetry, the unwritten equivalent of the creations of the pen, can be as mighty as the achievements of the sword.

Many other later poets almost automatically invoke the inspiration of *awen*. So, for instance, the anonymous author of *Armes Prydein* (*The Prophecy of Britain*) twice refers to the *awen*, 'the inspiration that foretells', although he attributes part of his prophecy to Merlin (Myrddin) and part of it to other 'druids' (*derwyddon*).[7]

In an early twelfth-century begging poem addressed to the poet Cuhelyn,[8] an anonymous bard implores God to send him *awen*. At the same time, quite unabashedly, he associates the inspiration of his *gwawd*, his panegyric, with the poetic tradition of the magical witch Ceridwen. Significantly, in keeping with this reliance on tradition, the term *gwawd* is cognate with other ancient Indo-European words relating to prophecy such as Irish *fáith* and Latin *vátes*:

> O Lord God, grant me inspiration [*awen*] . . .
> [To compose] a fervent panegyric [*gwawd*] . . .
> In accordance with the stately measures of Ceridwen
> For Cuhelyn the Bard.

---

[5] *Canu Aneirin*, ed. Ifor Williams (Cardiff, 1938), lines 548–552. See Kenneth H. Jackson, *The Gododdin* (Edinburgh, 1969), pp. 50–51, 134–135, for a somewhat different interpretation.

[6] *Poems of Taliesin*, ed. Williams and Williams, pp. lii-liii, p. 9 (VIII, 12–13), and pp. 96–97 (notes).

[7] *Armes Prydein*, ed. Sir Ifor Williams and Rachel Bromwich (Mediaeval and Modern Welsh Series 6) (Dublin Institute for Advanced Studies, 1972), lines 1, 107 (*awen*), line 17 (*Myrddin*), line 171 *derwyddon*.

[8] R. Geraint Gruffydd, 'A Poem in Praise of Cuhelyn Fardd', *Studia Celtica* 10/11 (1975/1976), 198–209 (specifically lines 1–3, 5).

Similar invocations paid simultaneously both to God and to the pagan Ceridwen, indeed, seem to have become a commonplace of Welsh poetry. Another poet, for instance, in pairing the sacred and the pagan, emphasizes the same sweetness of *awen* to which Gerald the Welshman refers:

> The Lord God will give me sweet *awen*
> Like that from the cauldron of Ceridwen.[9]

Even the 'Holy Bard of Brecon' (Gwynbardd Brycheiniog, fl. 1176) begins his *Ode to St David*:

> May the blessed Lord in the midst of night grant me
> Inspiration (*awen*) along with the breeze (*awel*) from the arising dawn.[10]

Dawn, incidentally, had provided the occasion for the completion of Aneirin's composition (see above).[11] And furthermore, in making his happy play on the phonological resemblance between the words *awen* ('inspiration') and *awel* ('breeze'), the Holy Bard with an uncanny instinct reaches back into the recesses of ancient tradition, for both *awen* and *awel* are words drawn from a common Indo-European root signifying 'breath'.[12]

Apart from what seems to have been the deeply entrenched belief maintained by the Welsh bards in mythic inspiration, the scribes have not recorded any large body of Celtic mythology (Category 1). The tales now known as *The Four Branches of the Mabinogion*, however, do at least supply a narrative that may well have been derived from a mythic concept of a divine family:

TIGERNONOS ═══════ RIGANTONA/MATRONA/EPONA
|
MAPONOS

The four tales preserve a distinctly recognizable reflex of a myth concerning the goddess Rigantona which has been transformed into a legend concerning Rhiannon, a tribal heroine who loses her son and then recovers him. The three-fold divine prototypes of the heroine, dimly discernable from archeological sources, possess complementary functions which are curiously and somewhat perversely represented in the narrative.

As queen, Rhiannon corresponds etymologically to the Celtic queen-goddess RIGANTONA, and as mother, she corresponds to the Celtic mother-

---

[9] *Llawysgrif Hendregadredd*, ed. John Morris-Jones and T. H. Parry-Williams (Cardiff, 1933), p. 305 (lines 1–2).

[10] *Hendregadredd*, ed. Morris-Jones and Parry-Williams, p. 197 (lines 1–2).

[11] See reference at note 5. Compare the Indian tradition of Ushás, goddess of dawn, who inspires poets.

[12] See Calvert Watkins, 'Indo-European Metrics and Archaic Irish Verse', *Celtica* 6 (1963), 216.

goddess MATRONA (later Welsh MODRON). In her association with horses and in her son's association with a colt which is born at the instant of his own birth, she corresponds to the Celtic horse-goddess EPONA. Her son Pryderi corresponds to the Celtic boy-god MAPONOS (later Welsh MABON). And the name of her son's foster-father, Teyrnon, corresponds etymologically to the Celtic god of chieftainship, TIGERNONOS.[13]

These mythic survivals of a divine family have been convincingly identified with place-names in Britain and with cult dedications both in Britain and on the Continent. In the *Mabinogi*, however, the significance of the myths has been reduced to the level of non-sacral legends (Category 2). Thus, for instance, in *Pwyll, Prince of Dyfed*, the first of the tales in the *Mabinogi*, Rhiannon graciously submits to an undeserved penance which requires her to sit by the mounting-block outside her husband's court, where she must recite her story to strangers and must offer to carry them on her back to the court. This strange perversion of a myth concerning a horse-goddess is delicately transformed by the sophisticated Welsh story-teller. 'Only rarely would anyone allow himself to be so carried,' he remarks.

Here and elsewhere, the story-teller preserves those miraculous elements of the tradition which he feels compelled to retain but glosses over them as if their original meaning were not his responsibility. At once a rationalist and a humanist, he specializes in refurbishing the old myths as living legends.

Within the realm of legend (Category 2) as distinct from myth, the Welsh story-tellers' favorite subject was clearly the British battle-leader, Arthur. If in historical fact he was a resistance-leader engaged in repulsing the invading Anglo-Saxons rather than – as some scholars have variously suggested – a mythological being (Category 1) or a totally fictitious character (Category 3), then it is easy to understand how his reputation may have inspired the British-speaking tribes during the remorseless spread of the Anglo-Saxons in the sixth century.

By the twelfth century, Arthur had, of course, become an international European hero, but in the meantime Welsh antiquarians had discovered a legitimate place for him in their genealogies (Category 2), tracing him through his father Uther Pendragon back to the divine being Bran son of Llyr, and through his mother Eigr (Igerna) to the legendary King Coel.[14]

---

[13] For a summary of scholarship regarding the divine family of Rhiannon, see Rachel Bromwich, *Trioedd Ynys Prydein* (Cardiff, 1961), pp. 458–497 (Pryderi), 433–436 (Mabon map Modron), 458–460 (Modron verch Avallach). In *The International Popular Tale and Early Welsh Tradition* (Cardiff, 1961), pp. 81–95, Kenneth H. Jackson warns the reader that the entire Rhiannon tale could have been drawn from international folktale motifs; but the fact remains that the protagonists were clearly identifiable by a Welsh audience as native to their own tradition.

[14] See Bromwich, *Trioedd*, pp. 274–277 (Arthur), 525–1523 (Uthyr), 284–285 (Bran), 366 (Eigr), 238, 266 (Coel). On the dubious historicity of Arthur, see David N. Dumville, 'Sub-Roman Britain: History and Legend', *History* 62 (1977), 173–192.

Passing by folktales (Category 3) – though not for lack of evidence – in this brief survey of poetic functions, we can turn to the role of the poet as supporter of regal order within the tribe (Category 5). Here the evidence is ample. The poetry attributed by tradition to the anciênt bards (the *cynfeirdd*, as they are called in Welsh) is parallel to early Irish bardic poetry, if we allow for the fact that the Celtic peoples in Wales and Britain, unlike the early Irish, were repeatedly exposed to alien invasion.

There are poignant signs of stress in the works attributed to Aneirin, Taliesin, and Llywarch Hen. Aneirin laments in *The Gododdin* the defeat of the loyal followers of his chieftain Mynyddawg Mwynfawr, 'Mynyddawg the Great-in-Wealth'. Mynyddawg bore a prestigious name meaning 'the Mountain Ruler', thought of perhaps as equivalent to the Romano-British title of 'Montanus', but at the end of the sixth century his warriors had attempted in vain to stem the spread of the Anglo-Saxon invaders into North Britain, and their bard was called upon to memorialize those who had fallen in battle.[15]

At about the same time, Taliesin dealt with the harsh realities of history in eight extant songs which celebrate two sixth-century leaders of the British resistance movement, Urien and his son Owain. His theme centers on the time-honored bardic topic of *clod*, 'fame, renown', a Welsh word derived from a familiar Indo-European root signifying 'fame', which appears also in such diverse forms as the German name 'Ludwig' ('one heard of in battle)' and the Greek 'Clio' ('the muse [of epic poetry and history] who records the famous deeds of ancestors').

Despite Taliesin's indirectness of expression, his primal theme is unmistakable in the repeated refrain with which he concludes seven of his eight poems of praise:

> And until in old age I die
> In death's inescapable grasp,
> I shall never be content
> Unless I have been singing in praise of Urien.[16]

The poems attributed to Llywarch Hen (Llywarch the Old), identified as the cousin of this same Urien, belong to a later date. These moving lyrics dwell upon the melancholy fate of an aging warlord whose sons are killed in battle. Thus, in a memorable stanza he ruefully remarks:

> This leaf, the wind whips it away.
> Alas for its fate –
> Old, born this year.

[15] See Kenneth H. Jackson, *The Gododdin* (Edinburgh, 1969). The equivalence between the titles Mynyddawg and Montanus is our own suggestion.
[16] See footnote 3. For translations of poems I–III, V–VI, IX–X, see Joseph P. Clancy, *The Earliest Welsh Poetry* (London, 1970).

Somewhat unromantically, recent functional criticism has argued, however, that these compositions were attached to the *persona* of the shadowy Llywarch for political reasons and that the compiler of these lyrics may very well have been intent on supporting and adorning the pedigree of Merfyn Frych (d. 844), the king of the realm of Gwynedd, who became the father of the powerful Rhodri Mawr (d. 877), King of Gwynedd, Powys, and Deheubarth.[17] If true, this argument underlines the difficulty of judging the real intentions of an poet who belongs to the misty past.

Ironically, evidence concerning the functions and intentions of the Welsh bards becomes more ample after the beginning of the invasion of the Normans who were destined ultimately to displace the power of the native Welsh rulers. At some time after this intermixture of cultures an anonymous author produced a fundamental document on 'the office and function of the bards'. This brief treatise, entitled *Y Tri Chof* ('The Three Memorials'), survives only in a seventeenth-century English version but clearly reflects memories of the ancient oral tradition. The bards must know by heart 'the history of the notable acts of the kings and princes'; they must be able 'to give account for every word and syllable' of the language of the Britons (that is, Welsh); and they must 'keep the genealogies and descents of the nobility, their division of lands, and their arms'. Even a bard so ancient as Taliesin would have readily assented to all three requirements, although he would be unaware of the significance of newfangled 'coats-of-arms'.

The additional stipulations enumerated in *The Three Memorials* are similarly traditional. As in Ireland and Scotland, the bard must always utter the truth, must make a visitation of the noble families within his circuit, and in exchange for a stipend must compose songs of praise (either eulogies or laments) for his patrons. Any noble whom he serves must be a *bonheddig* (someone of well-rooted pedigree) who is paternally (and preferably also maternally) descended from 'the kings and princes of this land of Britain'. A *bonheddig*, according to the treatise, brings his title with him into the world, and that title is not extinguished by death but remains 'in his blood to his posterity so that he cannot be severed from it'. Thus the bard must mystically sustain, not just a patron, but the entire lineage of his patron.[18]

The patronage system that operated in the period of the *cynfeirdd* ('ancient bards') still flourished in the later period of the *gogynfeirdd* ('less ancient bards'), as is evident from the eulogies, elegies, apologies, and contentions surviving from the twelfth and thirteenth centuries. The bards maintained the same occasionally arrogant pride in the privileges of their profession that the Irish bards displayed during this period. So, for instance, at times Cynddelw 'Brydydd Mawr' ('the Great Poet') of Powys sounds very much like O'Daly of

---

[17] See Patrick K. Ford, *The Poetry of Llywarch Hen* (Berkeley, 1974), especially pp. 25–32.
[18] G. J. Williams, 'Tri Chof Ynys Brydain', *Llên Cymru* 3 (1955), 234–239; also in *A Book of Wales*, ed. D. M. and E. M. Lloyd (London, 1953), pp. 104–108.

Meath (mentioned in Chapter 3). When he comes south to address the court of The Lord Rhys (ap Gruffudd) of Deheubarth, he demands a respectful silence from lesser bards and from nobles alike:

> Silentiaries of the court, call for silence!
> Silence, you bards! You're listening to a bard. . . .
>
> You noble falcons of Britain, I've wrought a prime poem for you.
> Your prime praises I sing.
> Your bard and justiciary am I.
> Your support is properly due me.[19]

And, on a different occasion, even when Cynddelw is cautiously addressing a poem of reconciliation to the same Lord Rhys, he does not hesitate to state the nature of the interdependence that knits the two of them together as patron and poet:

> You without me can but be silent.
> I without you can have nothing to say.[20]

That is to say, if we translate his intricate and yet unequivocal word-play even more freely: 'Without my services as a bard, you could not proclaim your own worth, and I myself as a bard would have no topic without you.'

As elsewhere, from the earliest recorded period the poets not only praised their patrons but also fulfilled the wider magical function of interpreting the future (Category 7). Most notably, the soothsayer Myrddin, otherwise known as Merlin, became associated with prophecies not only in Wales but eventually in all of Western Europe, including – as has been pointed out – the Highlands and Islands of Scotland. The earliest surviving example of Welsh vaticination, already mentioned in this chapter, is *Armes Prydein* (*The Prophecy of Britain*), ca 930, which is a model of optimistic soothsaying. In it, Merlin under the influence of *awen* predicts that the Welsh will be joined by the Celtic warriors of Ireland, Cornwall, Strathclyde, and Brittany and will defeat the hated Saxon invaders and expel them from Britain.[21]

2. INTERPRETING THE TRADITIONS

The fate of the early Welsh poetic tradition at the hands of its interpreters from the eighteenth century down to the twentieth century is remarkably similar to that of the Irish and Scottish traditions.

[19] *Hendregadredd*, ed. Morris-Jones and Parry-Williams, p. 151 (stanzas 4, 8)
[20] *Hendregadredd*, p. 113, lines 2–3.
[21] See note 7.

Thus, in 1792, an amiable antiquary named William Owen Pughe assisted in recovering from previously unread manuscripts the poetry associated with Llywarch Hen. Not content with publishing them, however, he also prepared a translation and constructed a biography of the legendary Llywarch, correlating the desperate chronology as best he could. The poet-warrior, he explained, spent some time at the British 'court of the celebrated Arthur', absented himself from Arthur's last battle, withdrew to the court of Urien, there to resist the Saxons, and finally retired to a quiet retreat in Wales, where he died at the age of one hundred and fifty. To these bold surmises, in a pioneering attempt at psycho-biography, Owen Pughe bravely added, 'It may be inferred that Llywarch composed most of his pieces now extant . . . to soothe his mind, borne down with calamities and the infirmities of uncommon old age.'[22]

It may be said of Owen Pughe that he was imaginative rather than dishonest, but the same can hardly be said of his collaborator, Edward Williams. Williams was a brilliant antiquarian and poet who wrote under the bardic name of 'Iolo Morgannwg'. Somewhat like James Macpherson in Scotland, he was eager to aggrandize his country's past, and so, finding the remains of early Welsh to be disappointingly scanty, he had already deliberately begun in 1789 to supplement them by publishing his own ingenious forgeries.[23]

These well-intentioned, patriotic Welsh counterfeiters were, however, merely products, albeit exceptional, of their age. In Cambridge, much earlier, Thomas Gray had already committed what might be called an unwitting forgery when the 'ravishing, blind harmony' of a Welsh harper inspired him to complete his stirring poem *The Bard* (1757) (which is discussed in detail in Chapter 9). And James Macpherson with his pseudo-Gaelic *Fragments* (already discussed in Chapter 4) had as early as 1760 enthusiastically adopted for his Ossian the histrionic postures, gestures, and stance of Gray's bard – chanting atop a rock, robed in melancholy garb, his eyes haggard, his beard and hair streaming in the wind, beneath the circling sun, moon, and stars.[24] Whether forgers or not, Gray and Macpherson and their followers had succeeded in inventing a new vision of the role of 'the ancient poet' – a decorative rather than a functional role – which early and pre-modern poets and their audiences would not entirely understand.

In the romantic period, writers redirected their attempts at translating and interpreting early Welsh poetry, but here in this brief survey their successes

---

[22] Relevant excerpts from Pughe may be found in Ford, *Poetry of Llywarch*, pp. 19–20.
[23] See *The Dictionary of Welsh Biography*, ed. Sir John E. Lloyd *et al.* (London: Honourable Society of Cymmrodorion, 1959), pp. 1033–1034 (under 'Williams, Edward', 1747–1826).
[24] *The Complete Poems of Thomas Gray*, ed. H. W. Starr and J. R. Hendrickson (Oxford, 1966), pp. 18–24, 208–211 (notes).

and limitations have perhaps already been sufficiently illustrated in Chapter 3 by the reference to Ernest Rhys.

The post-Romantic writers of the twentieth century offer a wide range of reinterpretations worthy of comment, and for present purposes, the works of David Jones and of Desmond O'Grady seem particularly instructive.

In his *In Parenthesis* (1927), David Jones, the Anglo-Welsh prose-poet, places his highly contemporary, non-antiquarian reminiscences of World War I against the background of the early Welsh *Gododdin*; and in his work he also echoes passages from *The Tale of Taliesin* and from *Culhwch and Olwen* and other Welsh sources.[25] But Jones is not attempting to reinterpret the *Gododdin*; he is using it as a frame into which he sets the searing recollections of a modern war imprinted in his mind as a poet and artist who was engaged involuntarily as a soldier. The work derives some of its resonance from the echoes of early Welsh poetry, but its real subject does not reflect the magical memories of the widely traveling bard Taliesin, surveyor of the past, the present, and the future. Rather, the poetry of the past provides a stable setting into which Jones place his own experience of a chaotic present.

At a more recent period, Desmond O'Grady has found inspiration of a very different kind in his version (1977) of *The Gododdin*. In the original poem, Aneirin fulfilled his traditional function as a poet on behalf of the victims of war by naming each one in turn and thus, in the bardic tradition, gained for them the *clod*, the everlasting fame, that was desired above all other rewards by Celtic warriors. O'Grady has omitted their names, substituting in each place an anonymous 'he', but he has retained the context of the disaster at Catraeth even though he has undertaken the composing of a modern poem in a current style and contemporary idiom, as if to say that it is now too late to celebrate the individuals by name but never too late to celebrate human valor.

O'Grady's version is, in his own words, a 'reading', and also, since he has arranged his lines on the page as a pattern, it is a 'transposition' of the original. Readers who wish to know precisely what each line of *The Gododdin* may have meant will, of course, be glad to consult Kenneth Jackson's scholarly translation and analysis (1969), but O'Grady in a most unobtrusive and non-egocentric way has undertaken to suggest '*one* way Aneirin might have written his poem today, did he live among us and write of local wars'.[26]

In citing examples here of poets who may have either coincided with or departed from the original function of the poet whom they have undertaken to reinterpret, we are not in any way suggesting that their deviation is 'wrong' or even that, if they had only attempted to fulfill the original function, then they would be a present-day success. Here reference has been made to modern

---

[25] David Jones, *In Parenthesis* (New York, new ed., 1963), title page (passage from *Gododdin*, ed. Williams, stanza xxvii); p. 207 (notes), quoting *Mabinogion*, trans. Lady Charlotte Guest (London, 1906), pp. 273, 98.

[26] Desmond O'Grady, *The Gododdin* (Dublin, 1977), pp. 75, 77, 78.

poets merely as indicators of the variability of our reinterpretations of the past. It is, however, literary historians and literary critics rather than modern, creative poets who must carry the burden of discovering the original functions of the early and pre-modern poets whom they interpret *before* they write their critiques.

CHAPTER 6

OTHER EARLY WESTERN EUROPEAN CULTURES: NORSE AND OLD ENGLISH

Among the earliest recorded Germanic cultures, Old Norse and Old English retain many of the features characteristic of what we have called the primal state. Indeed, even today English speakers unconsciously memorialize Germanic gods when they name the days of the week 'Tíw's day' (Tuesday), 'Woden's day' (Wednesday), 'Thor's day' (Thursday), and 'Fríg-day' (Friday).

1. THE NORSE TRADITION

The survivals of native religion, beliefs, rites, and cults among the North Germanic peoples of Scandinavia are particularly striking; and, because of their comparatively late acceptance of Christianity, the recoverable details of their pagan heritage are somewhat more extensive than are those, for instance, of the West Germanic peoples in England.

The great Icelandic historian and antiquarian, Snorri Sturluson, writing in the first part of the thirteenth century, warned his readers that Christians must not believe in pagan gods. Yet his own writings, along with the earlier fragmentary lays of *The Poetic Edda*, provide us with a revealing glimpse into the divine world (Category 1) as it was conceived of by the Norse – a world, somewhat like that of the early Irish tradition, which is divided by opposing forces including two kinds of gods, the Aesir and the Vanir, and by giants and dwarfs who are their enemies.

In his *Skáldskaparmál* (*Poetic Diction*, composed ca 1220) Snorri's protagonist asks the question, 'Where did that art come from that is known as poetry?'[1] The narration which Snorri provides by way of an answer is as detailed as

[1] Snorri Sturluson, *Edda: Gylfagynning og Prosafortellingene av Skáldskaparmál*, ed. Anne Holtsmark and Jón Helgason (Copenhagen, 1950), pp. 81, 83; *The Prose Edda of Snorri Sturluson*, trans. Jean I. Young (Berkeley and Los Angeles, 1954), pp. 100–102.

anything in the Welsh myth of Taliesin, which it resembles in several basic respects. The mead that inspires poetry was magically produced as a peace-potion during a meeting of truce at which the Aesir and the Vanir both deposited spittle in a crock. The Aesir transformed the contents into a human named Kvasir who travelled far and wide dispensing unlimited wisdom. Two dwarves killed Kvasir and mixed his blood with honey and thus produced the mead that turns the person who drinks it into a poet (*skáld*) or sage (*froetha mathr*). A giant extorted the mead from the dwarves. Then Odin in turn stole the mead from the giants and gave it to the Aesir and to those humans who can compose (*yrkia*, 'work') poetry.

The underlying implications of the myth, like those associated with the Welsh Gwion/Taliesin, are clear. Poetry is invented magically; it emanates from the divine; and it relies on the intoxicating power of a specially brewed liquor to transmit superhuman wisdom. Some intermediary donor may, wittingly or unwittingly, grant the gift to mortals, who thus acquire a power unique among humans to wield the wisdom that relates to the past, present, and future of their tribe. Poetry does not *originate* among human beings; it is a gift *acquired* by them through a special chain of events involving a mixture of trickery, deception, and occasional divine grace.

As might be expected from Snorri's attention to this myth, Norse poets frequently invoked the supernatural source of poetry (Category 4). So, the tenth-century Icelander Einar Helgason refers to his poem, *Vellekla*, as 'Kvasir's life-blood'.[2] And even in the highly realistic sagas, frequent reference is made to the mythic origins of poetry. At one tense moment in the *Gisli-Saga*, for instance, the hero composes a stanza in order to quiet his bondwoman. 'I pour forth the liquor of the dwarves,' he assures her. Then on another occasion when hard pressed, he composes a poem for his wife and similarly assures her, 'I pour forth the liquor of the dwarves.'[3]

The functions of the verbal artificer are as varied in the Norse tradition as in the other traditions which have been examined here. The poets preserved myths (Category 1), as, for instance, most notably in the Eddic poem called the *Volu-spá* (*The Sibyl's Prophecy*).[4] Because of its scope, this poem might better be entitled *The Prophetess's Cosmic Vision*, for it fulfills a wider function than that of merely prophesying the future.

The seer is interrogated by Odin, the supreme god of wisdom and poetry, and rather in the manner of the privileged Welsh bard Cynddelw, she calls for silence before she delivers her body of wisdom. In her opening response, she

[2] *The Skalds*, trans. Lee M. Hollander (Princeton, 1945), p. 104.
[3] *The Saga of Gisli*, trans. George Johnston and Peter Foote (Toronto, 1963), pp. 40 (chap. 26) and 55 (chap. 34); *Gísla saga Súrsonar*, ed. Agnete Loth (Copenhagen, 1963).
[4] *Poems of the Vikings*, trans. Patricia Terry (Indianapolis and New York, 1969), pp. 3–12; *Edda: Die Lieder des Codex Regius*, ed. Gustav Neckel, rev. H, Kuhn (Heidelberg, 1962), I, 1–16 (original).

claims kinship with the giants and undertakes to unveil past, present, and future. Like other seers, her utterances are recondite and obscure, but the sequence of her vision is relatively clear. She describes the evolution of the cosmos from the earliest beginning. She alludes to the role that is played in human affairs by the three Norns, Urd (fate – that which *has been* preordained to happen in the past), Verdandi (becoming – that which *is now* beginning to take place), and Skuld (necessity – that which *will inevitably* happen). She describes the past conflict of the gods and then foretells the impending destruction of the gods (*ragna-rok*) and finally describes the rebirth of the cosmos.

Then, in an ambiguous conclusion that is appropriate to a seer, she seems to say that her inspiration is now sinking, or in other words, that her trance has expired, and therefore she can tell Odin no more.

Apart from the superhuman seer in *The Poetic Edda*, an actual class of women variously called *volva* or *seith-kona* (spell-woman) or *spá-kona* (prophecy-woman) did in fact practise soothsaying (Category 7) in Scandinavian countries, just as their Viking descendants in Lowland Scotland perpetuated the tradition under the title of *spae-wife*.[5]

In *The Saga of Eric the Red*, for instance, on the occasion of a tribal emergency, a *volva* follows a ritual which is somewhat reminiscent of the Early Irish ritual of *imbas forosnai* (described in Chapter 3). The prophetess was seated upon a high-seat that was provided with a cushion stuffed with hens' feathers. She wore clothing that included materials such as lambskin, cats' fur, and calfskin – all presumably considered to be magically efficacious. She wore a decorated mantle, bore a pouch filled with charms, and carried an ornamented staff. Before the delivery of the prophecy which was desired of her, she was fed goat-milk gruel and animal hearts. An assistant prompted her *séance* by singing pagan 'fate-songs' (*varth-lokkur*), and, with the assistance of the spirits who had congregated around her, she was then able to interpret the future accurately, for, according to the saga, 'there were few things that did not turn out as she had prophesied'.[6]

The seer was said to be assisted by the ancestors of those families who were especially concerned with her sooth-saying, and she would customarily prophesy at feasts in the autumn and winter, relying perhaps on the belief that access to the spirits in the otherworld was at that time most available, as it was similarly thought to be in Ireland at Samhain and Wales at Calan Gaeaf – the ominous beginning of winter.

Despite the spread of Christianity throughout Scandinavia, the Norse

---

[5] For references to the Norse terms mentioned, see Richard Cleasby and Gudbrand Vigfusson, *An Icelandic-English Dictionary* (Oxford, 1874), and see *spae* in *The Scottish National Dictionary*, ed. William Grant and David D. Murison (Edinburgh, 1971), vol. 8.
[6] *The Vinland Sagas*, trans. Magnus Magnusson and Hermann Pálsson (Harmondsworth, England, 1965), pp. 81–83 (*Eirik's Saga*, chap. 4).

tradition-carriers transmitted not only their native mythology but also the Germanic legends (Category 2) which are reflected in the heroic lays of *The Elder Edda*. Even more, when the Norse settled in Iceland, where they developed a new form of democratic government, they also developed a new form of story-telling – the family saga (Category 3, the tribal past).

The older Norse sagas dealt with the ancient inherited heroic narratives concerning Sigurd and Brynhild and other legendary characters, and they fulfilled the same functions that the legends and lays of Cú Chulainn and of Finn mac Cumhail fulfilled for an Irish audience. The Icelandic family sagas, however, were, in a sense, a new invention in the Western European tradition. They cast the deeds of the enterprising settlers not into a heroic light but into a dispassionate and ruthlessly realistic perspective. In a remote way, they could be said to be akin to the settlement stories incorporated by the Irish antiquarians in *The Book of Invasions*, but they deal with the real-life founding families of Iceland rather than with abstract divinities and superhuman beings.

The problems that the sagas present are human problems. In *Njál's Saga*, for instance, the prudent hero Njál is potentially the ideal law-speaker, yet he is ultimately destroyed by the failure of his friend Gunnar to accept Njál's wise advice; and Njál's wife Bergthora is potentially an ideal wife, but she becomes fatally addicted to vengeance.[7] In *Grettir's Saga*, the truculent yet well-intentioned hero Grettir is the very reverse of the wise Njál, and he brings his own destruction upon himself.[8]

Thus the compilers of the Icelandic sagas interpreted their own web of family history against the background of the familial legends that had accumulated around the names of the leaders who had emerged during the great adventure of settlement in an undeveloped country – a challenge that had seldom in the same way, for instance, faced the Irish during the middle ages. The individuality of the settlers is clearly conceived, their very utterances are recorded, and – more than that – the dependence of the settlers upon the balance between human wisdom and human folly is dispassionately displayed. It may be said that these sagas are virtual case-studies in political science and that the tribal story-tellers have developed a new functional outlet for the exercise of their talents.

In the sphere of the poetry of praise and dispraise (Category 5), the Scandinavian *skald* as a court-poet is much more predictably traditional, even in Iceland, than are the authors of the sagas. Sigvat Thordarson the Icelandic skald, whose poems are quoted extensively by Snorri Sturluson in his

---

[7] *Brennu-Njáls Saga*, ed. Einar O. Sveinsson (*Islenzk fornrit* 7)(Reykjavík, 1954); *Njal's Saga*, trans. Magnus Magnusson and Hermann Pálsson (Harmondsworth, 1960), chapters 74, 75, 78.
[8] *Grettis Saga Asmundarsonar*, ed. Guthni Jónsson (*Islenzk fornrit* 7)(Reykjavík, 1936); *Grettir's Saga*, trans. Denton Fox and Hermann Pálsson (Toronto, 1974).

Heimskringla[9] obviously for their historical value – is an outstanding example.[10]

Poetry ran in Sigvat's family line, and the members of his family successfully devoted their poetic ability to the service of noble patrons. Sigvat's father had been a skald to an Icelandic jarl, Sigvaldi; Sigvat's sister's son Ottar was also a skald; and Sigvat himself, who reputedly could talk in rhyme as easily as if he were talking in the ordinary way, cherished particularly high aspirations. He had the gift, and he knew it! He introduced himself to Olaf Haraldson, the King of Norway, later known as St Olaf, and at once address a eulogy to him. The startled King – somewhat like a forerunner out of a Molière play – protested that he didn't understand poetry, but he soon became the persuasive Sigvat's chief patron and awarded him with a golden ring. Sigvat also received rings from Jarl Ragnvald and from Canute, the King of England, Denmark, and Norway; and, after composing an apologetic poem atoning for some offence like those current in Ireland and Wales, he was awarded a golden sword by St Olaf.

Sigvat's extant poems commemorate King Olaf's battles, eulogize the King's bravery in his last battle at Stiklastadar (AD 1030), report his death, lament his death, and celebrate the miracles associated with St Olaf. Moreover, as an instructive side-light on the function of the primal poet, the evidence shows that he served the King as adviser on diplomatic relations between Norway and Iceland, particularly as they related to Christian missions; and that he carried out delicate negotiations that assisted the King to win Astrid of Sweden as his bride.

Characteristically, just before his death, Sigvat the honest professional public-relations-expert advises St Olaf's successor, King Magnus, not to be offended by the true words of poets:

> Beware lest you are angered by warnings
> Frankly spoken by men of wisdom
> Whose chief concern is to uphold your honor.

Other examples of the central role played by the Norse custodians and masters of the verbal arts might be cited, particularly in the area of tribal law (item 5). Like their Irish and Welsh counterparts and like their Old English and other Germanic counterparts, they were expected to be able to recite their lore publicly and might be called upon to render judgments.

---

[9] Snorri Sturluson, *Heimskringla*, ed. Finnur Jónsson (Copenhagen, 1911); see index, p. 657, under *Sigvatr* for references; for translations, see *Heimskringla*, trans. Erling Monsen and A. H. Smith (New York, 1932), index, p. 762, under *Sigvat the Scald*; and Hollander, *Skalds*, pp. 147–176.

[10] Finnur Jónsson, ed., *Den norsk-islandske Skaldedigtning* (Copenhagen, 1908–15), pp. 223–275.

2. THE OLD ENGLISH TRADITION

The Angles, Saxons, and other Germanic peoples who first invaded Britain in the mid-fifth century were pagan, but the surviving Old English literature to which they gave birth is for the most part explicitly Christian in function. After the missionary visit of St Augustine of Canterbury in the year 597, Christianity spread rapidly throughout the English-speaking settlements. With the new religion came literacy, and the clerics who mastered the art of writing were understandably more concerned with the propagation of the faith than with the recording of their Germanic ancestors' pagan traditions.

The magnitude of the cultural change that is reflected in Old English literature is remarkable. Thus, in a poem entitled *The Gifts of Men*[11], when the author deals with poetic skill as one of the gifts, he does not attribute it to any pagan deity or associate it with any mantic practice. It is *God*, the poet says, who bestows gifts upon each and all, so that no one shall be utterly cut off either from mental skill or from deeds of might, although God will not allow anyone to advance his fame in the world excessively lest he despise the less-gifted.

Despite this major shift in attitude towards the source of poetic inspiration, however, the poet does mention some human activities that may have been derived from the pagan past. In his list of gifts, the poet includes several of the verbal arts, such as public speaking, the composing of lays, the performing of songs, the singing of divine songs of praise, the understanding of book lore, the craft of writing, and the councillor's interpretation of tribal rules and legal judgments. The references to 'lays' (*giedda*) and 'songs' (*léotha*) and 'tribal rules' (*folc-raedenne*) and 'judgments' (*dómas*) suggest that the pious author had not entirely separated himself from his Germanic roots.

Some Old English poems are more primitive, and none more so than the seventh-century *Wídsíth*, 'The Widely-Traveled One'.[12] This poem portrays the legendary career of a *scop* (equivalent to a bard) who departed from his kinfolk, the Myrgings of Saxony, in order to pursue his profession far and wide throughout the world. In the halls of kings he would sing to the accompaniment of a harp with such skill that the experts would declare 'they had never heard a better song'. In keeping with his traditional concept of his poetic function, the poet Wídsíth prides himself particularly in three accomplishments. He has acquired universal knowledge by dint of his superhuman travels; he has learned of the myths, legends, and history that are associated with the

[11] *The Exeter Book*, ed. George P. Krapp and E. van K. Dobbie (Anglo-Saxon Poetic Records 3)(New York, 1936), pp. 137–140; *Anglo-Saxon Poetry*, trans. R. K. Gordon, rev. ed. (London, 1954), pp. 316–317.
[12] *Exeter Book*, ed. Krapp and Dobbie, pp. 149–153; *Anglo-Saxon Poetry*, tran. Gordon, pp. 67–70.

rulers of the world; and he has been generously rewarded for the songs in which he has proclaimed their fame.

As to the first two topics, the basis of Wídsíth's claim clearly reflects the semantic development of a principal Indo-European verb relating to 'knowing' (discussed in Chapter 7). So, for instance, the Greek verb *(w)oida* means not only 'I have seen' but also by implication, 'I have a mental image – an idea', and hence 'I know'. Correspondingly, in the Old Norse *Sibyl's Prophecy*, the seer repeatedly utters similar claims: 'I remember', 'I know', 'I saw', 'I see'. And in *The Lay of Vafthrudnir*, Odin, the father of wisdom and of poetry, repeatedly boasts, 'Far have I traveled',[13] with the implication that his travels have provided him with wisdom.

These are the frequently echoed authenticating boasts appropriate to any sage, whether human or divine.So, for instance, in the Irish *Bricriu's Feast*, the semi-divine Curoi boasts that he is acquainted with Ireland, Scotland, Europe, Africa, Asia, Greece, Scythia, the Orkneys, the Pillars of Hercules, Brigantium, and Gades – place-names drawn from Irish antiquarian lore.[14] In the Welsh *Culhwch and Olwen*, Arthur's gate-keeper boasts – equally improbably – that he has acquired his wide diplomatic knowledge from having visited Caer Se, Asse, Sach, Salach, Lotor, Ffotor, India the Great, India the Lesser, Europe, Africa, Corsica, Caer Brythwch, Nerthach, Greece, Caer Oeth, Anoeth, and Caer Nefenhir.[15]

Wídsíth's claims are less droll than those of his Irish and Welsh competitors but are only slightly more restrained. He knows the more readily accessible Germanic peoples – the Goths, the Swedes, the Geats, the South-Danes, the Angles, and the Saxons; but he claims that he has come to know innumerable other obscure European tribes and even some who are much more exotic such as the Medes and the Persians. And – as scholars have pointed out – his chronological range is particularly startling: he has served Eormanric, King of the Ostrogoths, who flourished ca AD 375, and he has also accompanied Aelfwine, King of the Lombards, when he invaded Italy in 568![16]

Above all, however, Wídsíth is particularly proud of the rewards which he has received for his songs: King Guthere of the Burgundians gave him a jewel; King Eormanric of the Ostrogoths gave him a bracelet of pure gold 'worth six hundred pence by shilling-count'; the King's wife, Queen Ealhhild gave him another ring.

---

[13] For the *Prophecy*, see note 4 above. For *Vafthrudnir*, see Terry, *Poems*, trans., pp. 39–48; *Edda*, ed. Neckel, rev. Kuhn, I, 45–55.

[14] *Fled Bricrend*, ed. trans. George Henderson (Irish Texts Society 2)(London, 1899), chap. 93.

[15] *The White Book Mabinogion*, ed. J. Gwenogvryn Evans (Pwllheli, 1907), p. 229; *The Mabinogi*, trans. Patrick K. Ford (Berkeley, 1977), pp. 125–126.

[16] See *Widsith*, ed. Kemp Malone, rev. ed. (Copenhagen, 1962).

> Her praise was spread through many a land
> Whenever I should tell in song
> Where under heaven was the best
> Of gold-robed queens bestowing gifts.

When Wídsíth returned to his own tribe, he gave his precious bracelet to the King of the Myrgings, and the King in turn granted to the poet the land which earlier had belonged to his father. No doubt the gleemen who in later times sang Wídsíth's song to their new patrons hoped that these ancient examples of generous behavior might be infectious.

Deor's Lament[17] reflects, in the brief compass of forty-two lines, on the other side of the relationship between the lordly patron and the omniscient poet. Deor, a legendary *scop* belonging to an obscure South Baltic tribe, the Heodingas, laments that another poet 'skilled in song' has displaced him from the land that had once been given to him by his tribal lord. He enumerates a series of disastrous events, some legendary, some historical, that were familiar to him within the range of his Germanic repertoire of poetry, and between these references he reflects on his own situation. Six times he interjects the refrain:

> As that passed by, so may this.

Here the repetitive cry seems to suggest that the poet is invoking a charm (Category 9) in order to free himself from his misfortunes. Certainly the pattern of the refrain, '*Thaes ofereode, thisses swa maeg,*' reflects the internationally distributed formula of the charm, 'As X happens, so also may Y.' But if so intended, the Anglo-Saxon redactor of the legend of Deor counterbalances this pagan element by expressing in the concluding lines a pious acceptance of the divine will: the Lord works variously, granting favor to some, and 'a deal of woes' to others.

Generally speaking, it may be said that in comparison with Early Irish records, for instance, Old English literature provides a scanty representation of the survivals of a pre-Christian culture. In the realm of praise-poetry (Category 5), however, pagan patterns do persist in a religious setting. A celebrated example of this kind of survival can be discerned in the *Hymn*[18] attributed by the Venerable Bede to an Anglo-Saxon named Caedmon. His praise-poem, which is only nine lines in length, was composed perhaps as early as 680 or even earlier at the monastery of Whitby (in Yorkshire). The

---

[17] *Exeter Book*, ed. Krapp and Dobbie, pp. 178–179; *Anglo-Saxon Poetry*, trans. Gordon, pp. 71–72. See Morton Bloomfield, 'The Form of Deor', *PMLA* 79 (1964), 534–541; for a contrary but relevant view, see Norman E. Eliason, 'Two Old English Scop Poems', *PMLA* 81 (1966), 185–192.

[18] *The Anglo-Saxon Minor Poems*, ed. George P. Krapp (Anglo-Saxon Poetic Records 2)(New York, 1932), pp. 105–106; for a literal translation and discussion, see Stanley B. Greenfield, *A Critical History of Old English Literature* (New York, 1965), pp. 178–179.

monastery had only recently been established (in 657) in what were then the northernmost reaches of Anglo-Saxon Christianity, and there the untutored singer composed a spontaneous new song in praise of the Lord.

From the very first line, the poet follows the native patterns of praise poetry. Doubtless many pagan examples echoed in his ears, and yet he reversed their application, for he had presumably also heard a different form of laudation in his monastery: the *Te Deum laudamus*, the *Lauda anima mea Dominum* (Psalm 145), the *Lauda Jerusalem Dominum* (Psalm 147), the *Laudate Dominum in Sanctis eius* (Psalm 150), the *Laudate Dominum omnes Gentes* (Psalm 116), and the *Laudate pueri Dominum* (Psalm 112).

In reference to God as his patron, the poet plays entirely on the secular Old English terms conventionally used for 'ruler'. In the first line, with a marked emphasis on the newness of his theme, he sings: '*Now* we should praise. . . .' First he addresses this praise to the Warden (*Weard*) of heaven's kingdom'; that is, not to some earthly king who, as a patron greedy for fame, would purchase praise from poets.

We should praise 'the might of the Governor (*Meotod*)'; that is, the power of the being who metes out providence rather than that of a pagan god who must blindly yield to fate (*wyrd*). We should praise the Warden's 'bold plan' rather than rely on human plans. We should praise 'the achievement of the Father of Glory (*Wuldor-Faeder*)', not that of any mortal ruler.

The 'Holy Artificer (*Halig Scyppend*)' shaped earth for mankind with heaven as a roof; the 'Eternal Ruler' (*Ece Drihten*), the 'Almighty God-of-Love (*Frea Aelmihtig*)', prepared middle-earth as a habitation for human beings.

The *Hymn* is older than any other comparable Old English praise-poem; all of the key words and phrases are native Old English; and all of them subliminally would have carried pagan connotations, the significance of which only a missionary could have re-interpreted. Almost inevitably, while making the transition to a new faith, the poet is fulfilling his traditional function in a traditional manner.

Soon other Old English poets followed his path. In *The Dream of the Rood*,[19] an anonymous poet hails Christ as a 'young hero', who, in keeping with the Anglo-Saxon tradition of muscular Christianity, is 'strong', 'bold-minded', and 'brave'. In *Guthlac*,[20] the saint is 'bold' in the use of spiritual weapons, and the poet praises his might and his wisdom.

Secular Old English praise-poems, which resemble and yet differ from their Celtic counterparts, also survive. *The Battle of Brunanburh* (AD 937)[21] praises King Athelstan and his brother Prince Eadmund after they have routed the

---

[19] *The Vercelli Book*, ed. George P. Krapp (Anglo-Saxon Poetic Records 2)(New York, 1932), pp. 61–65 (lines 35–141); *Anglo-Saxon Poetry*, trans. Gordon, pp. 235–238.
[20] *Exeter Book*, ed. Krapp and Dobbie, pp. 45–188 (line 176); *Anglo-Saxon Poetry*, trans. Gordon, 256–279.
[21] *Anglo-Saxon Minor Poems*, ed. Dobbie, pp. 16–20; *Anglo-Saxon Poetry*, trans. Gordon, pp. 327–328.

Scots, Welsh, and Norwegians and have achieved the greatest victory that the Angles and Saxons have won since they settled in Britain. *The Battle of Maldon*[22] (AD 991) presents an even more dramatic encomium of the English warriors in their fatal stand against the Viking invaders who have landed at Essex.

Neither of these poems, however, is a praise-poem specifically addressed by a bard to his patron. In *Maldon*, the English hero, earl Byrhtnoth, refuses to settle for a truce that would require him to submit to the payment of tribute to the enemy; and the anonymous English poet expresses his admiration for the battle-leader's fortitude; but the poet is not personally Byrhtnoth's bard, nor is he a spokesman for the warrior class.

This latter distinction can be illuminated by Celtic parallels such as the Welsh panegyric 'Elmwood Edge' (ca 600) attributed to the historical Taliesin. This poem is one of the series referred to in the previous chapter which is dedicated to Urien, the Welsh warlord. In it, Urien's son Owain faces a challenge precisely like that facing Byrhtnoth. He proudly rejects the humiliating terms offered by the English invader, whom the Welsh have nicknamed 'Flame-thrower':

> Flame-thrower shouted a mighty boast:
> 'Would they hand over hostages, are they ready?'
> To him answered Owain, scourge of the English,
> 'They would not give them; they were not ready to,
>   and would not be.'
> And the army rushed forward with their leader.

In conclusion, Taliesin adds: 'I shall devise, the year long, a song for their victory', and then adds the refrain which has already been quoted acknowledging his bardic fealty to his patron Urien.[23]

In contrast with the Early Welsh praise-poets, the function fulfilled by the English composers of *Brunanburh*, of *Maldon*, and of the other poems entered in the *Old English Annals* seems rather to be that of monastic chroniclers. At the threat of invasion, they fervently expressed their patriotism by eulogizing the heroes who had saved the day and by condemning the deserters such as the wretched Godric in *Maldon* who had betrayed his people. Functionally, their poems might be said to be analogous to the war poems produced in Britain during World War I. Thus, for instance, *The Times* (London, August 9, 1915) issued a special supplement entitled *War Poems from the Times, August 1914–1915*, in which Rudyard Kipling proclaimed, 'The Hun is at the gate', and other

---

[22] *Anglo-Saxon Minor Poems*, ed. Dobbie, pp. 7–16: *Anglo-Saxon Poetry*, trans. Gordon, pp. 329–334.
[23] *The Poems of Taliesin*, ed. Sir Ifor Williams, rev. J. E. Caerwyn Williams (Mediaeval and Modern Welsh Series 3)(Dublin, 1968), poem 6; *The Earliest Welsh Poetry*, trans. Joseph P. Clancy (London, 1970), pp. 30–31. See chap. 5, note 16.

poets such as Robert Bridges, Thomas Hardy, and Laurence Binyon joined with him in patriotic fervor. Predictably, the poetic styles of the Old English and of the Modern English poets are very different, yet the poets in the *Annals* and the poets in *The Times* are performing essentially similar roles. The primal function can be fulfilled in many ways. In the face of a national crisis, all of these poets are attempting by means of their word-craft to interpret the emergency and to provide some appropriate and commonly acceptable sentiment for the occasion.

In the pursuit of further clarification of the Old English poet's function as a composer of praise-poetry, the great epic *Béowulf* offers the most abundant and yet ambiguous evidence. Unlike some of the early Celtic poetic traditions such as that of Cú Chulainn or of Taliesin referred to in this present study, the legend of Béowulf disappeared from oral transmission in England soon after the Norman Conquest of England. Today only one trace survives in written transmission – and that is the version recorded in a manuscript ca AD 1000, just shortly before the Normans began to superimpose their own alien culture on the English.

From the point of view of the later understanding of the poem, it is significant to notice that the text lay unnoticed until it was excerpted briefly in a catalogue of 'Ancient Northern Literature' published in 1705 and that it was not published *in toto* until 1815.[24] Consequently, the critical attention paid to the epic is of a comparatively recent period, and the earliest commentators were at a loss to deal with its significance. So, for instance, the French critic Hippolyte Taine in his *History of English Literature* (1863) esteemed Béowulf as a hero but said of the poem: 'Passion bellows forth like a great shapeless beast; and that is all. It rises and starts in little abrupt lines; it is the acme of barbarism.'[25] Subsequent criticism has been somewhat more perceptive in explaining the poet's function and technique, and comparisons with the heroic lays of the Norse *Edda* and other early Germanic heroic literature have clarified the nature of the poet's function.[26]

The *Béowulf* poet obviously admires the pagan ideals implicit in the narratives which he has inherited from the continental traditions of his Germanic ancestors. Just as the Norse poets admired Sigurd's heroic quest for fame, so too the Old English poet respects Béowulf's heroic impulses. 'Let him who can,' says Béowulf, 'win fame (*dóm*) before his death.' But, to a remarkable degree, the Old English poet emphasizes the importance of statecraft in the attainment of fame. Bravery and strength are not enough; altruistic wisdom is all-important.

---

[24] For the manuscript, see *Beowulf and Judith*, ed. E. V. Dobbie (Anglo-Saxon Poetic Records 4)(New York, 1953); for the present references, see text, bibliography, vocabulary, and notes in *Beowulf*, 3rd ed., ed. F. Klaeber (Boston, 1950).

[25] H. L. Taine, *History of English Literature 1*, trans. H. van Laun (New York, 1877), pp. 50–51 (bk. 1, chap. 1, section 5).

[26] See, for instance, Dorothy Whitelock, *The Audience of Beowulf*, (Oxford, 1951).

The word *fród* ('wise, mature, experienced') is used either alone or in compound form seventeen times in *Béowulf*; *snottor* ('wise, prudent') is used nineteen times; and *wís* ('wise, knowing') is used thirteen times; and all three terms are used especially in reference to the poet's paragons: to Hróthgár, the exemplary king of the Danes, who is presented as the antithesis of the unjust and unworthy King Heremód, and to Béowulf, the warrior and subsequent king and savior of the Géats.

The Old English poet has moderated the traditional Germanic emphasis on martial achievements by his emphasis on wisdom and has instead exalted the values of peace and friendship, as is particularly evident in any comparison with the attitude of the Norse poets towards the various degrees of wisdom. The Norse cognates of the three Old English words *fród*, *snottor*, and *wís* are used in quite different applications in the *Elder Edda*.[27] Fafnir, the dragon who guards the cursed hoard of gold, is *fród*, as are the gods Odin and Frey; the proverbial wise man characterized in *Hávamál* is *snotr*; and the gods are described as being *víss*. Other words than these, however, are used for the battle-hero Sigurd, such as *horskr* ('smart') and *spakr* ('perceptive'). The Norse poets conceive of their hero as possessing a kind of wisdom that might be described as 'expedient wisdom', 'appropriate *savoir faire*' – a concept underlying much of the motivation in ancient Germanic and Celtic narratives that have here already been discussed.

In the Norse *Hávamál*, the compiler of gnomic lore admits: 'Middling-wise should each man be; never look to be wise, for a wise man's heart is seldom happy if he is in fact all-wise (*al-snotr*).' In contrast, the Old English author of *Béowulf* seems to believe that human wisdom is indispensable, even though the truly wise man cannot outwit the inevitabilities of fate and of providence; and not only is wisdom attainable, but it is also essential for the welfare of society.

In both cultures, the functions of the poet are similarly tied to the obligation of transmitting tribal wisdom, but the composer of *Béowulf* – undoubtedly because of his contact with new Christian ideals – has acquired a complex concept of wisdom which rises above the older Germanic ideals of bravery, honor, and enduring fame. In other words, within the framework of the present analysis of 'primal' societies, it seems evident that some societies are 'less primal' than others. Nonetheless, even if this concession to the variability of human behavior is granted, it also seems true to say that the function of the poet is central to the functioning of the cultures that have here been examined. The poet is trusted as the potential savior of the tribe, for he has acquired traditional wisdom and can be expected to utter his potent judgments whenever he is called upon to do so.

---

[27] See *Edda*, II, *Kurzes Wörterbuch*, ed. G. Neckel, rev. H. Kuhn (Heidelberg, 1968), under the words discussed.

3. INTERPRETING THE TRADITION

As with the early Welsh poetry which has been discussed in the previous chapter, so with Old Norse and Old English poetry, later literary reworkings of the primal sources have produced entirely new interpretations of the meaning and significance that the early poets and their audiences attached to their native traditions.

Once again, as with Welsh, the redoubtable poet and antiquarian Thomas Gray clearly reflects the attitude of enlightened contemporary eighteenth-century readers towards what he calls 'the style [of poetry] that reigned in ancient times among the neighbouring nations or those who subdued the greater part of this Island'.[28] Gray did not deal with Old English literature, which was still in his day virtually unexplored, but he found poetic inspiration in Old Norse.

His *Fatal Sisters*, in which the Valkyries weave the web of fate for human warriors, is based on a poem preserved in the Old Norse *Njal's Saga*, and here he drew upon the pioneering Latin translation (1697) made by the Scandinavian antiquarian Torfaeus. His *Descent of Odin*, in which Odin queries a sibyl about the predicted death of his son Balder, is based on the Eddic poem, *Balder's Dreams*, and his version similarly relies on a Latin translation (1689) made by another Scandinavian antiquarian, Bartholinus. In 'translating' both poems, Gray does not indulge in quite the same embellishments that characterize his Welsh renderings of *The Bard* and *The Triumphs of Owen* (mentioned earlier) but reproduces his originals sufficiently clearly that his version at least reflects the sense as it is now understood by modern philologists.[29]

In the nineteenth century, romanticism displaced the antiquarian neo-classicism characteristic of Gray and his contemporaries. Myth and legend were transmuted in new and often strange ways. Medieval sources offered enticing plots, settings, characters, and imagery that invited reinterpretation; and soon anachronistic new meanings were attached to the originals.

Within the Germanic realm, Richard Wagner provides the extreme example of this kind of alchemy.[30] In *The Ring of the Nibelung* (1876) he drew eclectically upon the fragmentary and primitive Old Norse lays of Sigurd and upon the Middle High German courtly epic of Siegfried, *The Nibelungenlied*. His manipulations of the raw materials are complex, but an examination of his treatment of the death of Brynhilde may suffice to illustrate the process of his transformations.

[28] *Gray*, ed. Starr and Hendrickson. (See chap. 5, note 24.)
[29] Compare, for instance, stanza 5 of 'Balder's Dreams' as translated by Terry, *Poems*, p. 242, with Bartholinus's Latin as translated by Starr and Hendrickson, *Gray*, p. 216–217, lines 33–40, and with Gray's version in *Gray*, p. 33, lines 27–36.
[30] Richard Wagner, *The Ring of the Nibelung*, trans. Stewart Robb (New York, 1960).

For the Norse audience, the lays dealing with Sigurd the Fearless and Brynhild the Valkyrie unfold a tragic sequence of events originating in a crime committed by the malicious god Loki. As a consequence, a curse has been placed upon a supernatural treasure; the lure of this treasure gives rise to another crime; crime demands vengeance; and gods, giants, dwarves, and humans are thus swept inevitably into a disastrous sequence of obligatory acts of retaliation.

In the *Sigurd Lay* [31], when Brynhild learns that Sigurd has been killed, she laughs ominously and curses the slayers:

> Brynhild laughed – the whole hall resounded –
> Just once, with all her heart.
> 'Long may you enjoy your lands and thanes,
> You who brought down the bravest of men!'

Then, according to a manifestly pagan lay, *The Short Lay of Sigurd* [32], she has eight of her slaves and five bondsmaids killed so that they may provide her in Hel with a suitable retinue; she orders that her body be burned in a funeral pyre next to that laid out for Sigurd; and she kills herself. And, in sequence, according to *Brynhild's Journey to Hel* [33], she is transformed in the fire and rides in ghostly form on a chariot to Hel where at last she can be united with Sigurd.

The poet's bald recital of the passionate deeds that were once associated with, for instance, the Hindu ceremony of suttee suggests that his audience not only believed in the existence of supernatural valkyries such as Brynhild but also understood the traditional basis of the ancient rite of concremation. Cremation enables beings of exalted rank to continue their lives in the otherworld; and in order to maintain their happiness and their status they are expected to carry their favorite possessions – wives, horses, chariots, servants, weapons – with them. Even women such as Brynhild may enjoy this privilege, provided that they enter Hel by way of a violent death. [34]

The sophisticated composer of the Middle High German *Nibelungenlied*, on the other hand, treats his narrative materials as if they were part of a courtly romance. For his purposes, Brünhilt is a highly intractable character, and he therefore allows her virtually to disappear from his narrative after Sigfrit is slain, while he concentrates on providing his audience with a moving depiction of the sorrows, frustration, and indignation of Sigfrit's status-conscious wife Kriemhilt.

In reinterpreting the early sources of Germanic legend, Wagner had at his

---

[31] *Poems*, trans. Terry, pp. 174–176; *Edda*, ed. Neckel, I, 198–201.
[32] *Poems*, trans. Terry, pp. 182–195; *Edda*, ed. Neckel, I, 207–218.
[33] *Poems*, trans. Terry, pp. 193–195.
[34] Concerning concremation, see H. R. Ellis Davidson, *Gods and Myths of Northern Europe* (Harmondsworth, 1964), pp. 150–152, 157–158, and H. M. Smyser, 'Ibn Fadlán's Account of the Rus', in *Franciplegius*, ed. Jeff B. Bessinger, Jr., and Robert Creed (New York, 1965), p. 109.

disposal not only the original materials but also translations and commentaries, including such works of scholarship as Jacob Grimm's *German Mythology*, and brother Wilhelm Grimm's *Germanic Heroic Legends*, and the brothers Grimms' joint publication *German Legends*.

Wagner also had a talented and wealthy wife, Cosima, who could and did give him literary suggestions, and he had King Ludwig II of Bavaria as a patron. His relationship to the society with which he was involved was much more complicated than that of the Norse or the Middle High German poet. He believed as much as any Norseman that gold could be the curse of mankind, but his daring socialistic theories on the subject were not likely to gain acceptance from members of Germany's establishment. At the same time, though the sources of his operatic cycle were pagan, his faith was Christian, and his philosophy of life was tinged with Buddhist mysticism.

Predictably enough, in the *Götterdämmerung* before Wagner reaches the climactic scene of Brunnhilda's immolation, he crowds in a bewildering sequence of events. Brunnhilda removes the curse on the Rhine-gold by returning the ring to the Rhine-maidens; the villainous Hagen is drowned; and, in a scene suggested by the totally unrelated Norse lay (already discussed), *The Sibyl's Prophecy*, Wagner portrays the destruction of Valhalla, where the gods and the heroes are seated together. Moreover, Wagner implies that Siegfried through his death has in some Christ-like way redeemed Wotan. Only then does Brunnhilda ride into Siegfried's blazing funeral pyre on Grane, crying:

> On to embrace him,
> To live in his arms,
> Thus yoked to him ever
> In mightiest love.

Appropriately, Wagner's advice to the listener who would understand his work was that he must 'not cudgel his brains' but must 'let the events themselves work on his feelings'.

In the present study, which is intended to clarify the ways in which poetry functions in comparatively uncomplicated societies, it may seem inappropriate to set forth the Old Norse lay in contrast with Wagner's *Ring*, but the implication of this examination is that medieval literature should be read within its own terms, and here the contrast between tribal simplicity and operatic complexity is so striking that it sheds light not only on Wagner but also on the understated and anonymous Norse poets who crystallized in lays the traditions of their forebears – traditions which they understood and cherished and which indeed exemplified for their tribal audience the expectable course of human and divine events.

As a corollary, moreover, it may be suggested that Wagner in his *Ring* has created a magical forest that obscures the roadway leading back to the literature of earlier ages; and it is very difficult for us now to look behind that marvelous forest and discern the primal growth which seeded his trees. Those who undertake to read Old Norse lays, for example, whether in the original or in translation, are almost inevitably already aware of Wagner's Brunnhilda. The operatic heroine and the music associated with her have indeed penetrated to such a popular level that a parody of her has even appeared in television commercials. Yet the original Norse singer was presumably unaware of Christianity, Marxism, Buddhism, or the television version of Brunnhilda. To understand his lays, present-day readers must understand the singer's function and listen to him as if they had purged themselves of preconceptions and had been adopted through time and space into his tribe as voluntary exiles who had abandoned all associations that might be alien to his own culture.

The implications of the inevitable cultural distance that separates modern readers from ancient literatures have provided the major questions that have been dealt with so far, and they also provide the substance of the final chapter. In the meantime one basic aspect of the poet's role must be examined in greater detail, and that aspect is related to the poet's function as carrier of the inherited wisdom of his people. The poet is not just the adroit manipulator of traditional literary genres. Over and beyond that, in whatever culture we find him, whether ancient or pre-modern, he is in some way held to be the conservator and dispenser of wisdom.

CHAPTER 7

THE NOTION OF WISDOM

Central to all study of the function of poetry in early societies is the notion of what we call wisdom – the world-view of most traditional societies and the source of its practical morality. It is the framework in which the world is viewed. It is a concept which shows amazing similarities throughout the world and must go back to the earliest stages of human consciousness. There are of course differences in the concept of wisdom in various societies, but in this book we choose to emphasize the similarities. In our discussion we shall not make the distinctions which from another point of view than ours would be legitimate and indeed necessary.

It is hard to distinguish a universal subject, a notion which is built into so much of human thinking, from its surroundings. As has often been said, something which explains everything explains nothing. The notion of wisdom is so deeply embedded and so widely found in almost all early human endeavor that it is not easy to distinguish it from its ubiquitous background. Some overarching concepts are however needed, and wisdom certainly belongs to that category. It is one of the basic categories for our understanding of early thought and early action because it is at the base of so many instances of them.

In the past fifteen or twenty years, for the first time we believe, the full range of the early notion of wisdom is beginning to be identified and its widespread influence is beginning to be understood. This new understanding of the notion of wisdom is visible above all in recent Biblical scholarship.[1] Wisdom in the Bible cannot be confined to Proverbs, Job, and Ecclesiastes. It is ubiquitous. It

---

[1] See Walter Brueggemann, 'Scripture and an Ecumenical Life-Style: A Study in Wisdom Theology', *Interpretation, A Journal of Bible and Theology* 24 (1970), pp. 3–19, and R. B. Y. Scott, 'The Study of Wisdom Literature', *Interpretation, A Journal of Bible and Theology* 6 (1970), pp. 25–145. An earlier book, Johannes Fichtner, *Die altorientalische Weisheit in ihrer israelitisch-jüdischen Ausprängung, Eine Studie zur Nationalisierung der Weisheit in Israel*, Beihefte zur *Zeitschrift für die alttestamentliche Wissenschaft* 62 (Giessen, 1933), is still useful. For an introduction to Babylonian wisdom literature see Johannes Jacobus Andrianus Van Dijk, *La sagesse suméro-accadienne, Recherches sur les genres litteraires des textes sapientaux*, Proefschrift . . . Rijksuniversiteit te Leiden . . . (Leiden, 1953) and W. G. Lambert, *Babylonian Wisdom Literature* (Oxford, 1960).

is not accidental that both Jesus and the Father as well as the Torah itself were ultimately linked with wisdom. Logos is the principle of rationality that makes sense of the apparently irrational universe. Creation itself is the imposition of wisdom on chaos. In fact, the notion of wisdom pervades almost everything in the Bible.[2]

The new understanding of the importance of the notion of wisdom has also been manifested in the study of Old English and medieval literature. Bloomfield[3] and Shippey[4] have in recent years called attention to the importance of wisdom literature not only in all the older literatures of the world but above all in Anglo-Saxon poetry. As we explore other cultures and their art, more and more, we become aware of the importance of this concept. Nor is it merely confined to early societies. Most societies still take as one of their basic concepts the idea of wisdom. As a philosophy of existence in both an extended and general sense and in the form of practical advice, wisdom is found almost everywhere. It has long been recognized that literature teaches as well as delights, but in the West in the past 100 years or so, the delight has been the center of interest in literature and the teaching ignored, brushed aside, or diverted into 'how to' books. In most cultures, however, the didactic function of literature has not been ignored or brushed aside. Even in our Western popular culture, teaching is by no means ignored as comics, soap operas, popular songs all reveal. To be sure, the 'art for art's sake' movement of the late nineteenth century still flourishes in high-brow art and in the notion that art must not be useful. In modern times this notion arose with Kant's *Critique of Judgement*. This belief is not the assumption under which most of the world operates.

Wisdom is humanity's first and most basic step towards rationality, and it is important that it be seen in that light. Out of it came the fundamental world-view of science before statistical principles redefined the notion of science in our century. It was the drive to overcome the arbitrariness of things that led to the discovery and invention of order or laws underlying the apparent disorder and chance of the universe. Beyond and beneath the concept of method, which is usually considered the basic characteristic of science and rationality, lies the notion of what is the reality of the universe – both of man and of nature.

Rationality and reason have other significances, and these terms have been

---

[2] See Von Rad, *Wisdom in Israel* (Nashville and New York, 1972). The German original was published in 1970. See also Harvey H. Guthrie, *Israel's Sacred Songs, A Study of Dominant Themes* (New York, 1966), especially Chapter 4.

[3] See e.g. 'The Form of Deor', *PMLA* 79 (1964), pp. 534–541; 'Authenticating Realism of Chaucer', *Thought* 39 (1964), pp. 335–358 and 'Understanding Old English Poetry', *Annuale Mediaevale* 9 (1968), pp. 5–25 (The last two are reprinted in *Essays in Explorations: Studies in Ideas, Language and Literature* [Cambridge, Mass., 1970]).

[4] See *Old English Verse* (London, 1972) and *Poems of Wisdom and Learning in Old English* (Cambridge, England and Totowa, N.J., 1976).

used by philosophers as a principle of understanding since Plato. Plato, Aquinas, Spinoza, and Hegel above all emphasized the notion of reason as a cosmic principle. Modern science since the seventeenth century has made much of the rational or scientific method. But reason as the notion of order, which was first a discovery before it was a principle, has been much ignored. If G. H. Mead was right in his belief that one of the central questions of philosophy is the rise, transformation, and implications of the notion of reason,[5] then a basic element in this development has been ignored: the notion of wisdom. Although Mead's concept of reason was over-psychological and oriented towards man's use of symbols – both important aspects of the subject, of course – he did recognize the anthropological aspect of the question. He and others, however, have missed the fundamental role of wisdom in the formation and creation of reason, human rationality, and science. As a philosophical concept, reason and science came out of the older concept of wisdom.

Wisdom is the root of both scientific and humanistic thinking. All learning is at root and origin one. When we emphasize quantitative measurement, we come to a point of separation between the humanities and science; but when we emphasize their common origin in the notion of order and rationality, we tear down barriers and distinctions and see the unity of all human intellectual activity.

The ancient notion of wisdom then is the natural religion of early humanity. Their myths and tales have as presuppositions, no matter how fantastic the form, the idea of order and rationality. They attempt to answer the most basic question of all – 'why?' 'Why' cannot be asked unless there is present the assumption of order and rationality. In other words to ask 'why' assumes that there is a 'why'. It is this assumption that is basic and fundamental to all rational thinking, and it may be called wisdom.

When no simple universal answer is known or possible, myth and story fill the gap. Where they came from is of course another matter, but come they did. Wisdom is the root of all thinking about the universe whether propositional or metaphorical. It is the product of the earliest intellectual and rational attempt to master and understand the universe and the formulation of the results of that attempt.

Religion or indeed almost any other early activity cannot be separated in most early societies from the perspective of wisdom. It is so bound up within the culture of early societies that phenomenologically speaking, a division is difficult to make. Symbols help to maintain, as Dupré has remarked, 'the rationality of our action as something that is connected with the past and directed toward a future accomplishment'.[6] Without basically using the idea of

---

[5] See W. Kang, *G. H. Mead's Concept of Rationality: A Study of the Use of Symbols and Other Implements* (The Hague and Paris: Mouton, 1976).

[6] Wilhelm Dupré, *Religion in Primitive Cultures, A Study in Ethnophilosophy*, Religion and Reason 9 (The Hague and Paris, 1975), p. 63.

wisdom, he defines religion as wisdom and recognizes its universality. Religion in this sense is what Basil Bernstein would call a restricted code.[7] In this book, however, we use the word wisdom for those practical and theoretical ideas and attitudes towards the world which are at the basis of most early symbolic and conceptual thought in early societies. We are, however, in this chapter examining wisdom without the specific myths, symbols, and rites which make it concrete and alive for a particular people.

Although there is some overlapping, wisdom may, as we have said, be divided into two major divisions. The first and most basic, and indeed the one most ignored, is the fundamental outlook of most traditional societies – the rationale of the universe as they view it. The second is prudence, which presents practical advice for the understanding of man and nature and which enables humans to find a general principle for the explanation of particular actions or rules of conduct and to explain the past and guide the present and future.[8] When we speak of wisdom today we generally think of this latter division – practical homey advice for living or for reconciling humans to life. Wisdom as rationalizing philosophy is generally ignored or misunderstood. As we have said above it may be, as it often is, partially categorized under other headings as science or religion, but even these activities are different and have a slightly different focus. They, however, do rest upon the notion of a rational universe which is of the essence of wisdom in its first and broadest sense. We shall shortly look in greater detail at each of these two aspects of wisdom, remembering that one is essentially an outlook, a philosophy of the world, and the other, prudence, is implicit in a mass of stories, praises, blames, proverbs, gnomes, exempla, and so forth which apply that philosophy to concrete instances, either before or after the fact, or which inculcate the principles of that philosophy.[9]

The unappreciative view of wisdom is that it consists of a mass of old saws and proverbs which were popular with our ancestors and which are boring, repetitive, and useless. It is of course true that wisdom in one of its senses consists of proverbs, gnomes, meditations, and dialogues about human

---

[7] See Basil B. Bernstein, *Class, Codes and Control*, 3 Vols. (London, 1975–79), especially Chapter 5, Vol. I, pp. 76ff. We are grateful to Alan Gussin for this reference.

[8] See Gerard J. Dalcourt, 'The Primary Cardinal Virtue: Wisdom or Prudence', *International Philosophy Quarterly* 3 (1963), pp. 55–79.

[9] There is much confusion between these two aspects of wisdom, in the scholarship on the subject. See for example Dalcourt (note 8 above); Kieran Conley, *A Theology of Wisdom: A Study in St. Thomas* (Dubuque, Iowa, 1963); Robert Preyer, 'Victorian Wisdom Literature: Fragments and Maxims', *Victorian Studies* (1963), pp. 245–262 (who does recognize the distinction). The problem is the relation between *sophia* and *pro-esis*, wisdom and prudence, the one so high, the other so low and how both to unify and distinguish them. If Conley is right, Plato recognized their close similarity whereas Aristotle divided the sharply. They are different aspects of the same virtue. For a short but useful summary of the history of the notion of wisdom in the higher sense, see James D. Collins, *The Lure of Wisdom*, The Aquinas Lecture 1962 (Milwaukee: 1962).

conduct and that some of it is boring, contradictory, and repetitive. The moralizing which some moderns hate so much and which irritates those of the young who think it blocks merriment and joy is very characteristic of wisdom, for its subject in the narrow sense of the word is how to live so that one can get the best out of life as a whole. This is not a topic that appeals to those who are bent on immediate enjoyment or success. Perceptively, in one of his sequence of novels set in the 1950's, C. P. Snow portrays Lester Ince as an iconoclastic young Cambridge Fellow, who when asked what he has said to his students about Beowulf, replies: 'He was a God-awful bore.' Yet, for the Anglo-Saxon ancestors of these students, Beowulf had once been the exemplar of wisdom.

Iconoclasts aside, all cultures have praised and elevated wisdom and its manifestation in the sage. Perhaps the only subject which is universally admired is wisdom – not only by Hebrews or by Greeks, but also by Hindus and Chinese, Polynesians and American Indians, Hausa and Xhosa. All peoples without apparent exception admire wisdom, hypostatize and personify it, practice or say they practice it, teach it to their children, and use it to face or smooth away the irritations and dangers of everyday life. Perhaps the most admired man in all societies is the wise man, the Prospero who can explain and control things and who is the magician *par excellence.*

The notion of the wise man, in some cultures thought of as a type of holy man, is central to the notion of wisdom in both its senses.[10] The wise man is the vehicle of wisdom and preserves and disseminates it in oral societies. He may not always be a good man, although he frequently is, but he understands the ways of the world and of the universe and is usually willing or indeed anxious to share his understanding with disciples or colleagues. Some wise men are on the other hand difficult and hard to please. The wise man is a prime figure in oral societies. He may debate with us or deliver statements. One must visit him for help and carry out his commands if he issues them. In some cultures, the wise men are judges ('at the gates of the city' as the Bible puts it). In some cases they withdraw into the wilderness before they return, if return they do. Some mortify their flesh; whereas others live a relatively normal life. Some travel around from village to village spreading the good word, as that exemplar of such a wise man, Jesus Himself, did. Some can perform miracles but many just 'counsel', as we might put it today. Their life story is a model, or as it was called in Hellenistic literary terms, an *aretology.* On the other hand, some who possess exceptional powers of perception may be labelled 'fools' or 'jesters', but their aura is such that their utterances are respected.

A most important contribution of wise men to their societies may be their

---

[10] On the figure of the holy man see Peter Brown, *Society and the Holy in Late Antiquity* (Berkeley, 1982), esp. pp. 103–152.

Not all holy men are wise men but many are. Those who teach by word of mouth or example are wise. Those who are holy in other ways have the living power of God or the gods in them physically.

authorship, often anonymous, of wise sayings and proverbs. Without gnomes and proverbs, traditional societies cannot exist. A Luo woman who is writing a thesis on women in her society recently complained to her American director. She remarked that in order really to understand the Luo, one cannot get very far merely by studying their social structure, as she herself was doing: only by studying their proverbs and how they use them can their real life be uncovered. Proverbs put things into perspective. Proverbs solve differences of opinion. Proverbs raise the specific up to the general and make sense of the world to people. In another part of Kenya young Kamba people want to know from their teacher what proverbs the Americans use. To know a people's popular proverbs and when and how they use them is to begin to know that people.

Wisdom, however, as we have seen, consists of much more than proverbs, gnomes, dialogues, well-known to all medieval and Biblical students. It is the everyday philosophy inherited from earlier generations. Practical wisdom rests on a sapiential view of the world, the view that the world makes sense, possesses order, rules, and patterns to which individuals if they wish happiness must conform and that everything has its proper place and time. As the ancient maxim has it, 'sapientia est ordinare'.

The unexpected and the sudden are feared.[11] Wisdom, manifested in all that is best in life, including language and law, enables us to control by either action or understanding the arbitrary and the unusual. Language provides us with a set of rules and vocabulary which permit us to grasp intellectually the world and encompass its novelty. Law is the embodiment of general rules for conduct, and ideally lawyers are wise men. Schools traditionally have existed for the purpose of handing on wisdom and knowledge, and teachers are, also ideally, the guardians and transmitters of wisdom. Practical wisdom is prudence, which enables us to act and to choose so as to move in harmony with the world. The craftsman-artist is the pattern of the wise man. Bezalel, the ancient Israelite artisan who created the tabernacle according to the plans of God, is always referred to as a wise man. The smith who could work in various metals is the wise hero of many cultures, and his heavenly archetype may be found, for instance, in the Greek Hephaestus, the Roman Vulcan, the Irish Goibhniu, the Welsh Gofannon, and the Germanic Weland. The Sumerians believed all wisdom and science were gifts of the gods to men and hence sacred.

Poets in particular are regarded as the discoverers, preservers, and trans-mitters of wisdom because they, unlike ordinary mortals, have acquired wisdom by a unique gift of vision granted specifically to them as a super-natural gift. The striking range of this deeply imbedded concept is, for

---

[11] See David Daube, *Suddenness and Awe in Scripture* (London: Council of Christians and Jews, 1963).

instance, displayed by the many words which have come down from the Indo-European root *weid* (already referred to in the previous chapter), meaning 'to see' and thus 'to have been permitted to see' and thus 'to have come to know'. Hence in English today we still, without necessarily thinking about their source, use derivatives such as 'wis-dom' and 'wit' inherited through Germanic, 'vis-ion' through Latin, 'his-tory' and 'id-ea' through Greek, and 'Ved-a' (sacred lore) through Sanskrit. In all these words the first syllable carries the same connotation of having seen, and the vocabularies of other languages also reflect the same assumptions as to the poet's primary role. He may, incidentally, be referred to by words that signify 'maker' or 'weaver' or the like, but such words generally refer to his technique. He can, however, only be trusted to fulfill his true role when he demonstrates to the members of the tribe that he has, during his training, seen visions and has thus acquired more wisdom from that experience than any of the rest of them possess.

Creation itself is the divine imposition of order on disorder, cosmos on chaos. The Son is wisdom, and He is, according to the Christian tradition, the active Creator. The first verse of Genesis with its 'In the beginning' and the first verse of the Gospel of John, 'In the beginning was the word' gave the proof-texts to the Church Fathers that Jesus was the active Creator. The supreme artist is the Creator, and He, like his earthly counterparts, works all by wisdom. A knowledge of wisdom requires an initiation into immutable knowledge – not just into opinion.

The notion of wisdom in the Western world rests upon the idea of limits. Hell has no limits; heaven is limited. God made all, as the writer of the *Book of Wisdom* puts it (11:20), by weight, measure, and number. Things are normally located in their 'natural' place and happen in their 'proper' time or times. Mary Douglas has defined the primitive concept of dirt as matter out of place. The *kairos*, the right moment and the proper place, provide the basic framework of all wisdom. They dictate the proper times and places for celebrations, for deeds and events, for knowledge, for the criteria of the natural or proper, as may be seen in Chapter 3 of Ecclesiastes; for some things or acts, however, there is never a proper place or time – like the actions forbidden by the ten commandments. Hesiod's *Works and Days* especially gives us specific information of times – a tradition continued in astrology, in almanacs, and even in Aristotelian philosophy. St. Augustine speaks of everything in the universe as having its proper place and, if removed, as attempting to return. Love and gravity are both forces which attempt to put things and people back in their proper places.

The philosophy of wisdom teaches that ideally all things have their proper place and time. The religious law is the attempt to see that all is in its proper place and time and all done in its proper way. The Torah is the rule of how to do things in true wisdom – the proper holy times (the sacred calendar), the proper places for doing things that are pleasing to God (the holy places and buildings), and the proper modes of doing things, both ritual and moral. God manifested Himself to His people in Law and later, as many believe, in His Son. Both Law and Son are wisdom – the road to and model of right living and being.

Built into the notion of the world that wisdom presents is the idea that everything has its proper use or *areté*. The knife's *areté* is to cut; man's *areté* is to be just and merciful. Laws give man the details of his *areté*; and if God gives a law, that law is the wisdom of how a man is to live and is his *areté*.

The violation of wisdom may lead to disaster and requires external and internal purification. The Greek word for 'sin', *hamartía*, and the Hebrew word *chate* both come from roots which mean to miss the mark, to leave the right goal – in short to violate the dictates of wisdom. Ritual and ethical violations are both wide of the mark of the proper paths. Purification and confession enable people to return to the proper paths.

Traditional wisdom is based upon a rational view of the universe, but a rational view which encompasses the sacred. The ultimate rationality of things rests upon a notion of the sacred and the holy. Inasmuch as there is a 'right' way to do things and a 'right' way in which the universe is ordered, the 'right' is ultimately sacred. One is violating the order of the universe if one neglects the 'rightness' of things. The sanctions which this 'rightness' demands are the authority of the sacred.

At times there are serious conflicts. Job for instance raises the profound question of the irrationality of the rational. How can God justify a universe in which the righteous (those who are concerned with the 'right') are made to suffer and the wicked to flourish? What is the rationale of injustice? What the answer to this most burning of questions is, the question Ivan Karamazov wrestled with, no one knows for certain. Must we believe in rewards and punishments, cannot we know whether evil is a trial and a test for us? But the answer in the Book of Job is just the manifestation of the Holy and the Sacred itself. The Holy One does not answer Job's questions but refers to His power, to His imposition of limitations on nature. Job has previously heard of Him, but now his eyes see Him (42:5).

We are here reminded in a powerful way that the ethical is not enough. The power of the sacred is more important than the power of the good. Mystery must finally conquer reason. The realm of contemplation is higher than the realm of action, and the vision greater than the deed. Yet the deed cannot be by-passed. At the end of his speech, Job the rebel who has been rebuked is praised as 'my servant Job', and the justifiers, the three comforters, are then rebuked. God sympathizes with the rebel against Him and condemns his 'friends'.

The sacred has its paradoxes, and one of them is the necessity of wisdom, which leads man to the sacred and which balances the extravagances of the sacred. The sacred is ambiguous, the mysterious, which without the reins of wisdom leads us to madness. A dialectical relationship obtains between the two. The sacred without wisdom is madness; but wisdom without the sacred is barren.

Wisdom is both the practical aspect of religion available to rational determination and the world view which traditional religion assumes. It provides a common ground for the settling of disputes and debate and enables people to make some sense out of a complex and difficult world. It says that there is a right and wrong way, time, or place to do things and provides some guidance towards the determination of these. Children and princes must be instructed in its basic principles, and people must live by it, if they wish happiness or at least if they wish to know how to bear misfortune.

Divination and prophecy are considered possible because there is order in the universe and above all a proper place and time for everything. The present king of Nepal chose the date and time of his coronation, as his predecessors had done, only at the advice of astrologers who told him when to go ahead. The ancient augurs looked at bones and livers to determine the lucky, that is, 'proper' time. Only with a notion of some order in the universe can we assume that there are proper occasions and places. The assumption is almost universal even if there has been some skepticism as to whether any human can successfully predict with exactitude their occurrence.

Wisdom in its prudential aspect makes life bearable. One does not have to decide everything for oneself. There is, wisdom says, a traditional body of tested information which makes itself available for living. It enables people to avoid, as Kierkegaard puts it, 'the dread of infinite possibility'. It not only assures us that things have some stability, but that in spite of the unexpected and the new, things will basically continue in a rational manner.

Wisdom does not only pertain to human relations and self-development but also to nature, especially though not exclusively, as it affects people. There are, as Kenneth Jackson puts it,[12] nature gnomes as well as human gnomes, but the wisdom of nature is related to humans and is existential in import.

Closely connected with wisdom philosophy is, of course, the notion of tradition and ancestors. The degree to which ancestors are involved varies. In sub-Sahara Africa, ancestors are involved in almost every action, public and private. They are present and keep an eye on all members of the tribe, exhibiting pride or shame depending upon their descendants' actions. They may also punish misbehavior by bringing misfortune. The ghosts of Christmases past are always present, and they show their pleasure and displeasure. All people are fated themselves to become ancestors and hence must not neglect their own ancestors when alive. The degree to and the mode in which ancestors prevail in the world vary. We make diverse responses to this ancestral demand on us. In Japan, we find the notion of *on*, which is the code and obligation of conduct towards ancestors demanded of every human being. In Rome, Sallust, albeit in a rationalizing manner which distorts the full

[12] See his *Studies in Early Celtic Nature Poetry* (Cambridge, 1935), esp. pp. 127ff.

meaning of the act, speaks of 'Quintus Maximus, Publius Scipio, and other eminent men of our society' who 'were in the habit of declaring that their hearts were set mightily aflame for the pursuit of virtue whenever they gazed upon the masks of their ancestors'.[13] In the Judaeo-Christian tradition, we have Abraham, Isaac, and Jacob and the other saints who watch over the conduct of their physical or spiritual descendants, who plead to God for those of us who are at present alive, and who help us to resist temptation and difficulties. They may even bring us luck; and God may be called the God of Abraham, Isaac, and Jacob.

The subject of respect (and disrespect) toward the past and its relation to the present and to the tradition of wisdom has been much neglected by scholars, possibly because our Western society has primarily been future oriented. The subleties of influence and imitation have only recently been tentatively explored. The burden and help of the past create countless complexities to unravel. The use of the past for the present, both in the past and today, is an exciting field for exploration: the revolution which claims to return to the pristine state, the fear of and the pride in the past which motivates human conduct, the uses and abuses of the past (as Nietzsche puts it), these are a few topics about which little is indeed known.

It must not be thought, however, that wisdom and tradition are necessarily conservative forces. They may be radical as well as conservative. The attaining of harmony between the rules of wisdom and the way of the world may lead to strong changes as well as to the maintenance of the *status quo*. The history of the Church manifests in many ways this truth. Most Church reforms are made in the name of a return to the early Church. On this Langland, Luther, and Pope John XXIII stand together. At least two of these figures were revolutionary in their impact. The return to the past is not *per se* conservative; it depends where in the past one wants to go, how one interprets that past, and how one uses it. Usually it may be said that the further back one wishes to go (where in other words there is less accurate knowledge), the more revolutionary the changes are. The man who wishes the world to return to the conditions of his childhood is usually more conservative than the one who wishes to return to the golden age. In short, wisdom as a motive force is in itself neither reactionary nor radical. As in many matters, it all depends.

Besides tradition, the notion of truth is also closely connected with wisdom and specifically with rulers. The virtue of truth, for instance, was the highest royal virtue in ancient Ireland.[14] Why this elevation of truth? Truth is the quality which makes magic work and which enables a person to live up to his archetype and his ancestors. He must correspond to the pattern his social role

[13] Trans. J. C. Rolfe in Loeb edition of *The War with Jugurtha* IV (p. 136).
[14] See the discussion of the Act of Truth in ancient India and Ireland in Myles Dillon's 'The Archaism of Irish Tradition', *Proceedings of the British Academy* 33 (1947), pp. 245–264ff., and above, chap. 1, note 24.

sets for him; and he must reproduce in his own life what is set before him by his ancestors. The potent magic of his role will not work if it does not correspond to the archetype of its nature. The higher one's rank the more important it is that he live up to what is demanded of him. The truth of the king then is the most important truth because most depends on it.

We do not wish to minimize the economic aspects of culture nor their force in determining various aspects of early life. In many cases, however, economic analyses cannot explain the distinctive qualities of a culture. The Marxist assumption that economic factors are a determining force allows for the influence of the superstructure but does not prove their primacy. The problem, however, need not be solved here insofar as we may escape a crude economic determination that is certainly not necessary to any theory of human culture, including Marxism itself. We must at the least allow for the power of the religious and didactic functions of poetry. Wisdom cannot be reduced to a simple economic justification.

More difficult is the belief widely inculcated by the Romantic Movement and modern formalist theories that in explaining literary works the aesthetic function is primary. For early poetry certainly, and perhaps also for later pre-Romantic poetry in the West, the didactic and social functions of poetry are at least as important as, if not more important than, the aesthetic function. In early poetry there is, of course, an aesthetic element, and poems can be compared as to their beauty, but the aesthetic is not strictly separated from the social. The effectiveness of early poetry depends upon is truth and its magic as well as upon its beauty. The aesthetic element also varies from genre to genre and is probably more important in love poetry, for instance, than in charms.

In fine, neither the aesthetic nor the economic can be ignored in accounting for much early poetry, but on the other hand neither of these factors can be considered decisive in our judging its historical function or significance and in our understanding of it. Furthermore, these factors, the aesthetic and economic, vary depending upon the purpose of the poem. In charms or satire they are slight; in lyrics and praise-poems they are stronger. In both cases other factors are involved which are clearly important.

Early poetry is a crystallization of wisdom and magic; from the former comes its didactic element and from the latter its aesthetic element. Both are directed towards social and individual satisfactions. The didactic element includes the economic, historical, and moral goals; the aesthetic element includes the protection and power that well-ordered words can give. The didactic is rational; the aesthetic is magical. The magical promotes tribal and individual welfare by increase in wisdom, which is teachable and rational. But the rational will not work unless it has magical power, which comes from truth, and the correct arrangement of the right words in the right order, at the appropriate time.

The playful or humorous element in early poetry is not common, but it is there. A tightly structured, relatively unified, and public society has to have its necessary outlets for relief. These are indeed often public ceremonies like the fool's mass of medieval Christendom, or Mardi Gras of Catholic Christianity, or the feasts of Purim or the Rejoicing in the Law of Orthodox Judaism. They are officially approved occasions for the symbolic and active rebellion against the pattern. We find such occasions among almost all traditional societies.

There is, however, besides these public and official occasions for release of tension and for controlled rebellion and laughter, a strong subterranean subversion of order which often manifests itself in private humor. A highly structured society also makes possible 'jokes' about violations which only seem jokes to the insiders who know the proper procedure. These 'jokes', both subterranean and public, as well as the official days of licence provide the normal flow of humor which allows the pattern and structure to maintain itself in a satisfactory way.

Verbal art also contains humor, which is frequently in the form of exaggeration, distortion, verbal puns, and echoes. The humor is usually confined to tales, proverbs, and riddles and is rarely found among praise poems, satires, or charms, where the licence of humor would destroy effectiveness and possibly lead to dangerous consequences. The humor of these literary types – tales, proverbs, and riddles – is not often based upon a climactic point as in jokes but usually appears, if it appears at all, in an amusing ambience or in the pleasures of verbal resemblances. Humor does not normally translate well, but in traditional societies where the importance of both setting and language is great, the humor present is especially untranslatable.

Wisdom then is finally an outlook, a *Weltanschauung*, a world view, perhaps a paradigm in Thomas Kuhn's sense of the word, expressed particularly in admonitions and adages. It supplies perhaps the earliest religion of the world to deserve serious consideration, but it is not a religion by itself. It must be fleshed out with specific myths and supernatural beings. At the same time, it can be transmitted in various forms with an essential unity. It does not need any particular set of myths or gods. It can therefore be handed over from one religion to another. The ancient Hebrews can borrow some of their wisdom from pagans without affecting their own myths and deity. Or wisdom can in its turn effect changes in a religion that bring it closer to the universality of wisdom itself. Wisdom is supra-tribal and supra-religious, even if it is almost always closely united with a tribe, or a people, or a set of deities and stories.

Wisdom is supported by rhythm and repetition, and by these principles, understood in their broadest sense, man can imitate the wisdom of the universe. What essentially is law, what is a calendar, what is poetic meter but rhythm and repetition? The pattern of man's life imitates the pattern of the universe. The calendar marks the daily round of a year so that 'times and seasons' may be outlined. Poetry itself imitates the rhythm of the cosmos. History presents problems, but man's task is to find its rhythm. For most peoples, history is reduced to nature with its endless round.

When the term 'wisdom' is used in literary circles, it is, as we have stated above, often conceived of as referring to a limited number of certain obvious types of wisdom literature: proverbs, exempla, fables, moral meditations, dialogues, riddles, charms, and other similar forms. Generally considered to be dull and repetitious, these are usually passed over quickly, even if certain common wisdom forms are considered less dull than others. The commonly assumed forms of wisdom literature are usually prudential and practical in nature. Some are 'action' literature like charms, divinatory directions, or curses that are expected to bring results for the performer.

One must, on the contrary, emphasize that in one very important sense all early art and much action rests upon a basis of wisdom and is expected to reflect the order of the universe and often to bring about happy results for the commonweal. Epics and lyrics, hymns and eulogies, drama and fairy tales, are all in their way wisdom literature if they are looked at in terms of their social and cultural context and functions and of the presuppositions out of which they arise.

Wisdom then exists in many forms and is at the base of much that people in all societies do and think. Because of its ubiquity, it is often difficult to define and codify. For our purposes we may say that there are four main divisions: philosophical wisdom, prudential wisdom, scientific wisdom, and active wisdom. The first has been the main though not the only subject in this chapter. Prudential wisdom deals with and presents solutions to the problems of social existence. Scientific wisdom deals with rules of nature in various forms as it impinges on human life, and active wisdom deals with magic and entertainment. These four, especially in terms of their literary forms, will be the subject of our next chapter.

In order to articulate wisdom in a more specific way we must make certain distinctions. In terms of subject matter, practical wisdom deals with most aspects of human relations and self-development and with nature, especially in its impact on human living through weather, biological phenomena, simple physical reactions such as the boiling of water or the flooding of waterways, or plant growth. These perceptions are sometimes simply expressed and some-times presented in vivid or complex metaphors and similes which often make the information memorable. The commonest subject, however, is wisdom itself. Much of wisdom is concerned with wisdom's arguing for its own value, its ubiquity, its necessity. This self-referential quality is an outstanding feature of practical wisdom. If the purveyors of wisdom can convince others of its value, either by offering sage advice about living or by laudatory recommenda-tions, then it has justified itself. The practical everyday side of wisdom can only be effective if it is accepted and acceptable. This then is its main goal: to get humanity to acquiesce in it and accept it. In that case there is a harmony between its theoretical claims as a point of view and the humans who are being urged to accept it in order to obtain understanding.

Wisdom is abstract in order to put us into concrete reality. By realizing our human limitations, we learn to endure reality and to live in it with understanding, accepting the universe while we still recognize its insuperable difficulties. The fact that the favorite and highest form of wisdom literature is the dialogue, as in Plato and Job, is no accident; the man who tries to live according to the dictates of wisdom must also be in a dialogue, a dialogue with himself, with his neighbors, with the universe, and if he believes, with God or the gods. A dialogue never really finishes; it stops. It ends with the alternatives placed in position before us. This inconclusiveness is again and finally a part of wisdom. Not only is much wisdom about wisdom, but wisdom must acknowledge the limitations of wisdom. To be truly wise, one must possess wisdom, but one must also go beyond wisdom. The 'authors of proverbs and those who strive for understanding' (Baruch 3:23) must still learn the greater lesson – that wisdom, though absolutely necessary, is not enough. The road is through wisdom to get beyond it. Our greatest wisdom is to recognize its limitations while at the same time recognizing its truth. Wisdom should be the practical goal of mankind. The spiritual goal is religion, and those who disapprove of it should at least aim at wisdom as their goal.

CHAPTER 8

WISDOM GENRES AND TYPES OF LITERATURE

The notion of wisdom is so wide-spread in various cultures that it is almost a universal term and as such is not particularly helpful in the making of distinctions. It is therefore worthwhile to supplement the application of the term to poetry and literature by differentiating various categories of wisdom literature. 'Wisdom' alone is not enough. In Chapters 3 to 6 we have examined specific examples of 'poetic' wisdom within five early or pre-modern Western cultures. Now we turn to a much broader sample of the categories of wisdom literature. For purposes of comparison between these relatively familiar Western cultures and the cultures of the larger world, the Category numbers used earlier have been listed here when appropriate, and it will be noted that on a global scale the custodians of wisdom have varied their methods remarkably even when pursuing identical ends.

Poetry, especially oral or performance poetry, has important social functions in early societies, and in many of its manifestations it is recognized as a public activity. In this role, poetry may be summed up as the verbal accompaniment of many group activities and in some cases is itself the group activity. In the matter of prophecy, the poetry is the prophecy. On the one hand, public poetry creates the proper form of political and religious (not always separable by any means) acts and rites; and on the other, it affords the people an opportunity to celebrate various feasts, holidays, and crucial occasions such as going hunting or to war.

Besides these public and (if one may use the term) state functions, poetry in early societies has also personal functions which are harder to pin down but which do indeed exist. This poetry encourages the maintenance or the creation of order or wisdom in the individual in ways analogous to similar manifestations in society as a whole. It allows the comforting release of tensions and the subsumption of the particular under the general and universal. Besides these rational – that is, obvious and clear – functions, there is also present in both private and public poetry, an aesthetic element which links the forms employed to magical and contemplative purposes. By concentration on the form of the poetry one is captured by the words or chants themselves which are then enjoyed or contemplated for their own sakes. They help to bring about that of which they are signs. The power of the word is realized in action.

120

Both language and law, as we have seen in the preceding chapter, are particular manifestations of that drive for order which we call wisdom and which we find in every rational activity in early societies. Language by its very nature possesses the power of abstraction from the multitude of particulars and enforces a classification upon the world which gives the speaker and hearer the capacity for ordering experience by reducing multiplicity. Language uttered as law makes possible social action, both positive and negative, and binds society together by the power of communication. Language as message or precept, like law, can initiate action at a distance and control the wayward and that which is amorphous.[1] Language is both magical and commonsensical.

Furthermore, law as customary wisdom serves the common good, and its history in various cultures reveals its endless attempt to impose order on disorder. It is the concretization of social wisdom. The phraseology tends to win out over the spirit, but the perpetual modifications of law attempt to bring it closer and closer to the spirit so that adherence to justice may not be injustice. The words, however, at least keep us to the literal ideal of justice.

The principles of language and law are perhaps the two most important and basic elements in wisdom and are at the root of most other manifestations of sapience. Curiously enough language embraces most of these other manifestations and makes them possible. Language is basic in a very profound sense. Without language poetry would, obviously, be impossible. Law is more external, but it is the goal of order to which all early poetry in its social form aspires. But it too is dependent upon language. Language is both the presupposition of much in all cultures as well as a product of a culture.

Very important in most cultures, as we have already noted, are those ancestors who are thought to be especially concerned with their descendants and can seriously affect their lives. Recently Arthur P. Wolf has written, and his words apply to cultures other than the Chinese:

> Although the gods and ancestors differ in many important respects, they also have a great deal in common. The extreme contrast, from the Chinese point of view, is between the gods and the ancestors on the one hand, and ghosts on the other. The gods and the ancestors are granted the respect due social superiors; ghosts are despised 'like beggars'. Where the gods and the ancestors can be appealed to for protection and help, ghosts offer men nothing but failure of every kind.[2]

---

[1] See Wilfried van der Will, 'Name Semeion, Energeia: Notes on the Permutations of Language Theories', *Essays in German Language, Culture and Society*, ed. S. S. Prawer, R. Hinton Thomas and Leonard Foster, University of London Institute of Germanic Studies 12 (London, 1969), p. 213.

[2] 'Gods, Ghosts, and Ancestors', *Religion and Ritual in Chinese Society*, ed. Arthur P. Wolf (Stanford, 1974), p. 169.

Wolf had pointed out[3] that the essential difference between the gods and the ancestors is not that the former are punitive while the latter are essentially benevolent but rather that the gods represent public morality and are strong, while ancestors are concerned with their descendants and are relatively weak.

An individual is a link in a chain extending from his ancestors to his descendants. In secularized Western culture, this line through time is generally neglected, especially beyond one's grandparents and grandchildren, or at least it is left in a rather amorphous state beyond these limits. That one's ancestors were farmers or came from China or something of that sort suffices. Accuracy of knowledge of one's family in all cultures beyond a certain point is hard to retain. In the West we hesitate to believe in the continuing interest of our ancestors in our careers. In traditional societies, however, this chain of ancestors and descendants is very important and may be considered, so to speak, as a vertical one through time that may be set against the horizontal pull of an individual's contemporary society. But the vertical chain in these cultures not only includes the individual's own forebears but in some sense the notable ancestors of his tribe. In death, former chieftains are to some extent still the individual's chieftains along with the current chieftain – and former priests or poets still exercise their power over later generations and those still unborn.

Let us look at the various categories or genres of early literature in the light of the wisdom tradition and at what is associated with that tradition. The role of ancestors in the performance of poetry, for instance, as we have just seen, is especially significant and is extremely important in understanding the *Sitz in Leben* of public praise-poetry.

Aristotle wrote in the early part of his preserved *Poetics* that all poetry arises in praise or in blame. Whether this insight is literally true or not we cannot say, for there is no way of testing its accuracy, but it is certainly true that both are prime purposes of poetry in early societies, to which many poetic forms can be traced. They must certainly occupy a major role in any discussion of the forms of early poetry.

Public praise (Category 5) is the reward one seeks in occupying through luck, force, or heredity a certain elevated role in society and in carrying out its obligations. It is the public recognition of a public office and is that which is due to the holder of that office. It is his fame which must be publicly announced to 'live forever'. Unspoken praise is worthless and has no magic in it. True praise is a report, official and open, to the chief or notables for the praised one's contemporaries and even more for his ancestors. By praising the chief, the poet is calling the attention of the chief's society and of his and their ancestors to the recipient's merits so that both living and dead may be proud of, and reassured by, the achievements and qualities of their ruler. A main purpose of panegyric is not only to gratify the vanity of the recipient but also to

[3] Parts of this paragraph are paraphrased from *ibid.*, p. 168.

represent him as he wishes to be thought of by others.[4] Reassurance is also very important to *all* the tribe. The poet asserts the legitimacy and the appropriateness of the chief, and by the magical authority of his utterance he guarantees it.

In Southern Bantu society almost every one has a praise-name which may, if his family is distinguished enough, be his family's praise-name. When one of the authors of this book was introduced to Chief Burns-N^cmashe, he had been advised to call him Zilimbola, his family praise-name. One addresses in public and on public occasions a chief by his family praise-name. It not only recalls the memory of his distinguished ancestors to the listeners, but it also calls to the ancestors to be aware of their distinguished descendant or descendants. The fame only truly lives as it is being uttered. If a favor is desired, one praises in advance the ruler to whom the petition is addressed. Inasmuch as there is a personal element in ruling, favors and exceptions may be granted and are the prerogative of the ruler. In a relatively small society this prerogative is one of the ways equity is assured in the carrying out of justice and its rules.

Because the ruler possesses certain powers, often magical, granted him by virtue of his office and his ancestors, he may bestow blessings upon the petitioner, sometimes by words, sometimes by his touch, and sometimes by both. The root notion of blessing is closely connected to that of praise. The petitioner too may ask that blessings fall upon the ruler both before and after he presents his petition or request (Category 8).

To the ancient Semites, this magical power of blessing was known as *baraka* and is both in the power of the suppliant as well as in that of the ruler or leader.[5] This situation even applies to the divine level. We may bless (that is, wish all good things on) Him so that He may bless us.

Much of this mutual exchange relation is preserved for us in the West by the Judeo-Christian-Islamic tradition where we sing praises to God and even petition Him in certain controlled ways for blessings of various sorts. When we paraphrased Aristotle's *Poetics* above we omitted one further item from which all poetry is supposed to have evolved – hymns which are basically though not exclusively praise-poems to God or the gods. Early Greek hymns[6] and Biblical

---

[4] In this sentence, we are indebted to formulations in Alan Cameron's fine article, 'Wandering Poets: A Literary Movement in Byzantine Egypt', *Historia* 14 (1965), p. 502. We are also indebted to his whole article (pp. 470–509) for other insights as well.

[5] See, e.g., Giorgio Buccellati, 'Le Beatitudini sullo sfondo della tradizione sapienziale mesopotamica', *Biblia e Oriente* 14 (1972), 241–264. Buccellati sees in the Judeo-Christian blessings the new notions of messiah and the end of time.

[6] On Greek hymns, see Karl Keyssner, *Gottesvorstellung und Lebensauffassung im griechischen Hymnus*, Würzburger Studien zur Altertumswissenschaft 2 (Stuttgart, 1932). For praise in ancient Israelite song (and other aspects of the subject), see Claus Westermann, *The Praise of God in the Psalms*, trans. Keith R. Crim (Richmond, VA., 1966) and Harvey H. Guthrie, *Israel's Sacred Songs, A Study of Dominant Themes* (New York: Seabury Press, 1966) (the latter emphasizes the wisdom element). Raymond Schwab argues that all

psalms show a strong praise element throughout. God is praised as the source of all good, all power and wisdom. He is the imposer of wisdom (order) on chaos or order on the disordered.

Public praise-poems are part of wisdom because they accompany and pay tribute to the imposer of wisdom, the ruler, and because to praise that which should be praised is proper and orderly. Praise-poems are not only sung to gods or to their representatives on earth for personal reward (although that is certainly a major part of their function) but also because it is appropriate and suitable to the nature of things to do so. The public realm demands praise when it is due.

Even more, although of less importance to us because they are mostly lost, praise-poems are part of private life. They may be sung in self-praise to cheer oneself up, as with the jingle recommended by the French psychotherapist Émile Coué: 'Every day and in every way I'm getting better and better.' They may be sung in honor of a favorite object or person or place or animal. Love poems are frequently praise-poems, sometimes in whole and sometimes in part. Praise-poems also appear on other occasions of private joy.

Laments are praise-poems of either private or public scope. They are often addressed to the corpse or to the family or to the gods. They announce the arrival and elevation of a person to the role of ancestor. They praise the mourned one not only on behalf of the living but also on behalf of the already dead. People pass, but their praises (their history) remain.

Praises of places and times, especially sacred places and sacred times, are also found. They pay proper honor to that which should be honored. Cities or settlements as early impositions of order on existence, as embodied wisdom, are frequently praised. One also pays honor to an individual if one praises his city. Holy times and seasons are praised. Sometimes the instigator, whether divine or human, of a holy season or day is praised along with the season itself. The god is thanked for giving the people a holy season or holy day.

Ancestors are often praised, as for instance by the listing of ancestors and genealogies (Category 2). Among the Southern Bantu, the clan itself is praised, usually by women.[7] Clan praises are not thought of as chauvinistic but as giving the clan what is due it. The existence whether of an individual or a tribe is a holy event and deserves praise. The law or customary life of a tribe may be praised as the creation of a god or hero or as the imposition of order on disorder, or both.

The language of praise-poems, especially public praise-poems, is usually differentiated from ordinary language. Not only are formulas, repetitions,

---

literature begins with hymns. See 'Domaine orientale' in Raymond Quéneau, *Histoire des Littératures*, Encyclopédie de la Pléiade, Vol. I (Paris, 1955), p. 135.
[7] See David K. Rycroft, 'Southern Bantu Clan-praises: A neglected Genre', *Bulletin of the School of Oriental and African Studies, University of London* 39 (1976), 155–159 (and further references there).

epithets, rhythms, and even on rare occasions rhyme used, but also special effects. Zulu downtones, found frequently in normal conversation, are suppressed until the very final sentence in praise-poems.[8] Recitation with music or rhythmic instruments is common. Among the Southern Bantu, praise-poems are regarded 'as the highest form of literary art which they have produced, and praise-poets and reciters are in considerable demand, and are well rewarded for their work'.[9]

Among the Southern Bantu, a man, even if not a chieftain or ruler, assembles an *izibongo* (praise-poem) throughout his life. Unless he is a ruler, he composes most of it himself although he may have picked up some phrases in it from others. He utters this *izibongo* at times to himself. His children and neighbors hear it and know it more or less. 'The *izibongo* defines the person; initially it is the person.'[10] He recites, in times of stress or misfortune, the praise-poems of his ancestors.

The official *imbongi*, the poet of the chieftain among the Zulus, recites the king's or the chief's praise and that of his and his people's ancestors to bring the glories of the ruler-descendant to their attention. He does for the whole tribe what the father does for his household. The kingdom of all the ancestors is called upon by the present earthly kingdom in hope of their aid.

Praise-poems are, of course, not confined to the Southern Bantu; they are found in most cultures of the widest geographic distribution. Not only are they to be discovered in the rest of Africa,[11] and in Pakistan among the Pathans, for instance, but also, as we have seen in Western poetic traditions such as in Old Irish, Early Welsh, Old Norse, and to some extent Old English. These preliminary examples merely skim the surface of the wide sample of cultures which might be presented here from the past. Furthermore, in Western cultures they persist down to the eighteenth century[12] and on occasion, as we have seen (Chapter 4), to the present day.

---

[8] For this and other ideas in this section, we are indebted to the introduction to Trevor Cope, *Izibongo: Zulu Praise Poems*, Oxford Library of African Literature (Oxford, 1968).
[9] See G. P. Lestrade, 'Bantu Praise-Poems', *The Critic: A South African Quarterly Journal* 4 (Oct. 1935), 8. For other Bantu praise-poems, see I. Schapera, *Praise-Poems of Tswana Chiefs*, Oxford Library of African Literature, (Oxford, 1965), and Jacques Chileya Chivale, *Royal Praises and Praise-Names of the Lunda Kazembe of Northern Rhodesia: The Meaning and Historical Background*, Central Bantu Historical Texts III, Rhodes-Livingstone Institute, 1962). On the relation of African prayer to traditional praise poems, see Aylward Shorter, *Prayer in the Religious Traditions of Africa* (New York and Nairobi, 1965), pp. 1–25.
[10] From Professor Jeff Opland's speech 'Southeastern Bantu Eulogy and Early Indo-European Poetry' delivered at the Annual Meeting of the American Folklore Society, Salt Lake City, 13 October, 1978. We are much indebted to the whole speech in the present paragraph and indeed this book.
[11] See M. G. Smith, 'The Social Functions and Meaning of Hausa Praise-singing', *Africa* 27 (1957), pp. 26–43 and Francis Mading Deng, *The Dinka and Their Songs*, Oxford Library of African Literature, (Oxford, 1973).
[12] To take one example, see Alexander Sackton, 'The Rhetoric of Literary Praise in the

It is necessary once again to stress the fact that public praise-poems, even when addressed to the gods, are not all praise. They are frequently used as a vehicle of criticism, although it is normally necessary for the poet to phrase his criticism with care.[13] Furthermore, his praise must not be excessive. The demands of truth are by no means ignored. The danger of excessive and false praise of the chief is that the audience will regard such hyperbole as covert criticism of the chief and also that the panegyrist will lose his authoritativeness. In relatively small societies, as is the case with the societies we are considering, almost everyone is known personally, and his virtues and vices are public property. This situation is above all true of the chief and his council of wise men and their families. Praise-poems have to stay within certain rational lines, or they defeat their purpose. As Snorre Sturlason puts it in his introduction to the *Heimskringla* (c. 1230), 'It is the way of skalds, of course, to give most praise to him for whom they composed, but no one would dare tell the king himself such deeds of his as all listeners and the king himself know to be lies and loose talk; that would be mockery, but not praise.'[14] Private praise-poems, of course, especially those directed at oneself, one's beloved, or one's possessions, are not subject to these lines of containment. They are not public and usually have an audience of one or possibly a few more. Even here though, a private praiser, if he heavily indulges in hyperbole, may be considered to be somewhat odd or proud or selfish.

We are, however, mainly concerned with public praise-poems, poems or songs which are performed in public and often for public occasions. These poems are usually combinations of lyric and narrative elements. The hero or man praised is often addressed directly and his deeds and ancestors are recalled. Sometimes the poet directly addresses the audience and shifts from the second to the third person. His poem may be, on the other hand, entirely in one or the other person. Imagery and metaphors are freely employed which may make the poem difficult for an outsider to interpret but which give delight to the listeners. Tribal history as it is known may be drawn upon both to keep these events alive and to praise the hero or his ancestors or predecessors. Needless to say, these often present a tendentious view of history, usually favoring the present dynasty's view of things in the past. Comparisons are frequent, as in the Old Norse *mann-jafnadr* which uses comparisons to exult over competitors or possible competitors to the hero. Proverbs which occupy

Poetry of Raleigh and Chapman', *TSLL* 18 (1976), pp. 409–421. Sackton dates the use of the genre of 'literary praise' in England to the late sixteenth century!

For a history of an encomiastic tradition in medieval Latin and vernacular literature, see Annette Georgi, *Das lateinische und deutsche Preisgedicht des Mittelalters in der Nachfolge des genus demonstrativum*, Philologische Studien und Quellen 48 (Berlin, 1969).

[13] See Archie Mafeje, 'The Role of the Bard in a Contemporary African Community', *Journal of African Languages* 6 (1967), pp. 193ff.

[14] Edited Erling Monsen and trans. into English with the assistance of A. H. Smith (Cambridge, 1932), p. xxxvi.

an important role in these societies are freely drawn upon and appear in many praise-poems. Even riddles may on occasion be used. Catalogues as mnemonic devices are popular.

The praise-poem is regarded as a gift by the poet to the chief and must properly be rewarded by the recipient. This view of public praise is wide-spread, and the praiser expects gifts in return for his gift. Words with their powers can be a potent gift.

Praise-poems probably arose from simple praises uttered in succession or repeated. Then form was imposed upon them as a means of imposing order and memorability on praise. For variation and concrete detail, narrative began to be added and in some cases (and this is presumably one of the ways in which epic arose) took over to transform ejaculations of praise into descriptions of deeds done.

Rachel Bromwich puts it very well when speaking of the ancient Welsh (or Scottish) poem *The Gododdin*. She is discussing the two versions in which the epic exists and writes:

> We can observe the stages by which panegyric poetry, accurately preserved in the first instance as a 'correct record' and intended for recitation in the presence or in the immediate circle of the person eulogized, develops into epic by drawing to itself legendary features, and in doing so becomes subject to all the vicissitudes which result from improvisation at the hands of successive oral singers.[15]

Popular, folk, or national epics are praise-poems in which the narrative element has become predominant but which still preserve the primary function, no matter how subtly and complexly put, of praise of a hero. The fundamental social role of early epics and many later ones is to praise a hero or a band of heroes. In traditional societies, by praising one gives the hero his due in public, calls upon his ancestors to be aware of the deeds of their descendant, and in effect brings blessings upon him by the power of language and glory upon all successive generations. Short or crucial episodes from well-known heroic stories and epic-stuff are often recounted or sung as narrative lays in traditional societies. The medieval and indeed modern folk ballads go back to or are the content of this habit. We have, then, short sagas, tales, lays, and family romances such as *Guy of Warwick* and *Bevis of Hampton*, and beyond these, crucial episodes presented in either simple narrative or ballad-form, usually with the emphasis on human dilemmas but still with a poetic concern for all of those involved in the narrative.

In the early tradition (Category 4), Greek and Western among others, the appeal to the Muses (or the equivalent) is a call to supernatural beings to join in, in praising of the hero. The Muses whose task is to help poets and to praise

---

[15] See her review of Kenneth H. Jackson, *The Oldest Scottish Poem: The Gododdin* 1969 in *Med. Aev.* 39 (1970), 160–165. The quotation is from p. 165.

are called upon both to inspire the poet and the rhapsode and to sing through them and to sing themselves in the realm of the other world where they dwell.[16] In some cultures the gods themselves are called upon; in others the ancestors are either called upon[17] or recalled before the poet proceeds.

Not all cultures have epics or long heroic poems; many have instead praise-poems or a repertoire of short tales. The short sagas of the Book of Genesis are of such a type. The Chinese also do not seem to have long epics. Professor Daniel P. Biebuyck has been able to put short sagas together into a single epic in the *Mwindo Epic*,[18] which provides a modern example of an epic composed of, in this case, Nyanga tales about a hero. Animal epics which are either parodies of royal epics or epics of ancestor-animals may also be found.

History and genealogies (Category 2) are very important as the content background of praise-poems and epics. Especially notable are historic events of great significance, either for good or for evil. To the ancient Hebrews, the deliverance from Egypt and its consequence in the giving of the Torah is such an event. To the Xhosa people of South Africa the destruction of their power in the mid-nineteenth century due to a belief in a young girl's misleading dream is such a deed. In the presence of one of the authors of this book, the great Xhosa poet, Yali-Manisi, composed a poem orally for thirty-five minutes recalling that event and its tragic consequences. By the poet's retelling of the events, they became alive again and once again are capable of adumbrating the future or protecting a people from the future.

Genealogies are frequently listed. We may recall the genealogy of the Danish kings at the beginning of *Béowulf* or the genealogies in the early part of the Book of Genesis. In the latter we have the genealogy not of a tribe but of the human race. Genealogies in Genesis and elsewhere are of course not accurate, but in such cases they may carry some truth. Furthermore in various societies, they may give support to a ruling dynasty against its enemies. Such seems a major function in Old Irish genealogies.[19]

---

[16] On Homeric invocations to the Muses and their roles, see William W. Minton, 'Homer's Invocations of the Muses: Traditional Patterns', *TAPA* 91 (1960), 292–309.

The muses are the children of Memory and hence have a major link with the past. They are also the link to one's ancestors and one's people. This memorial role is not stressed by Minton, although one of their functions is to provide information. At the beginning of Hesiod's *Theogony*, lines 26–28, the Muses say to Hesiod that the vulgar think poetry is full of lies, but that they know how to tell the truth too.

[17] As in what would otherwise be a bizarre and functionless story, the Old Irish account of *The Discovery of the Táin* (in *The Tain*, trans. Thomas Kinsella [Oxford, 1970], pp. 1–2; ed. H. Zimmer, *Zeitschrift für vergleichende Sprachforschung* 28 [1887], pp. 433–434).

[18] (Berkeley, 1969).

[19] For comparable varieties and genres of poetry among some Turkish peoples, see Nora Chadwick and Victor Zhirmunsky, *Oral Epics of Central Asia* (Cambridge, 1969) especially Chapter 7 (pp. 171–195). Besides praise-poems and various related genres, this chapter discusses myth-poetry (also praise of the gods), poetry dealing with names and their origins, gnomic literature of various sorts, riddles, poetry of celebration (also a kind of praise-poetry), charms, and contests.

Public praise-poems are often called for in an oral society and are expected at certain ceremonies. Or they may be asked for at the whim of the poet. The poets may repeat formulas or phrases, but normally they are improvised with the help of these traditional units that may seem to be merely syntactic devices but are in fact important endorsements of the ruler's legitimacy. Occasionally the poems may be memorized, as is the case with many Irish and Scottish Gaelic bards. Some traditions, such as those of the Xhosa, do not seem to have genealogical or indeed syntactic formulas in the strict sense of the word, but they do have standing epithets and phrases which the poets often use in their relatively short praise-poems (the thirty-five minute one referred to above seems unique). This characteristic may possibly be due to their lack of meter and the employment, somewhat like the ancient Hebrew, of parallelism of clauses and phrases.

Private praise-poems will not detain us long. They are of great interest, of course, but they are hard to find. Occasionally it is possible to record one, but often they vanish even more absolutely than public eulogies. With the coming of writing, public praise-poems are now occasionally, and will be more frequently, written down or taped, but this recording will hardly touch private praise-poems unless they are the private praise-poems of public praise-singers. Yali-Manisi, for instance, has published some of his private and public praise–poems or approximate and reworked versions of them. With audio-visual technology, new possibilities open for the recording of performances.

Praise-poems to God are the only praise-poems Western worshippers are still actively involved in. Every Sunday or Saturday when they go to church they sing or intone praise-poems which have been captured in print and were originally composed either by a modern author or by an ancient Hebrew or Christian one. The book of Psalms contains praise-poems. Few actually continuously praise God; many, however, intersperse praise with narrative or descriptive statements or with requests as to His power and His love. Some of the so-called wisdom psalms such as Psalm 1 talk about the proper way to live. A few seem to have been composed for ceremonies like royal weddings or royal enthronements. Some specialize in celebrating or recalling special national or international events. These examples give a good picture of the various possibilities. Various literary forms may be used in praise-poems; hymns (as we have seen), aretologies, toasts, and even satires. Praise-poems contain many or parts of many other genres and embrace various sub-genres like laments.

Praise-poems as we have already seen are not all praise. They may criticize in a controlled way the object of their eulogies. So too, in some of the psalms, God is sometimes delicately criticized or seems to be criticized.

When a Xhosa poet is formally carrying out his role as a public praise-poet, he dons an outfit of fur, usually antelope or deer skin. Often at this time his chief is wearing, if he is a paramount chief, a garment of leopard skin, the royal accoutrement. Besides this outfit, the poet also takes up two assegais, and as he sings and performs he moves the assegais in a threatening way and shouts, as all praise-poems are recited among the Xhosa, in a loud and raucous voice.

These actions and dress indicate various things. A major reason originally for his loud singing and special voice was to indicate that the poet is being inspired by ancestors or ghosts or gods (a source which his audience cannot know). The special chant or shouting is characteristic of praise-poems of various peoples.

His garments and actions would also, however, seem to indicate that originally one of the functions of the praise-poet among the Xhosa, which we definitely still find in other cultures and to which Aristotle alludes, must have been satire, curses, and blame. The praise-poet, a professional satirist like Balaam, may be conceived of as going into battle with his chief, ready to hurl his curses at the enemy and miming their journey through the air with his assegais. Nowadays, however, the Xhosa praise-poet no longer acts in this way or even remembers his predecessors in such actions. Prolonged interrogation has produced no recalls. The present-day praise-singer will admit that such action was theoretically possible in the past but that he had not especially heard of it.

Robert Elliott in his *The Power of Satire* provides us, however, with much evidence of such activity. If words can soothe and glorify, they can also kill and maim. One curses one's enemies in order to defeat them. Any good tribal chief would take his cursers along with him into battle just as he would take his spear-throwers or his stone-throwers. In the West, the Celtic tradition in particular provides many examples of satirists though not necessarily battle-goers.[20]

Curses (Category 8) and satires (Category 5) are often no more direct than praise-poems are. Indirection and elegance of phrasing are in early poets' minds just as those of the poets of today. Zulu satiric poems, for instance, are often in question-and-answer form.[21] Satire may not be vicious or killing in intent but merely a form of criticism and may at times enter into praise-poems. Real satire is, however, more or less direct; otherwise it does not do its job, but the poet may use metaphors and epithets that to the uninitiated are not clear.

Curses are also used against internal enemies both human and animal. Rat rhymers, familiar to Shakespeare, are well known in Gaelic Ireland and Scotland and even today are not unheard of in Cape Breton Island. They would drive rats or mice out of a house by proclaiming, in the proper manner, the proper curses. Curses can be the verbal equivalent of human injuries when inflicted on special figures imitating the intended victim. Instead of personally sticking pins into a doll or an object owned by one's enemy, one could employ a professional curser or witch. Furthermore, one's ancestors can be irritated at a curser and bring him trouble. The witch doctor ('the doctor against

[20] See Chapter 3, discussion of Category 5.
[21] See Mazisi Kunene, *Zulu Poems* (London, 1970), pp. 15–16.

witches') or, as he is generally known today, the 'diviner' can determine the cause of the unpleasantness afflicting the individual who comes to him for help. Among the southern Bantu he or she may send the sufferer to a doctor (herbalist or physician), may indicate that an ancestor is the cause of the misfortune and must be appeased, or may identify the problem as due to an enemy or a witch or wizard employed by an enemy. It is difficult to find anti-curses strong enough to neutralize a curse, but it can be done. Sometimes a conversation with one's enemy will disarm the curses. In a few cases, one may try elementary psychiatry, that is, allow the patient to talk about his troubles. This procedure may by itself be effective. Quite often, the diviner is effective one way or another.

Tales and short narratives of various sorts are found in almost all cultures. They are more universal than epics, for, as we have seen, some cultures do not create epics, but all cultures possess stories. These literary forms comprise myths (Category 1), legends (Category 2), and tales (Category 3) about heroes, ancestors, or gods (sagas or epic lays one might call them), folk tales about representative human beings or animals, fables which tell short moral stories about animals or plants often with concluding morals, examples, and parables which are short tales with a clear point, or anecdotes which are very short tales with a point about great or wise men (philosophers, doctors, rabbis, teachers, and other great men). At one end of the scale, we find pure narratives with narrative development, and at the other the narrative becomes exiguous and the moral becomes important. Some of these have the role of praise or are partially eulogistic, but most are told for didactic and educational purposes.

Narratives are closely related to memory. Many are told by the tellers as true and are presented as a feat of memory. Memory is not, as one might think, necessarily a mechanical procedure but can be imaginative. Narratives are descriptions of several events, either real or imaginary, and when real, often rearranged for particular effectiveness. Serial reproduction is a common feature of memory of the past, and narrative seems especially close to the memorial process.[22] By recalling events, one relives them or enables others to experience them. The story must normally be thought of as true in order to be effective. The magic won't work if the story is not true.[23]

Elizabeth Stopp, speaking of folk tales or Märchen, writes:

> The mind which actually forms a Märchen is already looking back ('es war ein mal') from a higher state of consciousness than that described. An artifact is already to some extent replacing what was originally a live experience or a myth. By the fact of telling, the teller

[22] See F. C. Bartlett, *Remembering: A Study in Experimental and Social Psychology* (New York and Cambridge, England, 1932), Chapter 7, pp. 118–76. Memory, Bartlett argues (pp. 293–4) is related to the need for dealing with absent (past, present, or future) objects and hence related closely to language and tradition.
[23] See above, note 14

no longer sees the magical sphere naively as the only realm but as one existing in contrast to the ordinary world. Through the person of a hero, man comes to terms with the contrast between the two spheres. He attempts to reconcile them and the ensuing Märchen expresses two successive stages of consciousness constituting a simple epic artistic form.[24]

Although most traditional narratives may be put under the rubric of the didactic, what they do teach is diverse. Some are etiological tales, explaining the origin of something or some custom. Some praise heroes or tell stories about them. Some speak of the myths of the tribe. Some are especially for children and younger people. They may be any of the above, or what Soriano calls tales of warning devised to keep children away from water, wolves, woods, and so forth, or formulettes, or mnemonic stories, games, riddle stories, verbal games, tall tales, and so forth.[25] Part of the attraction of some of these tales and indeed of all tales is the sense of wonder they are meant to raise. Adults and children in tribal societies, except in emergencies, either do not travel or travel only to well-defined permissible places at well-defined seasons. Although this fixed condition is now changing, it is a slow process, and tales of strange worlds and strange deeds still fascinate listeners. The seven wonders of the world are enumerated for a non-travelling world as were other lists like the wonders of Ireland or the British Isles.

Whatever the function, whether it be ritual, didactic, or political, tales and stories in most cultures 'always contain an element of entertainment and relaxation'.[26] This element of pleasure, of relaxation, of wonder is omnipresent. These ends are, in most cases, however, subordinate to their serious purpose.

Stories must normally be recited as if they are true either by personal attestation, or by reliable authority. As we have pointed out, truth is necessary for their effectiveness. If they can be authenticated in some way, even if the authentication is not genuine, they should be. Many cultures, however, allow for relaxation of the demand for truth under certain circumstances which the whole tribe understands. On those occasions, made-up stories are told, and much merriment arises from the fantasizing which such occasions allow.

Sometimes the traditional tales, as in the Ifa cult of the Yoruba in Western Africa, are kept secret except on special occasions. Not all are narratives but many are. These contain Yoruba mythology, methods of divination, medicine,

---

[24] Review of Hedwig von Beit's *Das Märchen: Sein Ort in der Entwicklung* (Bern, 1965), in *MLR* 62 (1967), p. 752.
[25] Marc Soriano, 'From Tales of Warning to Formulettes: the Oral Tradition in French Children's Literature', *Yale French Studies* 43 (1969), pp. 24–43, trans. Julia Blech Frey.
[26] Daniel P. Biebuyck and Kahombo Mateene, *Anthologie de la littérature orale nyanga*, Académie Royale des Sciences d'Outre-mer, Classe des Sciences morales et politiques, NS.36.1 (Brussels, 1970), p. 9 (our translation).

magic procedures, observations about plants, rivers, or animals. The priests of Ifa are consulted just as diviners are consulted, and they often answer by telling stories.[27] Many traditional cultures on occasion, and even frequently, make use of secrecy to clothe the true meaning from the eyes of the vulgar or uninitiated.

One of the best reports available of the telling of tales is in Ruth Finnegan's *Limba Stories and Story-Telling*.[28] At evening sessions among these people, stories are told with vivid gesture and dramatic effect. Prose is used for the tales. They are admired or echoed by enthusiastic listeners. The narratives are interlaced with riddles and songs. During the day, proverbs and parables and occasionally a story embellish the speech of the elders. The language is formal only at law cases and funerals.

The Limba story is orally transmitted, and like all oral narratives it has no standard text. Music and dancing sometimes accompany the tales. As we have noted, historical or pseudo-historical tales are regarded as true, but fiction is allowed especially in humorous animal tales. The word in the Limba language for story (*mbara*) is of interest to us because it is connected with the root *bara* meaning 'old', just as the Gaelic *seanchas*, 'tradition, traditional recital', is derived from the word *sean* (cognate with Latin *senex*), meaning 'old'.

In the recitation, references or questions are often addressed to individuals in the audience. The audience interjects at times during the telling just as Xhosa audiences do during a praise-poem. Sometimes the whole audience joins in a song within the tale. Anyone can tell a tale if he wishes, but unless he is talented he does not hold his audience. Good tellers of tales are admired. The tales are told with a range of tone and speed. Often familiar stock characters, plot turns, openings, and conclusions recur. Formulaic phrases are frequent. Within a framework the performer continually improvises, expanding and compressing.[29]

Fables are also found in various cultures. If we include all animal narratives as fables, they are almost as ubiquitous as praise poems. Stories about animals in general are numerous, inevitably reflecting the close connection between animal and human life. Fables in the narrow sense of the word, those relatively short tales told for the most part about animals who are given human characteristics and which are specific about the lesson they inculcate, are rarer

---

[27] See Wándé Abímbolá, 'The Literature of the Ifa Cult', Chapter 4 of *Sources of Yoruba History* ed. S. O. Biobaku (Oxford, 1973), pp. 41–61. On folk tales in general, see Max Lüthi, *Das europäische Volksmärchen: Form und Wesen*, Dalp-Taschenbüxher 351, 2nd edition (Berne and Munich, 1960). First edition 1947. This book is slightly romantic and is limited to the European folk-tale, which has been influenced by sophisticated cultural elements. It does, however, present some universal qualities of folk tales.
[28] Ruth Finnegan, *Limba Stories and Storytelling* (Oxford, 1967). For Irish story telling, see James H. Delargy, 'The Gaelic Story-teller', *PRBA* 31 (1945), pp. 177–221.
[29] We are indebted to Ruth Finnegan's book for the three preceding paragraphs, at times echoing her language.

but are found in various cultures. They seem to have especially flourished in the Mediterranean area and in the Near East. Most of these particular fables are preserved in rather literary form [30] and go back to Greek models. They often present political protest; it is no wonder that the Russians use the phrase 'Aesopic allegory' to indicate political protest presented in a story. David Daube has called our attention to this feature of fable in his study of *Ancient Hebrew Fables*.[31] He finds three fables in the *Old Testament*, none in the *New Testament* (which has many parables, a related form), and some thirty-six in the Talmud and Midrash.

If we define the word fable strictly, there are not many Sub-Saharan African fables, but there are many animal tales, sometimes including human beings. Nor do we find many parables. Short tales, some of animals and some not, are frequently told, however, to entertain and teach the audience. They are similar to, but usually longer than, the medieval exempla which are told, often in sermons, to enliven moral and didactic discourse. The interpretation of these exempla requires a good knowledge of the culture out of which they come, and many need annotations and explanations to be understood. As in most stories, but especially in short moral tales, the ambient culture is taken for granted inasmuch as they are delivered orally within a closely related group of people. Proverbs are frequently used in these short tales, and exempla and riddles may be interposed. E. N. Obiechina well describes the world-view of most of the tribal societies although he is specifically referring to West Africa: 'The world of the traditional West African folk-tale is an undifferentiated world within which the dichotomy between the natural and the supernatural, the abstract and the concrete, the physical and the metaphysical does not exist.'[32]

Anecdotes, or, as the Greeks called them, *chreiai*, are a special kind of short moral narrative dealing with the acts or sayings in particular circumstances of men or women usually but not always considered wise. Occasionally the Greek *chreiai* are humorous and obscene. Many of our jokes would be considered *chreiai* of this sort. This specialized use of the term *chreia*, which normally has the neutral meaning of 'service' or 'need', in reference to 'an appropriate maxim' suggests the popularity of the genre among the ancient Greeks, and a few of their *chreiai* such as those concerned with Diogenes have passed into world culture. In Greek the genre existed at least as early as the fourth century BC[33] and soon became attached especially to the Cynic School of

---

[30] See for instance, Thomas Noel, *Theories of Fable in the Eighteenth Century* (New York and London, 1975). Lafontaine is of course the great poet fabulist of the modern era.

[31] The Inaugural Lecture of the Oxford Centre for Postgraduate Hebrew Studies, delivered in Corpus Christi College 17 May, 1973.

[32] 'Transition from oral to literary tradition', I, *Présence Africaine* 63 (1967), p. 155.

[33] See A. S. F. Gow in his introduction to his edition of *Machon, The Fragments*, Cambridge Classical Texts and Commentaries (Cambridge, 1965), p. 13. Some of Machon's fragments are *creiai*, but his are not in the least edifying.

Philosophy. From them, perhaps,[34] the Jewish tradition took the notion in order to characterize wise men, usually rabbis, and implant their teachings firmly in the minds of their hearers.

Comparable short anecdotes frequently used informally are told about great men in all cultures. They may be interjected into longer tales about heroes when some legendary saying of the hero is recalled. They are often in the mouths of the older men of the tribes and become known to all during childhood. Similar anecdotes are also told of wise men who were in fact entirely legendary, such as Boban Saor, the Gaelic master-builder, who in earlier times was called Goban Saor and is probably derived from Gobniu, the god of the smithy.

Wisdom, furthermore, may be diffused not only by narrative poems but also directly by theoretical wisdom poems and prose. These forms of gnomic lore (Category 6) may be divided into gnomes (comprising apothegms, maxims, and aphorisms), proverbs, counsels for rulers, meditations, and debates. Sometimes the term gnome is used to cover all such types of wisdom literature, but here we use it in a narrower sense. As we have already seen from the preceding chapter, gnomes and proverbs accompany an important role in all traditional societies. Parallelisms appear in both genres, but they differ to the extent that wit, rhetorical balance, and metaphor belong to the proverbial rather than the gnomic category. The gnomic style is usually direct, simple, and brief. It usually does not indulge in word-play and metaphor as is frequently the case with proverbs.

Proverbs and gnomes, like all wisdom literature, are based upon the notion of regularity and order both of the natural and of the social and individual world. There is a settled nature of things which it ill behooves one to neglect, and traditional aphoristic literature is there as a reminder. Aphorisms and gnomes have always appealed to philosophers and thinkers from earliest times down to Nietzsche and Walter Benjamin and with good reason. The subject matter of gnomes and proverbs is scientific (in the basic sense of the word), ethical, and prudential. Aristotle (*Rhetoric* 2:21) defines gnome as 'a statement not relating to particulars but to universals: yet not to all universals . . . but to all such as are the objects of action and are to be chosen or avoided in our doings'. Proverbs and gnomes normally apply to all units in a class or set even though in their phrasing they may be about particulars. Of course, their universality is limited by their appropriateness to the particular application. One must, for instance, sometimes go fast and at other times go slow. Perhaps this striving towards universalism is why scientists like Francis Bacon and philosophers have been attracted to gnomic lore. This quality also accounts for their similarity to the law. Philosophers have used them. Albertus Magnus

---

[34] See H. Fischel, 'Studies in Cynicism and the Ancient Near East: The Transformation of a *chria*', *Religions in Antiquity, Essays in Memory of Erwin Ramsdell Goodenough*, ed. Jacob Neusner, *Numen* Supplementary Volume 14 (1968), pp. 372–411.

defined maxims or gnomes in terms of the class of universal propositions which are not intuitively certain like axioms.[35] They provide a traditional culture with common ground for the settling of disputes and debates.

Gnomes of various sorts are found all over the world and have effectively made the transition to literary culture in writers like Gracian, Erasmus, Bacon, and Le Rochefoucauld.[36] Collections of traditional gnomes and proverbs are found in the *Hávamal* of the Poetic Eddas, in Greek anthologies of gnomes[37] known as gnomologies, in Old English,[38] the Bible, Old Irish and Welsh, and in Egyptian and Mesopotamian texts.[39] Sometimes gnomes are known as sentences or *sententiae*, and in the Middle Ages the *Sentences* of Sextus[40] were popular.

Proverbs are more difficult to define than gnomes. Although they largely exist for the same purpose, to teach wisdom, there is more of an aesthetic element in proverbs. There have been various attempts at all-encompassing definitions, but few seem to embrace all that we feel are proverbs.[41] They may operate as interruptions, confirmations, and opening or concluding remarks.

[35] See the reference in Monroe Z. Hafter, *Gracian and Perfection: Spanish Moralists of the Seventeenth Century*, Harvard Studies in Romance Languages 30 (Cambridge, Mass., 1966), p. 17.

[36] See Jonathan Culler, 'Paradox and the Language of Morals in La Rochefoucauld', *MLR* 68 (1973), pp. 28–39; Margaret M. Phillips, *The 'Adages' of Erasmus, A Study with Translations* (Cambridge, 1964); James Stephens, *Francis Bacon and the Style of Science* (Chicago, 1975), pp. 98–121; and Hafter above.

[37] See John Barns, 'A New Gnomologium; With Some Remarks on Gnomic Anthologies', *Classical Quarterly* 44 (1950), pp. 127–137; 45 (1951), pp. 1–19.

[38] See M. MacGregor Dawson, 'The Structure of the Old English Gnomic Poems', *JEGP* 61 (1962), pp. 14–62; Stanley B. Greenfield and Richard Evert, 'Maxims II: Gnome and Poem', in *Anglo-Saxon Poetry: Essays in Appreciation for John C. McGalliard*, ed. D. W. Frese (South Bend, Ind., 1975), pp. 337–354 and Blanche Colton Williams, *Gnomic Poetry in Anglo-Saxon*, ed. with an Introduction, Notes and Glossary (Columbia U. Studies in English and Comparative Literature) (New York, 1914).

[39] See, e.g., Johannes Jacobus Adrianus Van Dijk, *La Sagesse suméro-accadienne, Recherches sur les genres littéraires des textes sapientiaux*, Proefschrift . . . Rijksuniversiteit te Leidin . . . (Leiden, 1953).

[40] See Henry Chadwick, *The Sentences of Sextus, A Contribution to the History of Early Christian Ethics*, Texts and Studies, Contributions to Biblical and Patristic Literature, NS ed. C. H. Dodd 5 (Cambridge, 1959). Who Sextus was is quite a problem. These *sententiae* were translated from Greek *gnomai* in the late fourth century.

[41] See G. B. Milner, 'What is a Proverb? How Can We so Easily Recognize Something as a Saying Even When It's New to Us? The Answer May Lie in the Structure of the Phrase Itself', *New Society*, 6 Feb., 1969, pp. 199–202 (a structural analysis of statement parts) and Nigel Barley, 'A Structural Approach to the Proverb and Maxim With Special Reference to the Anglo-Saxon Corpus', *Proverbium* 20 (1972), pp. 737–750. These both have similarities. On proverb as metaphor, see Peter Seitel, 'Proverbs: A Social Use of Metaphor', *Genre* 2 (1969), pp. 143–161. For their role in preserving tradition and controlling society, see Leonard W. Doob and Ismael M. Huneh, 'Somali Proverbs and Poems as Acculturation Indices', *The Public Opinion Quarterly* 34 (1970–71), pp. 552–559.

They serve as a means of social control because they are used to settle disputes. A handbook of proverbs wrenched from their living context is scarcely interesting, for proverbs are made for the proper situations and operate best therein. They help us to cope with particular situations by raising them to a universal level, and in this they are like laws.

As we have seen, proverbs may sum up a culture and indeed provide clues to a culture.[42] They help us to understand a culture, and because of their memorial form or metaphoric structure they are ideal for teaching, as well as for encapsulating a situation and giving advice. They are the oil that keeps traditional culture moving.

Another well-known literary genre of counsels (Category 5) which purvey wisdom, this time to princes and rules, is what is generally known as 'Counsels for Rulers' or 'Mirrors for Princes' (*Specula principum*). We find advice to princes in various forms of literature, above all in praise poems, but we apply the generic term only to those works whose chief task is to advise the prince. We have a number of Old Irish forms of the genre, some indeed very old.[43] Here and in the corresponding Sanskrit mirrors, the emphasis is upon truth: that is, the ruler must model his acts and laws upon the way the universe runs or else he will destroy his realm. Throughout the Middle Ages various mirrors were compiled, and some, like the *Secretum Secretorum* falsely attributed to Aristotle, were very popular. A number of medieval Persian and Arabic mirrors exist.

In these works the poet was carrying out in a more systematic way an ancient function: to instruct the ruler or any ruler in the ways of wisdom, that is, the rational processes in the universe and society so that he may fit himself into the proper cosmic and social roles he assumed or is about to assume when he becomes a chief, ruler, or king. These early duties were probably carried out in many of his acts and in public, not to speak of private, speeches. The recognized poets had a certain leeway in criticism and suggestion, but they had to be careful. Their advice was presented both in direct and indirect speeches and poems. This function is also carried out in proverbs and gnomes, and the earliest *specula* were probably collections of these, as we may see in parts of the Biblical book of Proverbs.

Finally in this discussion of non-narrative theoretical wisdom genres let us turn to meditations and debates. These are often quite long and exist in various forms. They are not often recognized by literary critics as wisdom literature and may be found under various generic names. Old English meditations have for instance usually been called elegies by scholars. Strictly

---

[42] See Ernst Dammann, 'Die Religion in afrikanischen Sprichwörtern und Rätseln', *Anthropos* 67 (1972), pp. 36–48.

[43] See, e.g., Roland M. Smith, 'The *Speculum Principum* in Early Irish Literature', *Speculum* 2 (1927) pp. 411–445, and *Audacht Morainn* ed. trans. Fergus Kelly (Dublin Institute for Advanced Studies, 1976). For a history of the genre, see Lester K. Born, trans., *The Education of a Christian Prince by Desiderius Erasmus* (New York, 1936).

speaking the debate is not a genre but a form, but many longer wisdom pieces are put in the form of a debate or contest. When we come to riddles we shall refer to riddle contests or debates, but a fair number of meditations also appear as debates, either between warring aspects of the souls or between the soul and body (there is an ancient literary genre of the debate between these two), or between man and God or the gods, or between a king and a rival, or between a man and his friends, or between rival poets. Perhaps the most dramatic of all wisdom debates is to be found in the book of Job where Job argues with his friends and finally humbles himself before the majesty of God when He finally appears.

As we have said, 'meditation' is a classification based upon the nature and content of a wisdom work; 'debate' is a formal criterion. But the genres are closely intertwined. The debate has been recognized as a literary form, and indeed there is a considerable literature on the subject.[44] The 'flyting' or verbal contest maintained between poets, or between two men usually of distinction, until one puts down the other by words is a development of the debate genre, which we have discussed under satire to which it usually belongs.

Debates like those of Job are made up of various meditations. And within meditations like the Old English *Seafarer* and *Wanderer* or the Babylonian *Theodicy* and *Enuma-elish* we find internal debates. It is true that not all meditations are debates or are cast in question-and-answer form. *Ecclesiastes* is a true meditation without debate form unless we are to consider the speculative cast of mind seen there as questioning or debating with itself.

There are a number of question-and-answer examples of wisdom literature which have probably grown out of short question-and-answer oral situations. In the Middle Ages we find various literary kinds of this type. Often the questioner is a king or ruler, and the answerer is a poet or wise man. It is an ideal form for didactic purposes, especially if the wise man is a *Wunderkind*, as in the Hadrian and Epictetus debates in the middle Ages, or, as in the Satan (or Saturn) and Solomon debates in the same period. Class antagonisms (often wittily expressed) may be found in the wide-spread *Solomon et Marcolfus* debates found all over Europe. The Old English *Solomon and Saturn* debate belongs to this group with Saturn substituting for Marcolf. These are closely related to the *Speculum principis* form although only some are found in this latter guise. The question-and-answer format is usually more general than advice on ruling and contains information about nature and society. But these are not always absent from more particular *specula*.

Frequently the debate form or simple meditations are presented as a teacher teaching his pupils or as a father teaching his son or sons. Ideally the role of the teacher and father includes the instruction of those under his care, and these poems reflect such a real-life situation.

[44] See, e.g., Hans Walther, *Das Streitgedicht in der lateinischen Literatur des Mittelalters* (Munich, 1920) and Burghart Wachinger, *Sängerkrieg: Untersuchungen zur Spruchdichtung des 13. Jahrhunderts* (Munich, 1973).

The meditation has, as far as we are aware, been almost completely ignored although there are many examples in world literature, several of which are to be found in the Bible and Apocrypha (especially the Book of Wisdom, Ecclesiastes, and Ecclesiasticus). Meditations are rather loosely organized and follow the ramblings of a speculative mind. They seem to be based on what one might call intellectual speculation about the nature of the world and society. They are gnomes written large, sometimes very large; and they concentrate on social rather than natural wisdom, although parallels with the natural world are not unknown. These works when profound bring us into contact with the speculations of a wise and sometimes holy man, occasionally merely an experienced man, whose comments about life and human society are well worth attending to.

The next group of genres may be called meta-wisdom poems. They are closely related to the preceding group, but instead of purveying wisdom directly, these works deal with its means of communication. Needless to say, such poems are hard to classify exactly because they are often mingled into poems about wisdom pure and simple, as for instance in a collection of proverbs.

A relatively large segment of wisdom literature is about wisdom and the purveyors of wisdom. In fact, wisdom meditations such as we have discussed above are partly meta-wisdom meditations. Much wisdom literature argues that wisdom is important, and the first step in acquiring wisdom is to be wise enough to want to acquire wisdom. A wise man first knows or should know that wisdom is the highest goal of mankind. To attain an awareness of the superiority of wisdom is to have taken the first basic step on to the entrance of the temple of wisdom. The Old Irish poet who is quoted on the dedication page of this book appropriately declares that 'inspired poetry' (*aí*, cognate with the Welsh *awen*) is the daughter of wisdom and of prudence.

Besides the praise of wisdom (such as we find in Proverbs 8 or Job 28 and in many passages in Wisdom and Ecclesiasticus), we find many poems about those who purvey wisdom in traditional societies: praise poets, scops, and minstrels, and the like who write poetry about the hazards of poetic life and the necessity of being paid and rewarded. We also find eloquence about eloquence, a theme traditionally linked with wisdom.[45]

The kind of wisdom-poems about wisdom-poets may be found in begging poems in which the poet asks for gifts or money or in complaints about the hazards or miseries of minstrel life as in the Old English poems *Deor* or the *Wanderer*. In the latter, the *scop* remembers his happy days at the foot of his ruler, days which alas have now vanished. Begging poems are perhaps not so common as might be expected only because a gift from the chief is requisite as

---

[45] See above Chap. 2, reference to Cicero's *De Inventione* I (after note 29).

his due to the poet and need not normally be especially requested, although a reminder now and then might be useful. Contests between poets may be considered partly under this category and partly as satires. Jealousy is rife among traditional poets, and each is proud of his abilities whether real or imaginary. In a bitter quarrel, poets may hurl satires and curses at each other until one is forced to silence by the torrent and truth of words hurled at him. Germanic flytings and their Celtic counterparts belong to this category.

The last large category of wisdom literature may be called active wisdom literature. It is hard to find the proper characterizing noun or adjective for this group. 'Useful' and 'practical' are terms that might be used for those genres and literary forms which are not properly theoretical. Yet the use of these terms would imply that theoretical wisdom such as we have been discussing so far in this chapter is not useful or even practical. It is of the very nature of wisdom to be practical and useful no matter what genre is being composed. Some genres are more immediately practical and useful, but all are useful and practical insofar as they enable people to live in accordance with the 'laws' of the cosmos and of society.

The active group of wisdom literature may be divided into two, again with some reservations: those genres which are closely linked with magic or are magic themselves, and those which are simply practical or active in various ways. The first group consists of charms (Category 9) and divinations and prophecies (Category 7); the second of mnemonic poems and devices, work poems, petitions and prayers (Category 4), and games and riddles (Category 6). Let us look at each in turn.

Charms may be either objects which may be carried on one's person or attached to a dwelling (often called amulets and talismans)[46] or words which may be recited or carried around on amulets. Both object and words have the same purpose: to bring about a desired end such as cure of disease, a safe pregnancy and birth, cure of one's sick or injured animals, and so forth, or to develop an aura of defence and protection against the effects of an evil eye or ancestral irritation or malignant agents like demons, ghosts, elves, and so forth. Occasionally they may be worn in written form or recited for positive virtues: success in love or politics, for instance. They are usually partially written in formulas, contain foreign and meaningless words, repeat much, and often, though not always, argue from the past or assumed past in the form 'as x, so y' (if god or God preserved us or did such and such in the past, so He will

---

[46] Some scholars make a distinction between amulets and talismans, the former worn for defensive and the latter for positive and active powers. See, e.g., E. J. de Jager, 'Notes on the magical Charms of the Cape Nguni Tribes', *Fort Hare Papers* 2:6, November, 1963, pp. 291–309. De Jager also classifies charm objects into various sub-classes depending on their functions, e.g., love, protecting children in various ways and their mothers when expecting and nursing them, defense against animals, disease, nature, for fertility, success in hunting, good sleep, pleasant dreams and so forth.

preserve or do for us in the future if we remind Him of His deeds in the past).[47]

The charm is an attempt to control and to bind nature.[48] It is reflected in lullabies, invocations, elegies, and laments to help the dead soul pass safely the inimical powers of the air. Northrop Frye sees it in the repetitive incantations in modern advertisements. At the root of all verbal charms is the notion that words have magical powers and, if used properly, can control and bind nature.

Charms are found all over the world.[49] They are the quintessence of one of the fundamental roles of poetry: the magic power of binding and controlling. They are the most basic form of magic. From a literary point of view, their influence on other literary works is of more interest than the specifics of their own mumbo-jumbo. One of the authors of this book has argued elsewhere that the form of *Deor* owes something to the charm form especially in its 'as x, so y' arrangement.[50]

As we have noted, a characteristic of the wisdom point of view is the notion that time and space have their proper occasions and locations. Both divination and prophecy rest upon the notion of the power of language and upon the appropriateness of time and space to the recitation of the request for information or a wished-for event, or an appropriate location and time for something to happen. Prospero is the Shakespearean magician who knows the proper time. As he puts it (4.1.141–142) 'The minute of their [Caliban and his confederates'] plot is almost come.'

The Elizabethans used the word 'occasion' more or less as the Greeks used *kairos*, the proper moment, the exact moment, for action or for an event. In the Bible a term somewhat different from the common Hebrew word for time is used to indicate the 'proper time', as in *Ecclesiastes* 3 where a list of proper occasions is given us – a time to be born, a time to die, and so forth. The proper place is clearly demarked in English, but in older Hebrew[51] and other languages the notion of the proper place is reflected in the vocabulary.

---

[47] Prayers of petition in various Judeo-Christian Islamic sects still take that form. See what is known as St. Cyprian's Prayer in Joaquin Gimeno Casalduero, 'Sobre la oracion narrativa medieval: estructura, origen, supervivencia', *Anales de la Universidad de Murcia* 16 (1957–58), especially pp. 10ff.

[48] In his lecture to the Boston Area Stylistics Group on March 4, 1975, published in his *Spiritus Mundi* (Bloomington, 1976), pp. 123–147, Northrop Frye makes this point.

[49] For Central Asiatic charms, see Nora K. Chadwick and Victor Zhirmunsky, *Oral Epics of Central Asia* (Cambridge, 1969), pp. 164ff.

[50] See M. W. Bloomfield, 'The Form of Deor', *PMLA* 79 (1964), pp. 534–541, and above, Chapter 6, note 17. A recent edition of the Anglo-Saxon charms may be found in Heather Lesley Stuart's valuable *A Critical Edition of Some Anglo-Saxon Charms and Incantations*, Submitted for the degree of Doctor of Philosophy in the School of Humanities of the Flinders University of South Australia, 1974 (typewritten) in 3 volumes.

[51] The Hebrew word 'makom' is so used. In fact, God in Hebrew is sometimes called 'makom', the place (*par excellence*, the only One in His true place at all times). Cf. also 'Despise no man and deem nothing impossible for there is not a man that has not his hour, and there is not a thing that has not its place', Mishna, *Pirke Aboth* 4:3.

It is upon this notion that divination and prophecy rest, and the poet who is capable of divining and prophesying is often the shaman or the poet capable of being carried out of himself to obtain secret, divine information. The Romantic Movement made the divine or ecstatic poet (a most ancient idea) a basis of its poetic. In an earlier more restrained period when the question of the poet's function was not raised because it was taken for granted, the poet and the situation were recognized as inspired in most of his tasks. The audience and the utterance shared with the poet in the total poetic complex.[52]

The prophetic poet is the mouthpiece through which the god speaks. What comes out of the poet's mouth is the oracle, and in some cases, as in the prophetic books of the Bible, these oracles are collected by the prophet's pupils or disciples. They may differ in degrees of clarity. Obscurity or ambiguity is a well-known feature of prophecy, and lack of exactitude can obviously be a blessing to the prophet's reputation. Symbols and frequent gaps in expression abound in their messages. The injectionary and ejaculatory style is popular. Yet some prophecies are relatively clear, and the prophecy is of a general nature like 'the coming of the day of the Lord' or 'the coming of the days of wrath'.

Usually only prophecies to a whole people or to a ruler are preserved. The thousands of personal prophecies which must have been uttered have almost all vanished. The past is used as a storehouse of examples and parallelisms by many prophets. Often prophecies are clothed in enigmatic or Aesopic language to protect the prophet. If they are of public import they are usually chanted.[53]

Often the prophet or diviner makes a trance journey to the next world; and we find, as we have seen in the previous chapter, shamanistic journeys on a horse or up a great tree to the next world. They are often reported by travellers and indeed occasionally by the shaman himself. Vatic poetry in many countries assumes such a journey. Even when entrails, bones, stones, or cracks in the earth are read, a journey may often as well be necessary. In any case, it is a wise man who reads the signs.

The journey to the next world is not only a journey to the gods; it may often be a journey to one's ancestors who are wiser than we. Ancestors have a reason to protect one; a god or demon or ghost is more arbitrary. Ancestors are kinder.

One cannot make a strict division between divination and prophecy in their

---

[52] On the inspired poet, see Alice Sperduti, 'The Divine Nature of Poetry in Antiquity', *TAPA* 81 (1950), pp. 205–1240; Milton C. Nahm, 'The Theological Background of the Theory of Christ as Creator', *JHI* 8 (1947), pp. 363–372; Courtland D. Baker, 'Certain Religious Elements in the English Doctrine of the Inspired Poet During the Renaissance', *ELH* 6 (1939), pp. 305–1323.
[53] 'The poetry of the seer appears to be rarely spoken, but most frequently chanted', Nora Kershaw Chadwick, *Poetry & Prophecy* (Cambridge, 1942), p. 28. This is a most valuable book on the poet as prophet and diviner.

ordinary dimensions. Prophecy on its highest levels adds, of course, a new dimension to shamanism and, as in the Bible, creates a rich and notable literature of universal significance. Both divination and prophecy are based on the notion of 'occasion' and 'place'. The diviner himself must be in the right place and demand knowledge at the right time. And his information is usually concerned with 'when' and 'where' something is to be done, the proper 'occasions' and 'places' for it. Even public praise-poems often need to be sung in the right place and time. The place of the chief is often the right place, and certain kinds of meetings are the right times.

Frequently divination or prophecy is ecstatic, but divination can be divided into possession (ecstatic) and wisdom types.[54] The information the diviner utters may be produced, as we have noted, by a shamanistic experience, or it may be based on his past wisdom and common sense. Wisdom divination is impersonal and is based on the idea of order in the universe. The wise man claims no possession by spirits but draws upon his knowledge. There is a third type called by E. M. Zuesse intuitive in which the diviner uses no science and seeks no possession; simple common-sense is the source of the diviner's wisdom. It is, Zuesse argues, good for finding lost articles, and identifying witches and thieves.

Irish prophecies and divinations are numerous, and the druid's chief function was to serve rulers both as diviner and wise man;[55] and Roman and Greek divination are exceptionally well documented. There must have been some distrustful reactions against diviners in spite of the usual picture of Roman decadence after the second century AD[56] Yet in the West divination persisted in popularity.[57]

The idea of the poet as prophet has always had its believers, but the Romantic Movement raised the notion to a peak of intensity blotting out all the other aspects of the poetic situation. It is still with us, but its hey-day seems to be over.[58]

Let us now turn to various types of traditional poetry. Perhaps the most fascinating and best known of these are riddles (Category 6), which serve as games, amusements, and occasionally as part of religious or initiation

[54] See Evan M. Zuesse, 'Divination and Deity in African Religions', *History of Religions* 15 (1975–76), pp. 158–182. He also allows for an intermediate type which he calls intuitive.

[55] See the Appendix on Irish analogues in G. H. Huxley's *Greek Epic Poetry from Eumelos to Panyassis* (Cambridge, 1969), pp. 191ff., and Chapter 3 above.

[56] See Ramsay MacMullen, *Enemies of the Roman Order, Treason, Unrest, and Alienation in the Empire* (Cambridge, Mass., 1966) especially pp. 95–162.

[57] See Denise Grodzynski, '*Superstitio*', *Revue des études grecques* 83 (1970), pp. 333–350, and Robert Flacelière, *Greek Oracles*, trans. Douglas Garman (London, 1965) (Original Paris, 1961).

[58] Compare, for instance, Wagner's treatment of the Old Norse *Sibyl's Prophecy* in his *Ring of the Nibelung*, referred to above in Chapter 6.

ceremonies. There have been various attempts at defining a riddle, usually concentrating on the question part of the form and tending to ignore the social setting.[59] From one point of view they are the games wise men played in the teaching situation where questions are asked and answers are expected. A riddle tries to get a grown-up or youngster to see things in a certain way and hence is binding as well as liberating. Often the description in the question part of the riddle is capable of being misinterpreted so as to arouse the listener's attention.

In the sixties and early seventies, structural analyses tended to predominate in the explanation of riddles. Recently we have been told to look at the whole situation in which the riddle appears. In the earlier part of this century, Porzig emphasized the social aspect of the riddle. In keeping with modern emphases, although close to Porzig's approach, Alfred Schönfeldt emphasizes the riddle 'as a particular form of dialogue communication'.[60]

Northrop Frye contrasts the binding element of the charm with the liberating element of a riddle. The riddle serves as an escape. What you thought was A is really B. Images, he says, are close to riddles, and complex hermetic poetry like Mallarmé's rests on a riddle theory of poetry. This explanation is not, however, the whole story, for riddles can bind us as well as free us. Both qualities are part of their power.

Some riddles demand a single-word answer, usually a noun; some seek a cause or an interpretation. Sometimes the answer is a cryptic or riddle-like

---

[59] A very good introduction to the whole subject may be found in Mathilde Hain, *Rätsel*, Sammlung Metzler, Realienbücher für Germanistik Abt. E (Stuttgart, 1966). Claude Lévi-Strauss has some interesting and perceptive things to say about the riddle in *The Scope of Anthropology*, trans. Sherry Ortner Paul and Robert A. Paul, Cape Editions (London, 1967) pp. 34–39, inaugural lecture at Collège de France, Jan. 5., 1960. Jollès in his famous book on *Die einfache Formen* makes riddle a primary form. It is discussed by Archer Taylor, 'The Riddle as a Primary Form', *Folklore in Action, Essays for Discussion in Honor of MacEdward Leach*, ed. Horace P. Beck, Publications of the American Folklore Society, Bibliographical and Special Series 14 (Philadelphia, 1962), pp. 200–207 (Taylor questions Jollès' tendency to link myth and riddle by defining myth as an answer that contains a question). See also on riddles, Charles T. Scott, 'Some Approaches to the Study of the Riddle', *Studies in Language, Literature and Culture of the Middle Ages and Later*, ed. E. Bagby Atwood and Archibald A. Hill (Austin, 1969), pp. 111–127 and 'On Defining the Riddle: The Problem of a Structural Unit', *Genre* 2 (1969), pp. 129–142; Rudolph Schevill, *Some Forms of the Riddle Question and the Exercise of the Wits in Popular Fiction and Formal Literature*, U. of California Publications in Modern Philology 2, No. 3 (1911), pp. 183–237; K. Ohlert, *Rätsel and Rätselspiele der alten Griechen*, 2nd edition (Berlin, 1912); F. H. Whitman, 'Medieval Riddling, Factors Underlying Its Development', *NM* 71 (1970), pp. 177–185; and Frederick Tupper, Jr., 'The Comparative Study of Riddles', *MLN* 18 (1903), pp. 1–8.

[60] 'Zur Analyse des Rätsels', *ZDP* 97 (1978), pp. 60–73 (quotation p. 61). For Porzig, see Andre Jollès and Walter Porzig, 'Rätselforschungen', *Germanica, Edward Sievers zum 75. Geburtstag 25 November, 1925* (Hall a/d Saale, 1925), pp. 646–660 (in discussing the riddles in the *Rigveda*).

answer.[61] Sometimes it is a variety of *prosopopeia* as when the answer itself utters the riddle. These riddles often end with the question 'Who am I?' Some riddles are short narratives; others are pure static description either in third or first person form. Max Lüthi argues that part of the pleasure of the riddle lies in finding meaning in meaninglessness.[62] This insight should be pushed even further because solving a riddle really reduplicates the whole procedure of wisdom – the task of finding the pattern, the meaning, and the order in apparent disorder. The difficult metaphor is at the root of most, but not all, difficulties in riddles. Sometimes a riddle of a foreign culture reveals a new way of looking at something. A humorous example may be found in the Sotho riddle, 'We Basotho throw [it] down, but the Europeans fold it up.'[63] Riddles are of course closely linked to gnomes; and according to Nora Chadwick, among the Galla of East Africa gnomes of observation provide the answers to riddles.[64]

Riddles are found in most cultures. In Western Europe, there are notable collections preserved in Anglo-Saxon (in the Exeter Book) and in Old Norse (as in the *Saga of King Heidrek the Wise*).[65] Other riddles, and stories built around riddles, may be found in sagas, short tales, ballads, games, and so forth.[66] We must finally remember that the riddle process is the same as the attainment of wisdom process.

There are other verbal games associated with riddles which we shall pass over. Some of them are traditional and are cast in poetic form (as difficult as that type of composition is to define in early societies), but some kind of recurrent rhythmic or syllabic pattern may be found in them. Most of these games are the ephemera of oral literature. Survivals may still be found in modern children's games.

[61] Riddle 36 of the Exeter Book Old English collection gives the answer in a cryptogram. In this paragraph we are indebted to parts of a paper submitted to M. W. Bloomfield by his student, Joáquin Marinez Pizarro and entitled 'Observations on the Riddles of the *Exeter Book*'.

[62] 'Das Paradox in der Volksdichtung', *Typologia Litterarum, Festschrift für Max Wehrli*, ed. Stefan Sonderegger, Alois M. Haas and Harald Burger (Zürich and Freiburg i. Breslan, 1969), p. 472.

[63] The answer is nasal mucus or discharge. This riddle we have taken from S. M. Guma, *The Form, Content and Technique of Traditional Literature in Southern Sotho*, The Hiddingh-Currie Publications of the University of South Africa 8 (Pretoria, 1967), pp. 60–61 (where several others may be found).

[64] See Nora K. Chadwick, 'The Distribution of Oral Literature in the Old World', *Journal of the Royal Anthropological Institute* 69 (1939), p. 86. On the same page Mrs. Chadwick states that Tatar and Russian riddles are almost exclusively concerned with the universe, natural phenomena, and poetic diction. She also refers to the role of riddles (p. 86) in the bridal or betrothal ceremonies of various people.

[65] For English-speakers, see the edition edited by Christopher Tolkien, especially pp. 32ff. The bibliography on the Anglo-Saxon riddles is extensive. The most recent edition is by Craig Williamson (Chapel Hill, N. C., 1977).

[66] Some ancient riddles survive in children's games. See Willa Muir, *Living with Ballads* (London, 1965) pp. 38ff. on riddles in her Scottish childhood.

Other types of practical poems include work poems (Category 6) and petitions and prayers (Category 6). Petitions and prayers are often associated with, or arise from, praise poems, but they do exist in their own right regardless of their basis. In that case, they may be considered as a kind of practical poem, that is, a poem which has an immediate or useful goal. In this type of prayer, petitions and requests play the major part.

There is a large category of ritual poems and incantations which are also to be considered as practical poems. These tend to be rather fixed in form because of their sacred associations. In an oral culture, however, as Albert Lord has so notably shown, the reciter usually does not reproduce his traditional narrative exactly, although he may think he is doing so. In standard rites (sometimes partly narrative) there is more variation than the reciter thinks.

In their examination of the UNESCO collection of sacred texts from Africa, Germaine Dieterlen and her collaborators divide ritual and religious texts into two groups:[67] (1) prayers and incantations and (2) initiation texts. One can easily criticize this division on the ground that a different kind of criterion is used in each case and hence the divisions crisscross in some cases. This problem would probably arise in most attempts to classify sacred texts. Their book consists mainly of French translations of texts from various sub-Saharan peoples, and it includes Kirona initiation texts from the Doro ceremony in South Africa for young boys who reach puberty. Here proverbs are used to convey information to the young boys. Dogon initiation texts preserved in a rather special dialect (sacred dialects may be used for ritual texts) tell stories of creation and death and other myths interspersed with invocations and praises to the gods.

The Chagga people at the initiation of children into puberty sing a long incantation (pp. 257ff) in which part of a text is devoted to telling what is being done. The tswana of Shoshong (in Bechuanaland, as it was known) sing texts as they teach the young how to construct a new village. Some of the Xhosa people still perform the circumcision ceremony with texts. Wedding chants are often ritualistic and traditional. When the term 'initiation texts' is used as a category by Germaine Dieterlen and her collaborators, one can see that initiation is used in the widest sense of the word to include, for instance, initiation into marriage or house construction. Many events in traditional societies are accompanied by chants in the form of prayers. One can hardly say 'religious' because to many traditional peoples all of life is religious, but many of these events are special rites which require special words.

Finally we have a category of mnemonic and didactic poems. These poems or prose works exist for the purpose of enabling the traditions of the tribe to be handed on in easily memorized form. In one sense, of course, all wisdom

[67] *Textes sacrés d'Afrique Noire*, Collection Unesco d'oeuvres représentatives, Série Africaine (Paris, 1965).

literature is didactic, but this category comprises lists, names, genealogies, memorable events, or ritual directions presented in such form as to be easily remembered. Some proverbs fall into this category, and in particular it seems convenient to put the mnemonic and list proverbs in this category.

Some proverbs in the Book of Proverbs have the form, 'Three things, yea four things I do not understand,' followed by the four items. Normally various items are listed with or without an introduction. List-science, as it is sometimes called, is found in many cultures. In the later Jewish tradition, list-science is found in various forms,[68] and in the New Testament and early Christian moral writings we find lists like those of the seven or eight cardinal sins. When literacy is limited or when a culture is wholly oral, the listing of information in easily memorizable forms is very important. Rhythm and repetition in various forms help to make the information memorable. The verse structure depends of course on the dominant metrical mode of the language used. Repetition is a powerful aid to memory provided it is not so overdone as to become unbearable and dull. By repetition we mean 'the recognizable similarity, not necessarily the identity, of some element or feature within such a span of attention as may hold two or more items together in our regard'.[69]

Listing (Category 2) is one of the characteristics of wisdom literature[70] and probably arose in a school situation. Memorization is still a major form of learning, but in early societies that lack writing, memorability of the verbal form of the teaching is especially important.

Sometimes the information conveyed in mnemonic poetry is not merely local traditions and history, general wisdom, and knowledge but also knowledge of other peoples as far as it is useful. *Widsith* is a poem whose purpose probably is to teach its hearers about world history, particularly the world rulers ancient and modern of whom Anglo-Saxons might hear. We also have Middle Irish poems on world kingship which although certainly influenced by the Bible and Eusebian history and the literary tradition, have the same teaching function.[71] The best known are by Flann Mainistrech (died in 1056), who wrote seven of them, parallel to the seven poems he composed on the Kings of Ireland. These world-kingship poems contain more information than is provided by *Widsith*, but their purpose was probably the same. This type of

---

[68] See Wayne Sibley Towner, *The Rabbinic Enumeration of Scriptural Examples: A Study of the Rabbinic Pattern of Discourse with Special Reference to 'Mechilta d'R. Ishmael'*, Studia Post Biblica 22 (Leiden, 1973). See also the Talmud *Pesachim* 112a ff.

[69] Kathleen Lea, 'The Poetic Powers of Repetition', Warton Lecture on Poetry, *Proceedings of the British Academy* 55 (1969), p. 53. Roman Jakobson also makes clear that by his use of 'parallelism' he does not mean exact parallelism.

[70] See Hans Heinrich Schmid, *Wesen und Geschichte der Weisheit, Eine Untersuchung zur altorientalischen und israelitischen Weisheitsliteratur*, Beihefte zur *Zeitschrift für die alttestamentliche Wissenschaft* 101 (Berlin, 1966), pp. 95ff.

[71] See Seán MacAirt, 'Middle Irish Poems on World Kingship', *Études celtiques* 6 (1952–54), pp. 255–280; 7 (1955–56), pp. 18–455; 8 (1958–59), pp. 98–119 and 284–97.

poem rests on a long oral tradition which is no longer recoverable and falls into the tradition of the didactic practical poem.

The traditions of the culture to which the poet belongs provide the most frequent topic of the various subjects he sings about. As we have pointed out, all early poetry had a strong didactic element in it, but what we are especially concerned with here are those poems whose task is to make easy the ingestion of information. These may be about traditions, myths, commonsense wisdom, or nature wisdom. These are, of course, not scientific treatises, and they often betray strong political biases. Historians (poets) of this kind are not worried about objective truth. Their purpose is 'the inculcation of moral and spiritual' (and political) values, 'the elegant inspiration . . . to right conduct'.[72]

Nothing reveals these moral, spiritual, and political values as the dominating criteria more than genealogies. We are interested in traditional genealogies, not what Georges Duby calls modern reconstructions.[73] These genealogies establish ancestors of the important men and above all the chief of the society and help to support the legitimacy of the rulers. They display what J. A. Barnes calls 'structural amnesia'.[74] Jack Goody and Ian Watt write, 'Neither of these genealogies [Nigerian], nor the Biblical lists of the descendants of Adam, were remembered purely as feats of memory. They served as mnemonics for systems of social relations.'[75] These comments apply to all genealogies in early societies.

Only recently have Biblical scholars begun to understand the role of the Old Testament genealogies.[76] They serve to defend the authenticity of Israel's claim to God's blessing and even more to recall the ancestors of the tribe to the audience and the audience to the ancestors. They are conventional in number, often in ancient Semitic lands confining themselves to a fixed number, frequently ten. These are also either purely linear or are segmented at certain

---

[72] Donald J. Wilcox, *The Development of Florentine Humanist Historiography in the Fifteenth Century*, Harvard Historical Studies 82 (Cambridge, MA., 1969), p. 204 (written on what Wilcox calls 'rhetorical history' of the Renaissance).

[73] See 'Remarques sur la littérature généalogique en France aux XIe et XIIe siecle', *Hommes et structures du moyen âge: Recueil d'articles*, École Pratique des Hautes Études – Sorbonne VIe Section: Sciences économiques et sociales. Le Savoir historique I (Paris and The Hague, 1973) pp. 287–298 (Originally published in *Académie des Inscriptions et Belles Lettres*. Comptes rendus des séances de l'année 1967 [avril-juin], [Paris, 1967], pp. 335–345). This article is focussed on the Middle Ages and is not too useful for our purpose as it stresses the problems of modern historians in recreating the correct genealogies.

[74] Referred to in Jack Goody ed., *Literacy in Traditional Societies* (Cambridge, 1968), pp. 32–33 from Jack Goody and Ian Watt, 'The Consequences of Literacy', one of the essays in the book. The phrase of course refers to the forgetting that takes place in oral cultures either because of the amount of material memorized or because of political pressures.

[75] *Ibid.*, p. 31.

[76] See, e.g., Robert R. Wilson, 'The Old Testament Genealogies in Recent Research', *JBL* 94 (1975), pp. 169–189.

points which refer to a new and better known name or an actual shift in dynasty. Rival ruling lines as far as possible are omitted altogether. If one of the names cannot be omitted because of its fame, the true genealogical background may be obscured or erased. Other lists of ancestors are based on mythical heroes of the tribe.

With genealogies and other practical and mnemonic genres, we have come to the end of our listing, some consciously and some out of ignorance, but we think that those recorded here are a very representative group enabling us to see the background of the particular works that we have undertaken to discuss in this book.

One final point should be noted about this and our earlier chapters. G. L. Huxley cautiously remarks, 'Comparative studies of oral and written literatures are illuminating because they show that what has happened in one society may well have happened in another. What they can never show is that any practice observed in one society *must* have occurred in another.'[77] We are well aware of this problem.

Admittedly we have not made a strict division between oral and literate cultures. Much of our evidence has necessarily been derived from the written records that literate societies provide, and our reconstruction of the role of the 'primal poet' has had to be based on common sense and, to some extent, on analogies drawn from present-day oral societies.

Most surviving pre-modern cultures are now actually partly oral and partly literate, and in many cases one can only make tentative assumptions about a *purely* oral society. Analogy is a weak form of argument. No truth can be incontestably established only on the basis of analogy, yet when we have little other evidence and there seem to be some basic similarities, we can reasonably adopt certain conclusions. If, for instance, we find praise poems in the vast majority of early cultures, it seems not unreasonable to assume that they may be discovered in new cultures as yet unstudied and that they have already occurred in older societies which have now lost them.

One fact is clear. The actual genres discussed in this chapter belong to living oral traditions which have existed, with some changes, for centuries; and just as they substantiate our early Western literatures, so early Western literatures help to substantiate them.

---

[77] *Greek Epic Poetry from Eumelos to Panyassis* (Cambridge, MA., 1969), p. 191.

CHAPTER 9

PRIMAL POETRY AND THE MODERN AUDIENCE

In the preceding chapters we have for convenience occasionally used the term 'primal' in reference to the societies which we have been discussing. Here, as we draw from our findings some conclusions regarding their relevance to the modern reader, we emphatically reaffirm that we do *not* mean to imply by the use of the term 'primal' that these societies are 'primordial' or that they are 'simple' or that they are all 'much-of-a-muchness'. Nor do we mean to imply that their poetic traditions are of such transparency that they can be understood and appreciated effortlessly. On the contrary, we would suggest that any self-projection which modern visitors attempt to make into these unfamiliar cultures is likely to be bewildering and that any real appreciation of their 'literature' will require both patience and imagination.

To alien and uninvited visitors, unless they are trained anthropologists, any society which has retained a primarily oral culture may very well seem to lack anything remotely akin to 'literary' culture. Such visitors may indeed perceive no culture at all or, at best, may notice only the tribal songs that are the most loudly sung on some public occasion. Here even the perceptive Dr Johnson failed. Partly out of pique against James Macpherson's impudent Gaelic forgeries, and partly because of his eighteenth-century preconceptions, he felt compelled – in the very heart-land of Gaelic culture – to assert that, where there is no written language, there can be no poetry. Folklorists in recent times, however, have provided ample evidence to the contrary. How then can we rid ourselves of the misconceptions of this sort that may impede us when we attempt to understand and appraise cultures remote in time and space from our own, whether oral or literate, whether medieval or pre-modern?

There are many answers, all of them interrelated. In reference to the problem of orality, the answer is simple. Most cultures do perpetuate a considerable body of what we sometimes call 'folklore'. Generally, however, to call the primal poetry which we have been discussing 'folk poetry' is misleading. In many instances, at least, the kinds of oral traditions that have seemed worthy of being permanently recorded tend to pertain not to the 'folk' but to the rulers and leaders of the tribe. Thus, for instance, we must recognize that the complex – and, perhaps to a modern taste, somewhat tedious – Irish bardic praise-poems which have been reverently enshrined by scribes in family miscellanies are not the product of folk-singers who have undertaken to entertain powerless serfs or isolated hillbillies.

The primal poet fulfills his professional function by presenting, with appropriate ceremony at an appropriate occasion before an appropriate audience, his own appropriate utterances, and these are couched in a conventional form and idiom consonant with their acknowledged magical efficacy. The poet serves all the members of his tribe through a social contract that requires him to preserve and purvey the accumulated wisdom inherited from the ancestors of the tribe. Thus, far from playing the role of entertainer, he frequently fulfills a more serious and responsible role as priest and lawgiver and prophet, verbally mediating the past, the present, and the future.

The primal poet relies on his skill as an artificer of the kind whom the Romans called the *artifex* rather the *opifex*. That is to say, he is the constructor of the intangible rather than of the tangible. He is the creator of utterances wrought with words rather than of permanent monuments wrought from metal or stone. Yet, because of their importance in an oral culture, these potentially fragile utterances are stored, at least temporarily, not only in the memory of the poet but also in the memory of subordinate reciters, and thus they can be recalled whenever they are functionally relevant.

At a non-professional level, moreover, members of the tribe transmit orally the communal repertoires of traditional verbal utterances that they have personally gleaned from their heritage of wisdom – their own substratum of poetic lore. The repertoires belonging to this level of utterance may properly be called 'folklore', provided that the connotations of the term do not disguise the fact that the purposes of such lore were often essentially serious, even if ostensibly recreational.

Our own cultural heritage does not entirely prepare us for this kind of relationship between poet and audience. The modern poet writes for, and his works are read by, a very special, non-tribal audience of sophisticated individualists, often international in outlook and multilingual in reading. In this new setting the function of the poet is so different from that of his ancient predecessors who were appointed to serve the needs of an entire tribe that the simultaneous use of the same word 'poet' in reference to both types of professionals is easily misleading.

Members of a present-day audience are most unlikely to credit their favorite contemporary poet with magical powers, nor do they view themselves as patrons legally bound to him by a social contract, nor does he consider himself bound as a client to them as patrons. His unknown readers are not only faceless but also independent. They do not require his services at the regal, sacral, or tribal levels, for they already have easy access to the modern supports supplied by psychiatrists instead of druids, reference librarians instead of chroniclers, and security analysts instead of soothsayers. Intellectually, their minds are well stocked; they are capable of solving cross-word puzzles not only in the *New York Times* but also in the *London Times*: and they seldom yearn for the kind of assurance that is provided by simple oral wisdom.

How then can these modern readers bridge the gap between themselves and a poet remote from them in time or space? They can, of course, become collectors – as it were – of primitive poetry and live with it and come to love it. The art dealer counts on a similar possibility. To sell his client a Makonde sculpture, he assures him that this mysterious import from Tanzania possesses a universal aesthetic value, and if necessary he may also suggest that, in any case, it will flatter the decor of his client's dining-room.

Yet, to pursue this parallel, such simple solutions hardly suffice. Was the Makonde sculptor in fact concerned with universal aesthetic values? What, on the one hand, did the Makonde sculptor's magical art reveal to his tribe when, out of the inscrutable smoothness of a black-wood stump, he set free the intertwining bodies of their tribal deities and their ancestors and gave life to a vision of their history and their destiny? And how, on the other hand, can an alien possessor of the tribal statue understand the real meaning of the sculpture?

Unfortunately those who would glide culturally out of their present setting into other times and other places must recognize the fact that, even if poetry seems in some vague sense to be universal, it is in fact particularistic. To be sure, wisdom is universally esteemed, and poets as carriers of wisdom therefore, no doubt, deserve universal respect. Yet the poet, whether 'primal' or not, is always rooted in time and place and is consequently bound first and foremost to his immediate audience, no matter how transcendent his message may be, and his specific function may be far from universal.

Consider, for instance, two of the great 'universal' poets of Rome: Vergil and Horace. Functionally, Vergil himself as an epic poet can almost be described as 'primal' in the sense which we have attached to the term. Thus, as a poet-historian he glorifies his ruler (Augustus) and the legendary founder of the tribe (Aeneas of Troy) and the ancestral gods (in particular, Venus) and the tribe itself (the Romans). Yet Vergil's epic is certainly not a primal, native poem. In terms of its political function it is, to be sure, particularistic; Aeneas the legendary hero is the forerunner of Vergil's patron Augustus – an ingenious implication which any early Irish poet would have envied. Vergil, however, is an individualistic internationalist who borrowed his style and his main ingredients from the Homeric tradition of Greece, and he sheds such a Hellenic radiance and significance upon his *tour de force* that some of his own potential audience, ignorant of Greek, may have missed the literary brilliance of his epic.

Horace also is certainly not a primal bard. He does, of course, praise his ruler (Augustus), and he enjoys wealthy patronage (from Maecenas); yet Horace is not in any sense officially a public poet. Much that he says is individual and personal, often movingly so. He confesses the hope that his poetry will serve as his own perennial monument, enabling him to boast: '*I shall never entirely die*' – '*Non omnis moriar*'. Primal poets, in contrast, were expected to secure immortality not for themselves but for their patrons.

Primal poets were in essence valued because they were socially useful. Poets in sophisticated settings have not always been able to gain that kind of recognition. In his melancholy reflections entitled *Stello* (1832), Alfred de Vigny suggests that during the eighteenth century any poet who was at one and the same time both an individualist and an idealist was perversely turned by society into an 'eternal helot'. Nominally such a poet carried a 'blessing on his name', but antagonistic power-mongers placed 'a curse upon his life'.

Thus, as de Vigny points out, the French royalist poet Nicolas Gilbert was destroyed by the Encyclopedists because he supported monarchy; the young antiquarian poet Thomas Chatterton was driven to suicide because the English supporters of representative monarchy would not help him; and the classicist André Chénier was guillotined by the anti-aristocratic republicans because he did not support the French revolution. Thus, in the phrase made famous in the twentieth century by Verlaine, the individualistic poet became a *poète maudit*, a 'poet accursed', and ironically he was accursed by the very society which should have respected his primal wisdom.

Occasionally, it is true, even in the midst of the twentieth century a poet may emerge who seems to represent the tribal voice. So, on a rare and dramatic occasion, Robert Frost convincingly fulfilled the archetypal function of the public bard when on January 20, 1961, he recited on the steps of the Washington Capitol a poem specially composed for the Inauguration of the new chieftain, John Fitzgerald Kennedy. The wind blew auspiciously through his silver hair, and wisps of smoke (opportunely caused by a wiring short-circuit) curled mysteriously up from his podium. In his ode he remarked on the propriety of celebrating 'the august occasions of the state'. In the bardic tradition, he traced the history of his country; and, like a prophet, he predicted the 'glory of a next Augustan age', – 'a golden age of poetry and power'.

Rarely, however, do modern poets maintain such an archetypal role. More characteristic of what may be expected is the brief poem entitled *Inauguration Day: January 1953* by Robert Lowell. The occasion for this bitter and deeply felt personal utterance was the election of General Eisenhower as President. In retrospect the outcome of the vote may seem comparatively innocuous, but the choice of one so conservative was for Lowell anathema. Indeed, elsewhere (in a letter) he characterizes the new President of the United States as the symbol 'of America's unintelligent side – all fitness, muscles, smiles and banality'.

If Lowell had been a traditional tribal bard, he could still, even in defeat, have vented his personal bitterness by composing a satire against his victim, but the circumstances surrounding the utterance of a conventional bardic satire would have differed notably from the actuality of Lowell's lonely liberal isolation. If, in some old-fashioned realm, he had been the official bard for a group of disappointed clansmen who had failed to secure the succession of some favorite new leader, he could, for instance, very easily have composed a typical ready-made praise-poem in honor of the defeated hero – in this case,

153

Adlai Stevenson. Then, as a matter of course, he could have comforted not only himself but also all of his allies by inserting within the praise-poem a devastating satire of the unwelcome new chieftain – in this case, 'Ike'. For a modern poet, however, such poetic responses, which had once been automatic, were no longer satisfying. So instead Lowell composed his own unique sardonic sonnet.

His sonnet contains the conventional fourteen lines, but their beat is an idiosyncratic tetrameter rather than a pentameter. In the first part, which consists of nine lines rather than the usual octave, he deftly localizes his own immediate setting in New York by references to Stuyvesant, the El, Third Avenue, Manhattan, and Grant's Tomb, and he then emphasizes his reference to the unhappy General Ulysses S. Grant by the mention of Cold Harbor, the scene of the General's loss of 6,000 men in Virginia during the Civil War.

In the second part, which consists not of the usual sestet but of five lines, he deftly establishes the atmosphere of his monody by references to snow and ice. Then in a final devastating metaphor he juxtaposes the image of Grant in his Tomb and Eisenhower in the presidency: 'The Republic summons Ike, the mausoleum in her heart.' At this meditative moment of cold anger – as would happen with Lowell – even his intimate friends are scarcely included. Freed from tribal conventions, here the poet speaks entirely for himself.

THE AUDIENCE, UNIVERSAL OR PARTICULAR

As we have seen, poetry seems to be universally recognized as a special mode of utterance by human societies. One of its prime characteristics is that 'poetry' as we have defined it is in some way 'elevated' above the 'normal' mode of everyday utterances. The poet's tone, the audiences's expectations, and the poem's style together tend to differentiate poetry from prose in a clearly definable manner, no matter what the specific cultural background of the poetry may be; but other wide generalizations about the universal nature of poetry do not readily follow from this initial premise.

As a corollary, we may tend, for instance, to accept as a universal truth Wordsworth's eloquent pronouncement that poetry is the product of a 'spontaneous overflow of powerful feelings'. The gentle Wordsworth might very well have included the possibility that some poets may at times express violent feelings, but at the other end of the scale it is also possible that a poem may not necessarily reflect the poet's feelings at all. A Gaelic bard or an African *imbongi* may seem to praise a chieftain in the exalted language appropriate to the tribal poetic tradition and yet feel little personal enthusiasm for this obligatory expression of loyalty.

Since poetry is an elevated form of discourse, it may also seem to follow that poetry is therefore, in some loose sense, universally elevating and hence is beneficial to all humanity. In a famous assertion, Shelley declared that poets are 'the unacknowledged legislators of the world'. Ironically, the legislative function of the poet can scarcely be said to have received particularly widespread acceptance from parliament in Shelley's own day. Nonetheless such powers are often recognized, as we have seen, in primal societies. Indeed, sometimes the poet is, *de facto*, the *acknowledged* legislator of the tribe. The very fact that Shelley's wistful claim must be qualified again suggests that the universality of the role of poetry should be carefully defined. Primal, homogeneous societies may expect, or even require, the poet to legislate, and they may respond to what they have come to accept as the commanding voice of authority; but other more complex, heterogeneous societies are unlikely to assent unanimously to any one single voice.

That the role of poetry varies in various culture is also reflected in the multiplicity of the poetic genres that can be distinguished in any global survey of the devices of the poetic craft. Consider, for instance, the elegiac tradition. Every human society suffers from the sorrows of mortality, and it might therefore seem logical that, of all the conceivable genres of poetry, some standard form of elegy would occur almost universally. Yet, at least in our survey, such does not seem to be the case.

To be sure, Milton's *Lycidas*, composed in 1633, and Tennyson's *In Memoriam*, composed after Hallam's death two hundred years later, despite their considerable differences, reflect their kinship with a pre-established genre established in Europe as a heritage of Graeco-Roman literature. In both poems, the premature death of a close personal friend provided the subject matter of the elegies; grief provided the inspiration; and literary tradition provided a ready-made medium, which each poet shaped according to his own genius in his public expression of his private and individual grief.

By way of contrast, the medieval Irish bard (at least as far as surviving records show) seldom took advantage of the genre of poetic lament in order to express his *personal* grief. In some rare cases, the bard may in fact have been familiar with Greek or Roman elegies and may even have been tempted to imitate them, but traditionally as a bard he was required to respond neither as a person nor as a creative artist but as a supporter and sustainer of the members of his tribe. To satisfy their atavistic expectations, he must exercise his verbal craft in an acceptably traditional manner. Whenever they lost a leader who was important to them, he must conduct a communal exorcism of grief, and he must facilitate the supernatural transmission of ancestral powers and virtues from the deceased member of the tribe to the surviving descendants. Consequently, the bard's personal grief was irrelevant to his function; the genre of lament which he inherited allowed him only a tribal individuality and, stylistically, only a controlled range of utterance.

Hence to attempt to evaluate an Irish elegy within the usual concept of the elegiac tradition is a fruitless critical exercise. In comparison with Milton's *Lycidas*, for instance, we need say little more than that Milton felt free to utilize all the poetic machinery that he had acquired from his reading of the classics and yet was encouraged by the literary climate of his age to produce a uniquely personal work of art, in its particular splendor unlike any elegy composed before or since; whereas, for an Irish bard, convention precluded such possibilities. On the part of the bard, any blatant individuality would have been unacceptable, for magical utterances must be recognizably traditional and conventional.

The bard's one opportunity to achieve the kind of individuality that would be approved and, indeed, acclaimed by his audience lay in the ingenious application of permissible variations to the decoration of his poem. As a consequence, Irish laments are reminiscent of Irish manuscript illuminations in the brilliantly interlaced and decorated ornamentations which were permitted within the sacrosanct limitations of Irish art. Failure to recognize the peculiar restrictions so characteristic of Irish laments, as of bardic poetry in general, may leave the modern well-intentioned reader baffled. As a member of an uninvited audience his only solution is to undertake his own self-indoctrination, for the bards – dedicated poets who never aspired to become universal – now lie as silent as their chieftains and only their utterances survive.

The Audience, Universal or Particular

Any analysis of the function of poetry suggests not only that poets and poetry are universal but also that audiences are universal; but once again we must qualify the nature of that universality. Here it must suffice to discuss the nature of primal audiences and ignore the audiences acquainted with more sophisticated international literary traditions; and at the same time we must differentiate – as we have already done – between, on the one hand, what might be called the proper and intended audience who as auditors belong to the society for whom the poet composes and, on the other hand, what we have called the uninvited audience of readers, educated people possessed with a curiosity about the literatures of the world.

In comparison with the latter privileged group, the members of the primal audience must have been notably both willing and captive. To be sure, the human instinct that leads a satisfied audience to award their applause to a poem which they admire and to denote their disapproval by their boos may have played some part in the shaping of the primal poet's performance, but their influence on the content and form of their native poetry was probably minimal. Unlike the members of the modern audience who espouse educational broadcasting programs for a portion of their literary fare, the members of a primal society were not wooed by any promise of hearing either 'new voices' or unorthodox views 'which the management does not necessarily endorse'.

At least in the regal societies with which we have dealt here, the people of the realm must have realized that the poet's primary concern was to satisfy the king or chieftain by the *content* of his poem and to maintain the expected tradition by the *form* in which he cast the poem. In terms of freedom of choice, such an audience was in fact somewhat in the situation of those submissive members of the audience in a totalitarian state who are dependent upon the cynical rule of the political programmer, 'Show them what they should see.' Consequently modern readers must recognize that the primal poet knows and cares nothing about the preconceptions and expectations of alien intruders, remote from him in space, time, and culture.

Sometimes, moreover, our understanding may be confused by a misplaced assumption of familiarity with the kind of primal poetry that has inspired later antiquarians to rework, to expand, to refurbish, to modernized, and even to internationalize their primitive sources. Their well-intentioned endeavors are reminiscent of the familiar fallacy, 'If you've seen the movie, you don't need to read the novel.' Thus, quite excusably, the readers of James Macpherson's egregious misrepresentations of the Ossianic tradition mentioned earlier might not suspect that there could be any poetic virtue in the Gaelic heroic lays that he transmogrified into Fingalian pseudo-epics.

When Wordsworth suggested that the 'plaintive numbers' sung by a Highland reaper might well include 'old, unhappy, far-off things, and battles long ago', he presented an instinctive and much more accurate portrayal of Gaelic culture than anything to be found in Macpherson's works, but even his preconceptions need some emendation. The reaper's 'numbers' may well have sounded plaintive to Wordsworth as a devotee of the simple life, for the tune of an Ossianic lay gives the effect of a chant and is generally based on a pentatonic line that sounds not only unfamiliar but even barbaric to an ear that is unaccustomed to such exotic music. The spirit of the Ossianic lays, however, is not plaintive. Their sounds may be plangent, perhaps, but their spirit is prideful.

From at least the twelfth century to the end of the nineteenth century, heroic lays (which usually, but not necessarily, dealt with Ossianic legends) were particularly favored by Gaelic singers; and the obvious reason for the popularity of these narrative songs lies in the fact that they provided brief, moving distillations of the extensive heroic literature that was familiar to an audience accustomed to hearing the lengthy recitals of the shenachies. The listeners assumed that the heroes and heroines in the repertoire not only were real people but also were noble and exemplary ancestors whose lineage they shared. So, if, for instance, Wordsworth's solitary reaper was singing – as may well have been the case – the *Lay of Diarmaid*, she would of course have felt sorrow over the hero's death, but she might also have felt a personal pride in Diarmaid's heroism because he had heroically met his predestined destruction according to the ancient Highland code of honor and also, even more specifically, because in Argyllshire he was counted as the ancestral founder of Clan Campbell.

Despite the charm of their antiquity, Ossianic lays such as were sung by Wordsworth's reaper will admittedly never occupy some supreme niche in the annals of world literature. Yet the sensitive reader or listener who understands their function will appreciate their peculiar excellence in contrast with Macpherson's misty transformations of the traditional lore of the Highlands. So too, the modern reader of the terse, stark Norse lays that portray the fate of the heroic Sigurd must consider their function lest he be overwhelmed by Wagner's apocalyptic vision of Siegfried as he is engulfed in the Germanic twilight.

Paradoxically, it is sometimes poets themselves who impede our attempts to understand the cultures which lie behind them in time and space; and the more authoritative and eloquent they are, the more we are misled. So, for instance, Wordsworth provides us with his own historical reconstruction of the ancient world of Stonehenge. It is invested by the 'Briton clothed in wolf-skin vest, with shield and stone-axe, . . . of barbaric majesty', and supported by Druids, 'long-bearded teachers, with white wands uplifted, pointing to the starry sky . . . and plain below'. Such airy visions scarcely assist us archaeologically in contemplating the stone-age, pre-Celtic circle at Stonehenge, nor do they clarify our understanding of the earliest survivals of Celtic-British literature.

Tennyson also can be misleading. He did, it is true, contribute to our understanding of the Anglo-Saxons by producing his pioneering modernization of the Old English poem *The Battle of Brunanburh*, but in his poem *Boadicea* he perpetuated the aura of misty glamor that had been cast over the ancient Britons in the nineteenth century. In it he reconstructs what the defiant British queen might have said in the face of Roman oppression:

> 'Me the wife of rich Prasutagus, me the lover of liberty,
> Me they seized and me they tortured, me they lash'd and
>   humiliated,
> Me the sport of ribald Veterans, mine of ruffian violators!
> See they sit, they hide their faces, miserable in ignominy!
> Wherefore in me burns an anger, not by blood to be satiated.
> Lo the palaces and the temple, lo the colony Camulodune!' . . .
> So the Queen Boadicea, standing loftily charioted,
> Brandishing in her hand a dart and rolling glances lioness-like,
> Yell'd and shriek'd between her daughters in her fierce volubility.

Judging by what we know of the Celtic-British poetry attributed to Aneirin and Taliesin in the sixth century, we may reasonably guess at the nature of the unrecorded Celtic-British poetry composed in the era of Boudicca (alias Boadicea) in the first century, and we can perhaps be justified in suspecting that the rhetoric of Tennyson's voluble Queen is totally anachronistic both in style and content. So too, for that matter, modern archaeologists complain about the anachronism associated with the famous Victorian statue of the triumphant British heroine who drives eternally forward in her familiar war-chariot poised on the edge of the Thames. The menacing scythes attached to her hub-caps, we are now told, lack historical justification.

Such objections may seem pedantic – indeed, even philistine – yet they relate to the problems faced by all non-specialist readers no matter how intuitively brilliant they may be as literary critics. So, for instance, the comparatively recently discovered Celtic-British poems of Aneirin and of Taliesin require of the modern reader an understanding of the bardic function just as unclouded as that essential for the comprehension of any other unfamiliar primal or pre-modern poetry. The poems may stir the critic's heart and excite his analytical faculties, but the critic's comments can scarcely be considered relevant until he has discovered why the poems were composed.

The essence of the problem associated with our understanding of the role of the poet is, in short, closely connected with the gradual disappearance of the bardic poet and the emergence of what may for convenience be called the personal poet. Such a shift is subtle and imperceptible. It does not occur universally at some one moment. It does not even complete a tidy cycle at some given moment within any one homogeneous cultural community.

Where the shift occurs, bardic poets may still be singing for a listening audience while personal poets are addressing a different kind of reading audience. Sometimes a poet such as, for instance, Robert Burns, may quite unconsciously perform in both roles. Thus on the one hand we find Burns – like any 'obscure, nameless bard', to quote his own phrase – composing a new version of the old, traditional Scottish ballad *Lord Gregory*, while at the same time publishing his entirely self-centered *Farewell*, which is addressed to the brethren in his Masonic Lodge at a time when he was planning in despair to emigrate to Jamaica.

Modern-day readers, of course, will find nothing particularly surprising in this dual role exercised by Burns, nor did he. In his age Burns happened to be able to serve not only as a folk-poet but also as a drawing-room poet. In many of the cultures which have been surveyed in this book, however, such a range of function would not have been conceivable. In particular, during the long history of poetry, probably few cultures have encouraged poets to engage in self-expression, for members of a tribal audiences were more interested in what the poet could do for them than in what he had to say about himself.

The historical discontinuity between the bardic role and the personal role of poets is, of course, a matter of great complexity, and this book has merely attempted to present from a philological point of view some relevant illustrative materials, leaving the literary-critical implications to the reader. Here, however, by way of illustration it does seem appropriate to examine in some detail one final example of the kind of cultural discontinuity that may be said to separate the old world from the new.

In England an obvious choice of period is provided by the eighteenth century, and a convenient focus for comparison is furnished by Thomas Gray's poem 'The Bard' (1757). This striking work has already (in chapter 7) been cited as having established the official eighteenth-century English image of the ancient tribal bard. In it the poet invents his own private vision of what a Welsh bard in the thirteenth century would have looked like and how he would have behaved. His bard is a fierce patriot who curses the invading Anglo-Norman King Edward I and predicts the coming of a glorious new age of Tudor monarchs and poets and then commits suicide.

Gray's poem is of especial relevance for several reasons. First it should be noted that, to some extent, the poem contains a touch of verisimilitude, for Gray, through his academic contacts at Cambridge, had become acquainted with the work of the first Welsh literary historian, Evan Evans, who eventually in 1764 published a pioneering study, *Some Specimens of the Poetry of the Antient Welsh Bards*, and thus through Evan's translations he knew something of the early warlike poetry of Wales.

In this respect, however, it is instructive to compare the eighteenth-century invention of Gray with the actual Welsh bardic poetry produced during the era of King Edward's invasions. Gruffydd ab yr Ynad Coch ('son of the Red Judge'), for instance, composed a famous lament for Llywelyn ap Gruffydd, the last Welsh Prince of Wales, who was slain in a skirmish in 1282 by one of Edward's soldiers. His head had ignominiously been brought in triumph to London; the effect wrought upon the Welsh by the loss of their Prince was shattering; and Gruffydd's lament poignantly conveys across the centuries the magnitude of the grief felt by himself and by his countrymen.

No matter how profound Gruffydd's personal grief may have been, his utterances are, however, strictly modeled on the conventional patterns of lament that the examples of Celtic laments already mentioned would lead us to expect of a professional bard. Clearly his lament is composed not for himself but for all of the Prince's people, and his technique is entirely traditional and conventional.

Thus, the sorrows of the people recall to his mind King Arthur's disastrous final battle at Camlan – a stock comparison:

> As at Camlan, many are the miserable cries,
> Many the tears trickling down cheeks.

The bard, drawing on the familiar bardic phraseology customarily applied to rulers, praises the 'golden-handed' Prince as 'an oaken door', 'a hawk', 'a lion', 'a candle among kings'. The Prince was of distinguished descent, he was generous, he was brave, he was handsome, as the patrons of bards always should be. Because of his death all nature is perturbed; and the world, as the bard says, – in this case with considerable justification – is now coming to an end.

In short, the entire poem is completely predictable, as a good bardic poem should be, and it merits its place in the annals of Welsh literature primarily because of the virtuosity of Gruffydd's rhetorical variations and because of the national importance of the subject.

The merits of Thomas Gray's poem, on the other hand, accrue for very different reasons. His poem is highly imaginative and, indeed, idiosyncratic, and he follows no model. His own insatiable academic curiosity, his own scholarly reading, and his personal contacts with the work of Welsh scholars have lead his imagination to recreate what he feels to be the spirit of ancient Wales. He composes his poem with a calm detachment even though his hero is defiantly nationalistic, and, as he develops the poem, he somewhat surprisingly allows his Welsh bard to end up by predicting the future accomplishments not of Welsh but of English poets such as Shakespeare and Milton.

Furthermore, it is striking to study the genesis of his poem. He began to write the poem in 1754, but he found difficulty in completing it, even though in its final version it was only 144 lines long, and he did not publish it until 1757. In a letter he suggests that the conclusion of his poem was in part inspired by his fortuitous meeting at Cambridge with a visiting Welsh harper, John Parry:

> Mr Parry has been here and scratch'd out such ravishing blind harmony, such tunes of a thousand year old with names enough to choak you, as have set all this learned body a'dancing.

In the light of the rather flippant tone of his remarks it seems evident that for Gray the writing of the poem was somewhat of an antiquarian *jeu d'esprit*. Having invented a tale of a noble savage, he wished to distill from his poem the highest dramatic force and immediacy that he could attain. To provide a satisfactory ending he therefore allowed the Bard to exit from the stage by leaping 'headlong from the mountain's height'. The final words of the poem were, at Gray's first working: 'he sunk to endless night', but to increase their histrionic force, he even substituted the appropriately histrionic revision suggested by his friend David Garrick, the actor: 'he *plung'd* to endless night'.

The possibility that Welsh bards were not accustomed to committing suicide was not a matter of concern to Gray. He simply let the noble Welsh savage end his life in very much the same way that an antique Roman in similar circumstance might have done, for the poet was writing for his own time and place, and he could have felt no reason to project himself backwards in time far from the neoclassical setting of Cambridge into the undocumented world of tribal bards.

The difference between the two worlds – one, the imaginative world of the eighteenth-century university poet, and the other, the practical world of tribal bards – is further illustrated by artistic representations. Gray's poem inspired a Welsh artist, Thomas Jones, to commit his impression of the Bard to canvas (ca 1774), and this painting presents a striking contrast to the representation of a medieval bard already referred to in Chapter 4. The latter is an illumination in a manuscript of the *Scotichronicon*, an historical work compiled by John Fordun in the latter part of the fourteenth century, which was subsequently revised and extended down to the year 1437 by Walter Bower.

Medieval portraits of bards in action are not common, but the business-like Illuminator of the Fordun-Bower manuscript provides an eminently satis-factory example (Illustration 1), for he clearly understands the actual function of the bard whom he represents. Equally interestingly, the eighteenth-century Romantic Welsh painter, Thomas Jones, faithfully captures in paint Gray's inspired poetic vision of the ancient 'bard' (Illustration 2). Each portrayal is unmistakably marked by the style of the period in which the work was produced, and each in a very satisfying way reflects the assumptions of the artist concerning the function of the bard.

The reasons for these differences in representation are obvious. The medieval Illuminator is aware of the fact that a bard customarily serves as an intermediary in public ritual, and he knows that the purpose of his art is to recreate history. The eighteenth-century painter views the bard as a remote, theatrical character belonging to an almost unreal world, and he recognizes that his subject presents an ideal topic for a Romantic painting. The Illuminator follows the Fordun-Bower text fairly closely but with intelligent selectivity. He represents a particular event that occurred during the inauguration of the eight-year-old Alexander III in 1249 at Scone (in Perth) . The ceremony as depicted takes place on the inaugural mound (center) next to Scone Abbey; the cross (upper right) stands nearby in the cemetery. The King is seated (center) on the Stone of Destiny (later removed in 1296 by King Edward I to England), wearing the crown and the mantel of state and holding the scepter adorned with a lily. At the King's right stands an unidentified nobleman holding the sword of state, and at the left stands a figure probably representing the King's widowed mother Marie de Coucy.

The features mentioned so far correspond somewhat to the official representations of the King that appear on his various royal seals, but the Illuminator has emphasized in particular the 'Highland Scot' (near left) who, according to the text, after the ceremonies of inauguration 'suddenly fell on his knees before the throne and, bowing his head, hailed the King in his mother tongue'. The Highland bard wears a sword as a sign of his status, and he is dressed in what may be intended as a distinctive Highland plaid wound around him and Highland shoes on his feet. Acting the part of the shenachie or tribal historian, he utters the Gaelic beginning of a royal genealogy: 'The blessings of God, O King of Scotland, Alexander, son of Alexander.' Every feature of the illumination is in keeping with reality, including even the implication that the bard is reciting and not reading his address.

So far, the Illuminator follows the written text closely, and in one respect the exigencies of art happen to bring his representation particularly close to the essence of the bardic tradition. The annals record in detail the long genealogy which the bard recites after his preliminary blessing. Predictably, this *tour de force* follows the familiar pattern of such utterances. It counts ancestry backwards in time through Alexander's verifiable historical progenitors and then attaches his line to misty creations of legend and shadowy relics of forgotten mythologies. It then concludes with a prefabricated coda, deliberately invented long since for bards by pseudo-historians, and this fiction triumphantly demonstrates that the King is directly descended from Gaidheal Glas, who is claimed to be the eponymous ancestor of the Gaels of Ireland and Scotland.

It is a minor matter, to be sure, but the historian is probably wrong when he reports that the bard 'read' this pedigree aloud. The historian was writing long after the event and perhaps did not, as a Lowlander, quite comprehend the extraordinary facility with which Highland bards could weave a genealogy out of the materials stored in their memories. Somehow the Illuminator, though also far removed from the era of Alexander III, perhaps comes closer to representing what may very well have been the case when he portrays the kneeling bard as one who is ready to release an irresistible flood of names from his memory. A genealogical scroll is represented on one of Alexander's official seals, but bards do not need scrolls. In any case, both the historian and the artist convey a clear representation of the function of the bard. What concerns both of them is that the King's claim to legitimacy must be supported by the authority of the inherited wisdom of the past.

Not surprisingly, by way of contrast, Thomas Jones's painting *The Bard* (ca. 1774) conveys only the faintest of memories of the basic Celtic bardic function. Jones, though born in Wales, was educated at Oxford, had studied art in Rome, and was a friend of members of the contemporary literary set, including David Garrick, the actor. One of Jones's older contemporaries who had preceded him at Oxford was Evan Evans, with whose literary-historical work Gray himself – as has been remarked – was well acquainted. Obviously, however, in dealing with the Welsh past Jones the artist was inspired less by 'antient' Welsh specimens than by Gray's own romantic English poem, and, indeed, the painter excels even Gray in converting the bard from public functionary into theatrical performer.

Thomas Jones enthusiastically replicates in paint almost every vivid word of Gray's poem. The Bard holds a lyre and stands on the haughty brow of a rock frowning o'er the Conway River on Mount Snowdon's steep. Affrighted ravens sail aloof, and in the foreground a famished eagle screams. The Bard's beard streams in the troubled air. Giant-oaks enclose the scene. Three corpses (presumably those of Cadwallo, Urien, and Modred, referred to by Gray?) lie behind the Bard. The invading English king, Edward I, winds his long array down a diagonal mountain pass in the distance toward the point in the foreground where the Bard will call down ruin upon the ruthless king just before he plunges into the roaring tide.

Jones does, it is true, depart from Gray's script in that his Bard does not turn his gaze defiantly towards the ruthless King but, rather, stares towards

1. (p. 164) A Gaelic bard authenticates the claims of Alexander III as King of Scotland in 1249.

2. (p. 165) *The Bard*, a Romantic view of the solitary poet painted by a Welsh artist, Thomas Jones (1742–1803).

the middle-background where megalithic monuments not mentioned in the poem loom out in dramatic *chiaroscuro*. The artist's contemporaries, of course, would have seen the relevance of these archaeological remains, which, though actually pre-Celtic, they would have thought of as 'druid circles', and they would no doubt have assumed that the Bard was momentarily preoccupied with this focus of some ancestral cult.

In the main, however, the artist completely reinforces the poet's conception of the primitive bard. Eighteenth-century observers could view the ancient Welsh Bard in the painting as a Noble Savage who had been initiated into the mysteries of the druidical tradition and had gained enlightenment in the realms of Natural Religion. They could also count on him as a man of action who, when Edward appeared, would hurl the appropriate words of defiance: 'Ruin seize thee, ruthless King! Confusion on thy banners wait!' And they could imagine him to be an impassioned, self-expressive poet who would perfectly reflect the preconceptions of their own age. It would have been hard for them to imagine how coldly political and opportunistic the professional bards had once been.

Illustrations of the contrasts between the world of the bards versus the world of self-expressive poets could be multiplied indefinitely. The details would vary considerably, but the division is inescapable. Every culture, moreover, sustains its own preconceptions; and – as a corollary – the bard may well encounter just as much difficulty in penetrating the world of the self-expressive poet as the poet will encounter in the reverse direction. The primary purpose of this book has been to suggest merely one practical solution for one practical problem. To understand and appreciate the poetry of the functional bard, modern readers must be able to cross backwards over cultural divisions. They must enter into the bard's society not as missionaries or preachers but as submissive listeners and observers. Their personal whims, tastes, standards, criteria, and even their longing for novelty are all irrelevant until they become no longer uninvited strangers but members of the tribe.